The Manresa Method

The Manresa Method

An Ignatian Approach to Philosophy, Jungian Psychology, and the Enneagram

STEPHEN J. COSTELLO

CASCADE *Books* · Eugene, Oregon

THE MANRESA METHOD
An Ignatian Approach to Philosophy, Jungian Psychology, and the Enneagram

Copyright © 2026 Stephen J. Costello. All rights reserved. Except for brief quotations in critical publications or reviews, no part of this book may be reproduced in any manner without prior written permission from the publisher. Write: Permissions, Wipf and Stock Publishers, 199 W. 8th Ave., Suite 3, Eugene, OR 97401.

Cascade Books
An Imprint of Wipf and Stock Publishers
199 W. 8th Ave., Suite 3
Eugene, OR 97401

www.wipfandstock.com

PAPERBACK ISBN: 979-8-3852-5723-2
HARDCOVER ISBN: 979-8-3852-5724-9
EBOOK ISBN: 979-8-3852-5725-6

Cataloguing-in-Publication data:

Names: Costello, Stephen J. [author]

Title: The Manresa method : an Ignatian approach to philosophy, Jungian psychology, and the enneagram / Stephen J. Costello.

Description: Eugene, OR: Cascade Books, 2026 | Includes bibliographical references and index.

Identifiers: ISBN 979-8-3852-5723-2 (paperback) | ISBN 979-8-3852-5724-9 (hardcover) | ISBN 979-8-3852-5725-6 (ebook)

Subjects: LCSH: Jesuits—spirituality. | Ignatius, of Loyola, Saint, 1491–1556. Exercitia spiritualia. | Religion—Philosophy. | Philosophy and religion. | Religion and psychology.

Classification: BX4700 C678 2026 (paperback) | BX4700 (ebook)

01/15/26

Unless otherwise noted, Scripture quotations are from the Jerusalem Bible, copyright © 1968 by Darton, Longman & Todd LTD and Doubleday and Co. Inc. All rights reserved.

I dedicate this book to my amazing parents, Val and Johnny, in loving gratitude, admiration, and respect.

Contents

Preface	ix
Acknowledgments	xiii
Introduction	1
Chapter One: Pilgrim's Path: Accompanying Ignatius of Loyola	21
Chapter Two: Considering the *Spiritual Exercises*: The Perspective of Five Jesuit Thinkers	43
Chapter Three: Conversion in Charles Taylor and Bernard Lonergan	82
Chapter Four: Consolation in Boethius	98
Chapter Five: Desolation, Dark Night, and Depression in Guardini, John of the Cross, and Hopkins	110
Chapter Six: The Examen of Consciousness in Wittgenstein	139
Chapter Seven: Imagination in the Works of Carl Jung, Ira Progoff, and James Hillman	152
Chapter Eight: The Enneagram and Christianity	176
Chapter Nine: Care of Creation, the Great Chain of Being, and Catholic Social Teaching in E. F. Schumacher, *Laudato Si'*, and Simone Weil	198
Conclusion	217
Bibliography	227
Index	237

Preface

My interest in at least three of the thinkers who feature prominently in this work—St. Ignatius of Loyola, C. G. Jung, and Bernard Lonergan—dates to school days and university. I discovered St. Ignatius of Loyola in fifth year in boarding school and wrote a church history essay on Ignatius and the Catholic Counter-Reformation. Spanish was one of my leaving certificate subjects, so Ignatius, who was born in the Basque region of Spain, appealed to me for a number of reasons. I continued with my studies in Spanish language and literature at University College Dublin, together with philosophy. Decades later, I would make the Ignatian Spiritual Exercises.

I had intended to become a psychologist first, then a barrister-at-law specializing in criminal law. However, things didn't turn out as I expected. I got a rude awakening when I discovered that psychology was not about Freud and Jung or depression and schizophrenia but concerned itself more with brain physiology, animal behaviorism, and mathematical statistics. I switched niftily to philosophy, where I felt immediately at home and continued with the subject up to doctoral studies, specializing in Freud and hermeneutics. In the library at UCD, there were shelves devoted to both Freud and Jung, and I devoured these volumes with increasing interest. I graduated with an honors bachelor of arts degree in 1988 in philosophy and Spanish. While I was doing my master's degree in philosophy by major thesis during the day on the problem of personal immortality in the theistic existentialism of Miguel de Unamuno and tutoring in the Departments of Metaphysics and of Logic and Psychology, at night I was studying law at the Honourable Society of King's Inns. Something had to give, and my love of philosophy overshadowed any lingering interest I had in law; and so after graduating with an MA in philosophy in 1990, I carried on in the Department of Philosophy, which culminated in a PhD in 1994 with a thesis entitled "Hermeneutics and the Psychoanalysis of Religion: The Ethical Implications of Ricoeur's Reading of Freud," supervised by Prof. Richard Kearney, which was later published as a book. I had the honor of meeting French phenomenologist Paul Ricoeur a few times during this period. Feeling that my knowledge of psychoanalysis was theoretical and looking to have another option and occupation outside of academia, I initially enrolled in psychosynthesis, but the director suggested I apply to do an analytic training at the newly founded Irish Institute of Psychoanalytic Psychotherapy (now housed in St. James's Hospital, which is aligned with Trinity College Dublin, though the Jungian component has been completely dropped since) since I really wanted to become an analyst. I was accepted as one of the first intake of students and embarked on a rigorous three-year training that included theory, individual analysis (two to four times a week), group analysis, infant observation, and two theses. Equal weight was given to Freud, Jung, Klein, and Lacan. I had previously, during my undergraduate and postgraduate years, undergone a relatively short Lacanian analysis, which I very much took to and returned to some years later. As I was already familiar with Lacan, for my analytic training, I underwent both a Jungian and Kleinian analysis. (Perhaps another time I will discuss the merits and demerits of these approaches.) My thesis brought these schools together on the subject of criminology, which was later published as a book: *The Pale Criminal: Psychoanalytic Perspectives*. For many years, I was associated with the Lacanian movement, which was brought to Ireland by Dr. Cormac Gallagher, an ex-Jesuit who had studied in Paris and translated a vast amount of Lacan's works. I attended his Wednesday seminars in St. Vincent's Hospital and gave lectures to members of the Association for Psychoanalysis and Psychotherapy in Ireland (APPI), as well as writing for *The Letter* (Lacanian journal). I had set up the BA in philosophy at Dublin Business School (DBS) and co-ordinated its MA in psychoanalysis. The college, where I was senior lecturer for many years, had a strong Freudian and Lacanian component. One of the few groups to be active in Dublin at this time was the Lacanian one; it had a presence in both the undergraduate and postgraduate levels in DBS College. The annual meetings and conferences at the Education and Research Centre of Vincent's University Hospital attracted analysts of all orientations. Interestingly, there is still no official and accredited Jungian training in Ireland. There was—and still is—the Irish Psycho-Analytical Association, based in Monkstown and known as the Monkstown Group, founded by Jonathan (Jonty) Hanaghan, who was analyzed by Anna Freud and who wrote a book on Freud and Jesus. I also gave a few papers to this group.

Having also been influenced by Bernard Lonergan and Viktor Frankl on the subject of meaning, I felt the need to add this dimension to my work in philosophy and psychoanalysis. So many years later I would find myself in the USA finishing the clinical part of a diplomate in logotherapy, which I received in 2009, the same year that I founded the Viktor Frankl Institute of Ireland, precisely to introduce Frankl's work into Ireland. My practitioner's diploma in logotherapy and existential analysis from the International Association of Logotherapy and Existential Analysis in Vienna was bestowed on me in 2012. I retain close ties with Vienna and have regularly participated in and contributed to their existential analytic conferences.

My clinical approach draws on both psychoanalytic and existential traditions. This book, then, reflects the prism and perspective with which I (presently) see the world, grounded as it is in philosophy, depth psychology, and mystical theology. Despite the plurality of themes present, the unity, I hope, is also apparent throughout these pages, as St. Ignatius's method is the fulcrum around which the concepts I consider rotate.

Acknowledgments

I WOULD LIKE TO express deep gratitude and love to my parents, Val and Johnny, first and foremost, for their constant curiosity, enthusiasm, and encouragement. Huge thanks must also go to my friends, especially Darren Cleary, Tom O'Connor, Cathal O'Keeffe, and to Patrick, Linda, and Josh Treacy, for their uplifting presence in my life, and with whom I have enjoyed deep and delightful discussions, as well as to Duncan Reyburn for our philosophical engagement and friendship over the last couple of years.

Introduction

MANRESA

MANRESA IS IN CATALONIA, which lies in the northeast of the Iberian Peninsula, to the south of the Pyrenees Mountains, the capital of which is Barcelona, the largest city in the region. Crossed by the Cardoner River (*El Cardener*), it's an industrial area that features the well-known Basilica of Santa Marta, a Romanesque-Gothic church. Manresa is also the place where St. Ignatius of Loyola, SJ (1491–1556), the Spanish mystic and founder of the Jesuits, stopped to pray on his way back from Montserrat in 1522.[1] A cave near the town, where St. Ignatius experienced a series of mystical visions, contributed to the formulation and fundamentals of his famous book *The Spiritual Exercises*, which would be published in Latin in 1548. As such, Manresa is a place of pilgrimage. Ignatius's text, comprising a set of contemplations, meditations, and prayers, was composed between 1522 and 1524, though later refined by him in Paris when he was studying there. The principal aim of his manual is to help retreatants to order their lives and discern the divine will.[2] The exercises form the cornerstone of Ignatian spirituality.

---

1. See Costello, *Ignatian Mysticism*.
2. See Thibodeaux, *Discern*.

METHOD

A twentieth-century son of St. Ignatius, Canadian Jesuit philosopher Bernard Lonergan (1904–84), identified, five hundred years after Ignatius, four cognitive operations that he deemed to be constitutive of the psychological subject, namely, experiencing, understanding, judging, and deciding.[3] We can characterize and classify both his and Ignatius's project and approach as an exercise in the self-appropriation of interiority, as the personal discovery of the dynamic structure of inquiry. Drawing, as I do in this book, upon Ignatius and Lonergan, among a number of others, I felt that the title *The Manresa Method* was an appropriate one. A method is not a plan or program; it's a normative set of operations that can anticipate unknown goals. It's a way of discovering what you do not know. A method (*met'hodos*) is a procedure or process for attaining an object; it can also be a technique or mode of reflection. It's our performing mind in action. It's not simply a mental exercise but a way of life. Method—the life of theory (*bios theoretikos*)—is less about abstraction and more about attunement as well as attention to the real. It is openness to the way things are—a heightened sensitivity; it is living in the truth of being. It seems obvious that when we've reached a certain point, we need guidance in discerning our deep desires in the labyrinth of our lives to gain much-needed insight in terms of its direction and our evolution. Lonerganian philosopher Joseph Flanagan defines method as "a procedure for discovering an unknown," which "leads to results, not only once but repeatedly."[4] Indeed, method is a form of conversion.[5]

THE MANRESA METHOD

We have the scientific method:

- Observe
- Hypothesize
- Experiment

We have the phenomenological method:

---

3. Lonergan, *Insight*; and *Method in Theology*.
4. Flanagan, *Quest for Self-Knowledge*, 4.
5. Flanagan, *Quest for Self-Knowledge*, 262.

- Indicate
- Return
- Explicate[6]

We have Lonergan's transcendental method:

- Experience
- Understand
- Judge
- Decide

It struck me that we could do with a method in the spiritual life, and we have one with Ignatius:

- Consider
- Imagine
- Contemplate

In this book I deploy a number of Ignatian themes such as consolation, desolation, conversion, consciousness, and imagination, which form the basis of the exercises and on which the saint wrote while he sojourned in Manresa. I call it the Manresa Method. When I later Googled the term, I came across an article by Irish Jesuit Brendan McManus, entitled "The Manresa Method: Praying with Your Desire." However, I mean the term in the above, much broader way. The Manresa Method is, thus, an Ignatian-inspired path and practice of examination, reflection, consideration, conversation, imagination, conversion, and contemplation. I take the method out of the explicitly Ignatian register in applying and amplifying it as it becomes embodied in and exemplified by various thinkers. To this extent, Ignatius acts as a springboard. Method, of course, should never be at the expense of mystery.

THE LABYRINTH OF LIFE

In Greek mythology, the Labyrinth was a structure devised by Daedalus, the artificer, for King Minos of Crete. Its function was to contain the minotaur—the half-man, half-bull monster, who dwelt at the center of the

---

6. See Engelland, *Phenomenology*.

maze. The minotaur would eventually be killed by Theseus, the Athenian hero. If a maze has many branches, a unicursal labyrinth has a single path to the center. Examples of such archetypal patterns can be seen on Cretan coins, while Chartres Cathedral is the most famous medieval example of this design.

Our path through life to our center may be viewed as a structured labyrinth gesturing to deeper meaning and fulfillment, fullness even. There are, assuredly, twists and turns, culs-de-sac, crossroads, and T-junctions, all of which represent the ebb and flow of human existence. Our life is a path as much as it is also a puzzle, a mystery to be lived more than a problem to be solved, something to be experienced rather than explained. The path may be circular and convoluted, but it has one way in (birth) and one way out (death). The labyrinth symbolizes our journey of spiritual growth. An itinerary is a planned route or journey; ours is an Ignatian one that goes to the center of the person and addresses his/her vital, ultimate concerns, offering spiritual signposts along the way from an array of thinkers.

Antonio Machado (1875–1939), a leading member of the Spanish literary movement known as the Generation of 1898, penned the following lines, which comprise stanza 29 of his *Proverbios y Cantares*: "Caminante, no hay camino / se hace camino al andar," which I translate as "Traveler, there is no path; you make your path by walking."[7] We are wayfarers in search of wisdom. The path appears as we set out on the search. As we glance back over our shoulders, at the trodden terrain, and see the trail that we will never tread again, we encounter the trace—a faint outline—of the presence of Someone or Something, vestiges of meaning amid the remnants and ruins. This "journey to the center of the earth," as Jules Verne called his 1864 adventure novel, is a venturing inward that can be captured by another beautiful symbol deployed by Plato in the opening lines of his *Republic*—*kateben* (I went down)—which marks the descent into the depths of ourselves; indeed, it is the same verb that is so prevalent in book 11 of the *Odyssey*, which describes the exploits of Odysseus.

On our travels through life with their travails, sometimes we're driven forward by a momentum not of our own making, a propulsion or compulsion; other times, we are dragged kicking and screaming; occasionally, we become aware that we are also drawn upwards/downwards

---

7. Machado, *Poesías completas*, 223.

(indeed, as Heraclitus recognized: the way up and the way down are the same), into "the dearest freshness deep down things"[8] where we discover the divine as the ultimate source of order in society and psyche. It is this particular pathless path of self-understanding and self-transcendence that I indicate here by expounding on such Ignatian topics as accompaniment (ch. 1), spiritual exercises (ch. 2), conversion (ch. 3), consolation (ch. 4), desolation (ch. 5), consciousness (ch. 6), imagination (ch. 7), an Ignatian interpretation of the Enneagram (ch. 8), and care for creation in its relation to the great chain of being, together with the church's social teaching, with special focus on the question of human rights (ch. 9). I do so by refracting such themes through the lenses of Ignatius himself in chapter 1; by five Jesuit thinkers in chapter 2; by philosophers Charles Taylor and Bernard Lonergan in chapter 3; by Boethius in chapter 4; by Romano Guardini, St. John of the Cross, and Gerard Manley Hopkins in chapter 5; by Ludwig Wittgenstein in chapter 6; and by depth psychologists Carl Jung, Ira Progoff, and James Hillman in chapter 7; while in chapter 8 the relationship between the Enneagram and Christianity is explored, before concluding in chapter 9 with the papal encyclical *Laudato Si'*, Catholic social teaching, and the work of E. F. Schumacher and Simone Weil, with a Platonic position on the polis being briefly articulated. The conclusion raises the vexatious issue of clerical sex abuse, together with some criticisms of the Society of Jesus articulated by one of their own and the suggestions of a remedy.

First, though, we must say something about the unique charism of the Jesuit Order. I will do so by drawing on two important documents: the *Formula of the Institute* and the *Constitutions*.

FORMULA OF THE INSTITUTE

What is known as the *Formula of the Institute of the Society of Jesus*, approved by Pope Julius III in 1540, is a foundational document, the rule, one could say, of the Jesuit Order, which sets out the structure of the Society, based on the Five Chapters of 1539.[9] *Exposcit Debitum* is the papal approval of the formula from 1550. In chapter 1, the formula refers to the Jesuit being a soldier of God beneath the banner of the cross of Christ whose job is the defense and propagation of the faith for the progress of

---

8. "God's Grandeur," in Hopkins, *Selected Poems*, 20.
9. See Portal to Jesuit Studies.

souls in Christian life and doctrine, preaching, serving those in prisons and hospitals, the education of children, giving the Spiritual Exercises, and consolation through the sacraments of the church, for the common good and God's greater glory. In essence, this is the life of the Jesuit. In chapter 2, it states that the task of all professed members of the society is to campaign for God under obedience to the pope as vicar of Christ. The fourth vow taken demonstrates this devotion to the Holy See—to be free to be missioned anywhere in the world where the need is greatest. The question each member needs to ask themselves is whether they have enough spiritual capital to complete this task/tower. The words employed are militaristic, in keeping with the time and occupation of St. Ignatius, such as "enlisted," "militia," "clad for battle." Chapter 3 stresses the importance of obedience to the father general, who is in charge of the society, and is elected by a majority of votes. Chapter 4 counsels against avarice and enjoins evangelical poverty. Moreover, the order's houses should act as a kind of seminary for the society for those who will labor in the vineyard of the Lord. Students deemed to be suitable for the society should be possessed of intellectual ability and moral character. Chapter 5 stipulates that the Divine Office be said privately, not in common or in choir. The conclusion calls this short document a sketch and plan of life to guide men who should be both humble and prudent. In short, the formula is an articulation of the purposes of the society.

THE CONSTITUTIONS

The *Constitutions of the Society of Jesus and Their Complementary Norms* is an explication of the *Formula of the Institute of the Society of Jesus* and an expression of the foundational spiritual and apostolic experiences of the first companions, which should inspire the lives of contemporary Jesuits. In 1550, Ignatius showed the constitutions he had written, originally in Spanish, to nearly all the society's professed fathers who had come to Rome and solicited their criticism. The year 1553 saw them sent to Spain for their promulgation, and final tweaks were put to them in 1558 when the entire society gathered in Rome to elect a superior general to succeed the departed Fr. Ignatius. The constitutions were confirmed with unanimous enthusiasm. They are quite a long document (the text itself, before the index, runs to over four hundred pages) and are concerned with things like the detail of the probation period, the formation of novices, electing the general, running the houses associated with the society, community life, the profession of vows, the mission and ministry of members, etc. Like the Franciscans, who describe themselves as the Order of Friars Minor (OFM), Ignatius calls his society the "least congregation,"[10] which was first approved by Pope Paul III in 1540 and dedicated to the "salvation and perfection of the members' own souls."[11] Attention is always paid "to the greater service of God."[12]

New members to the society are to make the Spiritual Exercises for a month, then work in a hospital for a month serving the sick; they are then to go on a pilgrimage for another month without money, begging door to door, getting accustomed to discomfort (and keeping the fact that they are a member of the society secret). Another month after this experiment will be spent in humble employment, and another month is to be spent teaching Christian doctrine to boys. This is a period of probation. After these two years of novitiate, an oblation of three vows is taken. The charism of the society is anchored in the Spiritual Exercises.[13] Emphasis is put on enculturated proclamation of the gospel through (interfaith) dialogue with followers of other religions, as well as on "the faith that seeks justice."[14] The objective is, to repeat, "to benefit their own souls and those of their neighbour."[15] Value is placed on their vocation; "motivated by the internal law of love, will more and more embrace our way of proceeding,"[16] as Ignatius calls it. The importance of "discerning love"[17] is highlighted, as well as "the mystical dimension of Christian faith and of our spirituality,"[18] not forgetting discernment over concrete choices. What is looked for is "the balanced development of the spiritual, intellectual, and affective life"; through such balance, "the maturity of the whole person will be achieved."[19] *Cura personalis*. Such a maturational process within the society will see "every trace of egoism removed."[20] In terms of

10. Padberg, *Constitutions*, 23.
11. Padberg, *Constitutions*, 24.
12. Padberg, *Constitutions*, 25.
13. Padberg, *Constitutions*, 59.
14. Padberg, *Constitutions*, 60.
15. Padberg, *Constitutions*, 132.
16. Padberg, *Constitutions*, 142.
17. Padberg, *Constitutions*, 143.
18. Padberg, *Constitutions*, 144.
19. Padberg, *Constitutions*, 145.
20. Padberg, *Constitutions*, 145.

study, there will be lectures in languages, logic, moral philosophy, metaphysics, and Sacred Scripture,[21] as well as an awareness of transcendent values. Scholastics should study philosophy for at least two years, while four years should be devoted to theology (though the last year might see a pastoral application).[22] Those who show academic aptitude should continue to higher (postgraduate) degrees. And one modern language (other than one's native tongue) is stipulated.[23] The purpose of all these studies is "to train Jesuits to proclaim and transmit the truth revealed in Christ and entrusted to the Church."[24] Jesuits must also show "solidarity with the poor."[25] The young Jesuit will also need to gain practice in giving the Spiritual Exercises to others, as it is a "spiritual weapon" to be deployed accordingly.[26] In philosophy, the doctrine of Aristotle "should be followed," just as the Scholastic doctrine of St. Thomas is mandated in theology.[27] This traditional Aristotelian Thomism characterizes both the Jesuits and the Dominicans (and arguably the Carmelites) and stands in marked contrast to the Platonic Augustinianism of the Franciscans. Spiritual direction is likewise required. By the time one is to pronounce the final four vows, the candidate should have spent at least ten full years in the society and be "outstanding in the following of Christ."[28] To be admitted to solemn profession, the candidate must have obtained an outstanding level of virtue, sound judgment, and prudence; have a talent for the society's ministries as demonstrated for at least three years; possess complete availability and mobility for mission and ministry; and have reached an outstanding (this word is used a number of times) level of learning, preferably equipped with a higher degree; he will also not be one who will strive for promotion to prelacy or seek any preferment.[29] He will be driven on, rather, by love and will live more for Christ and his body, which is the church.[30] The embrace of obedience is singled out as a distinctive charism conferred/bestowed by God and the society but is

21. Padberg, *Constitutions*, 149.
22. Padberg, *Constitutions*, 153.
23. Padberg, *Constitutions*, 155.
24. Padberg, *Constitutions*, 156.
25. Padberg, *Constitutions*, 168.
26. Padberg, *Constitutions*, 172.
27. Padberg, *Constitutions*, 185.
28. Padberg, *Constitutions*, 200.
29. Padberg, *Constitutions*, 209.
30. Padberg, *Constitutions*, 201.

always an act of faith and freedom.[31] Jesuits, moreover, preach in poverty, following the example set by Our Lord. The preferential option for the poor has been proposed by the church and one "which the Society wishes to make its own."[32] What is stressed is the "service of faith and the promotion of justice" and to "find God in all things."[33] The Jesuit apostle goes forth from his experience of the Spiritual Exercises, which is a school of prayer, as a man called to be "a contemplative in action."[34] He will spend at least an hour a day in prayer (mental or vocal), attend daily celebration of the Eucharist, and make the twice-daily examen of consciousness.[35] The Jesuit will also be devoted to the Sacred Heart of Jesus. All the above, for, as the *Constitutions*' concluding sentence puts it, "the praise and service of our God and Lord Jesus Christ, and the help of souls."[36]

This should provide a comprehensive enough précis and picture of the type of society that Ignatius envisaged, as well as what is looked for in a budding Jesuit. In the words of Bernard McGinn, Ignatian spirituality, in short, is a "mysticism of apostolic service."[37] Let us now look at the various spiritual influences on Ignatius and his school of spirituality.

FRANCISCAN INFLUENCES

If it was a Franciscan pope—Clement XIV (1705–74)—who suppressed the Jesuit Order, it took a Jesuit pope (Jorge Mario Bergoglio) to assume the name of Francis after the founder of the Franciscans. The arrival of the Jesuits on the religious scene in Europe in 1540 sparked much jealousy and animosity among various religious groups, and rivalry quickly set in. Historically, there has always been some conflict (mainly of a theological nature) between the Jesuits and the Dominicans, a controversy thought to have begun in 1581 when the Spanish Jesuit Prudencio de Montemayor defended certain theses on grace that had been vigorously attacked by the Dominican Domingo Bañez. In 1607, an exasperated Pope Paul V informed the two parties that the name-calling between the two orders

---

31. Padberg, *Constitutions*, 222.
32. Padberg, *Constitutions*, 229.
33. Padberg, *Constitutions*, 261.
34. Padberg, *Constitutions*, 262.
35. Padberg, *Constitutions*, 264.
36. Padberg, *Constitutions*, 418.
37. McGinn, *Mysticism in the Golden Age*, 62.

had to stop. The Dominican Melchior Cano (1509[?]–60) defeated the wish of the Jesuits to establish themselves in Salamanca.[38]

There are some similarities between the Jesuits and Order of Friars Minor (Franciscans). Both Ignatius and Francis came from wealthy families of the minor nobility. Both founded missionary orders. Both, before their conversions, enjoyed fancy clothes, gambling, womanizing, and fighting. In terms of spirituality, both encouraged engaging the senses and imagination in contemplating scenes from the Gospels. The Franciscan St. Bonaventure had employed the discernment of spirits centuries before Ignatius (influenced by Bernardino of Siena, who was an Italian Franciscan friar); the latter, indeed, had *HIS* as his emblem before it became the logo of the Jesuit Order.[39] Both orders were missionary and cared for the poor and marginalized, though Jesuits were known as the educators and spiritual directors of Europe shortly after their inception. The phrase "contemplatives in mission," so reminiscent of the Ignatian "contemplatives in action," was coined by Bernardino (1380–1444). One contemporary author compared the Spiritual Exercises of Ignatius with those of Francis of Assisi through Bonaventure's life of St. Francis, *The Major Life of St. Francis*, where Bonaventure writes of the "striking similarities" between them.[40] Both Francis and Ignatius withdrew to pray—Francis to a grotto, Ignatius to a river and cave (the Cardoner near Manresa). If Bonaventure delineates Francis's life according to three stages—purgation, illumination, and perfection (unity)—Ignatius's exercises are divided into four weeks but structured within the same three stages of the spiritual life; week one being the purgative, week two corresponding to the illuminative, and weeks three and four inviting transforming union. Both orders have active-contemplative dimensions. What the poetic canticle is to St. Francis, the *contemplatio* (in the exercises) is to St. Ignatius. When recuperating on his bed from battle after a cannonball shattered his leg (1521), Ignatius fantasized about all the good deeds he would do like St. Francis and St. Dominic. Ignatius sought to imitate Francis; indeed, there were many Franciscan influences that marked Ignatius's boyhood in Azpeitia. An observant Franciscan from the Convent of Bermeo (Biscay) came to Loyola to receive two ladies as tertiaries in the order, the elder of whom (Doña Maria) was Ignatius's cousin. There was a Franciscan friary (the Convent of the Immaculate Conception) in Azpeitia. Her profession

38. Volz, "Melchior Cano."
39. Casey, "Was St. Ignatius a Franciscan?"
40. Purfield, "Call and Response."

ceremony was attended by Martin de Segura, a Franciscan of the Cisnerian reform. Ignatius brokered reconciliation between his brother Don Martín with the Franciscans of Azpeitia. Ignatius imitated Francis's love of the humanity of Jesus and Lady Poverty. And like Francis, Ignatius also stripped off his clothes and put on a sackcloth of penance as he ventured forth from Montserrat monastery to visit the poor and sick in hospitals (at the time he was writing his *Constitutions*, Ignatius consulted the constitutions of the Friars Minor). Like Francis's paean of praise and prayer to sun, moon, and stars, Ignatius would emphasize finding God in *all* things, including nature. Ignatius loved to look at the stars. Both men enjoyed the solitude and beauty of the countryside. Both orders highlight the importance of the renewal and reform of the church. There is a mutual respect and admiration between the two orders. Pope Francis's encyclical *Fratelli Tutti* ("On Fraternity and Social Friendship") from 2020 is Franciscan at heart with his interest in the care of creation and the climate crisis. In a talk on November 6, 2019, at Boston College, Franco Mormando made some historical and biographical connections between Francis and Ignatius, one of which was that St. Francis Borgia, SJ, ordered Franciscan depictions in the Church of the Gesú, which is the mother church of the Society of St. Jesus. He cited the influence of Franciscan Cardinal Ximenez de Cisneros on the Ignatian exercises, especially with regard to the composition of place and application of the senses (originally derived from Franciscan image theory; the Franciscans popularized the living nativity scene and the visual Stations of the Cross). He stated further that Ignatius's confessor in Rome was a Franciscan.[41]

So, we can see from the above the many commonalities between the Jesuits and Franciscans even if, it is also true to say, there are some quite substantial differences too that can't be underestimated. One comment that is worth citing: in an interview, Franciscan sister and scientist Ilia Delio remarked: "One can see why Teilhard spoke of Franciscan theology as the 'theology of the future'!"[42]

CARMELITE CROSSOVERS

I will cite just four Carmelite crossovers with Ignatian spirituality. First, Hans Urs von Balthasar (who spent most of his life as a Jesuit) wrote *Two*

---

41. Mormando, "Ignatius the Franciscan."
42. Delio, "Atonement and Evolution."

Sisters in the Spirit: Thérèse of Lisieux and Elizabeth of the Trinity, which, as the title makes clear, concerns itself with these two Carmelite nuns, whom he praises for their contributions to and insights into the contemplative life. Balthasar writes that "representatives of other [religious] orders and of the secular clergy were able to feel at home and close to the Carmelites."[43] In this work, he brings these two saints together, believing that no one "is so much himself as the saint, who disposes himself to God's plan for which he is prepared to surrender his whole being, body, soul and spirit."[44] Second, Teresa of Ávila was influenced by Ignatius's Spiritual Exercises and consulted with Jesuit fathers who had a house in Ávila, one of whom greatly encouraged her in spiritual direction—Fr. Juan de Pradanos.[45] Third, theologian John Betz (who was one of the translators of Jesuit philosopher and theologian Erich Przywara's *Analogia Entis*) wrote to me, saying, "It's shocking but true, that Przywara's immensely complicated *Analogia* is really about Therese's way and that combined with the method of her sister in Carmel, Elizabeth." Fourth, the great Carmelite philosopher Edith Stein's confessor and confidante was none other than Erich Przywara, SJ, who emphasized the role that an early reading of Ignatius's exercises had "on the spiritually questing young soul."[46] Tyler goes on to say that Carmelite John of the Cross's anthropology of the symbolic dark night grasps the psychological dimension as much as his contemporary Ignatius Loyola.[47] The dark night is, in Tyler's words, "no cold wet Northern night" but "the warm erotic, sensual Southern night full of the smells, sounds and touches of a hot land baked by sun during the day and now at peace and rest in itself."[48]

Another interesting connection to note is the presence of Catholic philosopher Rudolf Allers (1883–1963), who was associated with psychoanalysis, then Adlerian psychology, before distancing himself from both. Allers was a mentor to both Viktor Frankl and Balthasar as well as a friend to Edith Stein. Psychotherapist and playwright Elizabeth Clark-Stern wrote a play, *Timeless Night*, based on Frankl and Stein, which has them meet in an old storage shed in Auschwitz to discuss the deepest longing of their souls before the dawn that brings liberation or

---

43. Balthasar, *Two Sisters in Spirit*, 12.
44. Balthasar, *Two Sisters in Spirit*, 21.
45. McLean, *Towards Mystical Union*, 62.
46. Tyler, *Living Philosophy of Stein*, 27.
47. Tyler, *Living Philosophy of Stein*, 136.
48. Tyler, *Living Philosophy of Stein*, 138.

extermination. The play premiered on February 1, 2014, in Washington, DC.

There has also been a critique of Ignatian spirituality from David Torkington, who describes himself as a spiritual theologian in a blog post entitled "Ignatian and Carmelite Spirituality—Complementary or Contradictory," where he favors Carmelite spirituality. Even though it reads, unfortunately, more like a rant, I wanted to tackle it head-on, as I think it deserves a robust response. I summarize below the main points of his tirade:

- There is no true discernment in the exercises, as they are based not on mystical theology but human anthropology (it is anthropocentric, not theocentric). He maintains that the Jesuits have no mystical tradition.
- Jesuits have rejected contemplative prayer.
- Ignatian spirituality is nothing more than devout humanism.
- The exercises are a beginner's guide to prayer and not a pathway to union with God, as they exclude mystical theology.
- Jesuits have no knowledge of the mystical way such as one finds in the "great Carmelite saints."
- What Ignatius calls contemplation is really (only) meditation.
- Despite their reputation for intellectual brilliance "that dazzles their devotees, Jesuits are by training no more than spiritual adolescents. They are therefore unable to lead and guide others into contemplative prayer that is totally alien to their tradition."
- Jesuits make others feel spiritually inferior.
- For four hundred years Jesuits have been preventing the Holy Spirit from raising up great saints.
- Jesuits have spent their time harnessing "their own unpurified mental and emotional powers to misunderstand and misapply whatever the current secular 'wisdom of the world' happens to be for the benefit of the Church, and often . . . with disastrous consequences."
- Ignatian spirituality "is all but totally different from the Carmelite Mystical Spirituality that is needed more today than at any time before."

- Ignatian spirituality represents the Stoic philosophical tradition.[49]

What are we to make of this? The first thing to note is that Torkington offers absolutely no scholarship to back up his claims. Indeed, he doesn't cite any academic articles or even citations from the exercises themselves, which is extraordinary. Moreover, he seems to be writing with a high-feeling tone. One would have to wonder whether an unconscious complex is being triggered. What is his motivation here? It reads like a very personal and embittered invective. To try to answer some of his outlandish claims: First, it is true that some Jesuit theologians such as Karl Rahner and Bernard Lonergan start from a philosophical anthropology; others, like Hans Urs von Balthasar, do not. But why does this matter, as both perspectives lead to God? It is possibly true that a traditional Thomist might object, but at least one would hope he would do so philosophically rather than emotionally. Second, one might very well argue that Ignatian spirituality comes from the Stoic philosophical tradition, but in being Christianized the exercises represent a significant departure from this tradition of thought. Third, to say that the Jesuits have no mystical tradition is absurd, as I have made clear in my book *Ignatian Mysticism*, to which I would refer the reader. It could be the case that Torkington doesn't understand the mysticism that animates the exercises—has he even read them or experienced them firsthand? It is doubtful from what he has written. Perhaps Ignatian mysticism is different from the mysticism of other religious orders, and this has confused him. It is hard to know. Fourth, yes, there is a humanism running through Ignatian spirituality, but it is a Christian humanism, one that has contemplative prayer at its center. It is hard to take Torkington seriously here, to be honest. Fifth, it is true that, in the main, the exercises were addressed in Ignatius's time to young men entering the society, but one would have to ask Bernard Lonergan, Karl Rahner, Henri de Lubac, Hans Urs von Balthasar, and Pierre Teilhard de Chardin, to name but a few of the greatest theologians of the twentieth century schooled in the Spiritual Exercises, whether they think the exercises are a "beginner's guide." Many Carmelites have been impressed and guided deeply by Jesuit confessors into the heart of contemplative prayer and transforming union. It is a shame Torkington seems to want to pit one mystical pathway over another. Sixth, Ignatius does distinguish between meditation and contemplation in the exercises. People use these terms in all sorts of different ways; conceptual confusion can abound

---

49. Torkington, "Ignatian and Carmelite Spirituality."

due to different language games being deployed, as Wittgenstein makes clear. Seventh, as to the ad hominem comment about Jesuits making people feel intellectually inferior, I have little doubt Torkington may well feel intellectually inferior. Eighth, what can one say to his assertion that the Jesuits are actively preventing the Holy Spirit doing his work and that by implication Jesuits suffer from some sort of mental disorder? It is so bizarre that one must simply pass over it in silence. Perhaps this is a projection from Torkington, in which case it would be kinder not to say anything else. Perhaps he has experienced desolation at the hands of Jesuits; perhaps it is a projection from an unintegrated shadow. It is saddening that a self-described spiritual theologian feels the need to lambast in the most extraordinarily unintellectual and un-Christian way another mystical tradition in the church. In Ignatian terms, it is evident that the bad spirit is at work. I don't suppose his views are accepted or taken too seriously by Jesuits or by Carmelites, for that matter. It is certainly a missed opportunity for creative dialogue and constructive disagreement between these two great orders. Indeed, both the Jesuit and Carmelite Orders derive from the soil and soul of sixteenth-century Spain and have much in common even if their emphasis and language differ. To counter the above, I refer the reader to a talk from the Carmelite Institute of North America, where the two spiritualities are discussed, in contrast to Torkington, both reasonably and responsibly.[50]

A CARTHUSIAN LINK

Let us note, en passant, that the Jesuits have a unique relationship with the Carthusian Order, which not many people know about. St. Ignatius wanted to join the Carthusians after his conversion. He held the order in high esteem. When writing the *Constitutions* for the Society of Jesus, Ignatius discouraged any Jesuit from transferring to a different order; the only exception was to the Carthusians.[51]

---

50. McDermott and Fitzgerald, "Teresian and Ignatian Spiritualities."
51. Minnich, "Early Jesuits' Relations."

IGNATIAN WOMEN

The Ignatian charism has many congregations. We may mention the following female religious orders that are indebted to Ignatian spirituality: the Congregation of Jesus (CSJ) founded in 1609 (formerly known as the Sisters of St. Joseph), the Congregation of Saint Joseph (CSJ) founded in 1650, the Congregation of the Religious of the Virgin Mary (RVM) founded in 1684, the Society of the Sacred Heart of Jesus (RSCJ) founded in 1800 (formerly the Madams of the Sacred Heart), the Congregation of the Religious of Jesus and Mary (RJM) founded in 1818, the Faithful Companions of Jesus (FCJ) founded in 1820, the Congregation of Our Lady of the Retreat in the Cenacle (RC) founded in 1826, the Sisters of St. Joseph of the Apparition (SJA) founded in 1841, the Missionary Sisters of the Sacred Heart of Jesus (MSC) founded in 1877, the Handmaids of the Sacred Heart of Jesus (ACJ) founded in 1877, the Missionary Sisters of St. Peter Claver founded in 1894, La Xavière founded in 1921, and the Servants of the Lord and the Virgin of Matara (the Serviadoras or SSVM) founded in 1988. The Institute of the Blessed Virgin Mary, whose members are commonly known as the Loreto Sisters (IBVM), founded in 1609 by Englishwoman Mary Ward, was hugely inspired by the Spiritual Exercises of St. Ignatius Loyola.

THE ORATORIANS

The Catholic Church seems to be increasingly polarized between progressives and conservatives. It is hard for the center to hold. Most hover hermeneutically in the middle space. The Jesuits are seen by many (especially traditionalists) as liberals, more so in the light of Pope Francis's decision to restrict the Tridentine Mass in his apostolic letter of *Traditionis Custodes*, issued motu proprio and promulgated on July 16, 2021. The Oratorians, founded by St. Philip Neri in the sixteenth century (the same century as St. Ignatius), with St. John Henry Newman being its most famous member, continue to celebrate the Latin Mass while also offering the Novus Ordo (Mass of Paul VI). They have sung Vespers, hymned in Gregorian chant, and emphasize the place of liturgical beauty. In the United Kingdom, aside from established houses in Birmingham, London, and Oxford, new communities have sprung up in Manchester, York, Cardiff, and Bournemouth. In Dublin (Ireland), there is an oratory in formation at St. Kevin's Church on Harrington Street. Like the Jesuits, Oratorians do not seek ecclesiastical preferment (their phrase is *amare nosciri* [love to be unknown]), and also like the Jesuits they combine the active and contemplative life. They too have their brand of spiritual exercises, which is the distinguishing mark of the secular oratory. Contrasted with the Ignatian exercises, the Oratorian exercises include mental prayer, spiritual reading, cultural and intellectual endeavors, convivial conversation, discourse on the lives of the saints, moral exhortation (virtue ethics), etc. Theirs is a school of prayer, known for emphasizing the importance of sacramental confession, spiritual direction, eucharistic devotion, splendor in liturgy, joyful piety, intellectual rigor, communal prayer, personal sanctity, a blend of tradition and adaptability, and the integration of faith and reason. Unlike the Jesuits, who are a missioned order and always *on the road*, the Oratorians promise to remain in the community they join for the rest of their lives (much like monks), with their room being their *nido* (nest).

In his dissertation "Newman the Priest," the late Dom Placid Murray, OSB, of Glenstal Abbey (whom I knew), records St. John Henry Newman's observations and comments on the differences between the Oratorians and the Jesuits.[52] Newman makes the point that the Oratorian is almost the reverse of the Jesuit, contrasting obedience to the superior, characteristic of the Jesuits, to the personal influence of the Oratorian. I have summarized Newman's main points in these fifteen relevant pages thus:

- St. Philip Neri's undertaking is more original than anything in the Rule of St. Ignatius—the oratory is a return to the very first form of Christianity (corrective: St. Ignatius didn't write a rule as such).

- By contrast to the Jesuit's vows, the Oratorian takes none. St. Philip wrote no constitutions—the Oratorian's rule is the Rule of St. Philip himself. St. Philip formed a community without vows and almost without rules. An Oratorian is a law unto himself.

- The outward look of a Jesuit, showing the influence of the long Spiritual Exercises and the military usages of their tradition, depicts someone whose "look is imposing, whose speech is measured." He is a "staid and upright figure, his eyes downcast or uplifted, his

---

52. My thanks to Fr. Gerard Deighan for bringing this to my attention and to Dom Henry O'Shea of Glenstal Abbey for sending me Murray's dissertation. See Murray, "Newman the Priest," 202–16.

abstracted countenance; and his high biretta" is in contrast to the Oratorian, who "sits in an easy chair, in a lounging posture, one hand stretched on a table, with bright sparkling eyes and a merry countenance."[53] The "pleasant, brightfaced, modest looking youths" who are the Oratorians have nothing of "the external gravity, composed attitude and reserve of a Jesuit novice."[54]

- The Jesuit "does not know what tact is, cannot enter into the minds of others, and is apt to blunder in most important matters from this life of habit of mechanical obedience to a Superior and a system."[55] It's important to remind the reader that Newman's oratory papers, from which these quotations come, were penned in January/February of 1848. Aside from certain gifted men such as Francis Xavier, Newman contends, there is in the Jesuit a want of sagacity and mental dexterity in meeting the age. The founder of the Jesuits, he reminds us, was a soldier, and their order is a military body. He writes: "They are the Knight Templars of modern history." These hard-working and devout Jesuits "are often little more than mechanical instruments."[56] Their renown is far higher than that of a humble oratory.

- Just as the Rosary is to the Dominican, the scapular to the Carmelite, and the "wonderful Exercises"[57] are to the Jesuit, the oratory is distinguished by the exercises of St. Philip. Nowhere does Newman find among the Oratorians of the seventeenth century "traces of the use of the Exercises of St Ignatius in their retreats."[58]

- Music is a study in the oratory whereas it is excluded from the occupation of the Jesuit.

- The Jesuits do not know the word "home"—they are strangers and pilgrims upon earth whereas the word *nido* produces a soothing influence and arouses fraternal feeling in the heart of an Oratorian. The Jesuit meets and parts with Jesuit "in resigned, mortified, I will

---

53. Murray, "Newman the Priest," 207.
54. Murray, "Newman the Priest," 208.
55. Murray, "Newman the Priest," 210.
56. Murray, "Newman the Priest," 210.
57. Murray, "Newman the Priest," 212.
58. Murray, "Newman the Priest," 212.

add, cold spirit, which becomes those who have emphatically put off all earthly feelings and ties."[59]

Newman is certainly forthright here, and his slant on the subject is evident. Whether it is accurate is another matter. So, while Newman "never warmed to the idea of becoming a Dominican,"[60] considering them intellectual but too technical, doctrinaire, and too much of a closed school, and despite having been acquainted with and practiced the exercises, according to Murray, making a real attempt at apprenticeship, indeed of discipleship, he abandoned interest in the Jesuits later.[61] Newman did write a memorandum on the exercises, but there was "nothing original in these notes" and he did not consider the Ignatian exercises as suitable for Oratorian spirituality.[62] Newman was on friendly terms with the Jesuits, whom he genuinely admired, but never took steps to apply for admission to the society, despite an article published in *The Quarterly Review* that erroneously asserted that he had applied but was refused.[63] What stopped him was a personal feeling, contends Murray, which he describes as "that of safeguarding his own personality."[64] Murray transcribes Newman's words from a letter written to J. D. Dalgairns on December 31, 1846: "As—Jesuit, e.g., no one would know that I was speaking my own words."[65] Newman had already compared the Jesuits to the Greek phalanx and the Oratorian to the Roman legionary. Though Newman was favorably disposed to the Vincentians, he shrank from what he considered "Dominican rigorism and Jesuit corporate conformism."[66] Some, such as English Oratorian and Newman scholar Fr. Henry Tristram, wonder why Newman didn't become a Benedictine.[67]

---

59. Murray, "Newman the Priest," 215.
60. Murray, "Newman the Priest," 78.
61. Murray, "Newman the Priest," 79.
62. Murray, "Newman the Priest," 79.
63. Murray, "Newman the Priest," 79–80.
64. Murray, "Newman the Priest," 80.
65. Murray, "Newman the Priest," 80.
66. Murray, "Newman the Priest," 81.
67. Murray, "Newman the Priest," 82.

CHAPTER ONE

Pilgrim's Path
Accompanying Ignatius of Loyola

> The geographical pilgrimage is the symbolic
> acting out of an inner journey.
> THOMAS MERTON, *MYSTICS AND ZEN MASTERS*

WE SET OFF ON our pilgrim path with Ignatius as we explore the journey he took as reflected in his autobiography and spiritual diary. Ignatius was born in Loyola on October 23, 1491, the son of the lord of Loyola, Beltrán Ibáñez de Oñaz, and of Marina Sánchez de Licona, member of an important Biscayan family, in the municipality of Azpeitia, in the Basque Country. Ignatius died on July 31, 1556, in Rome. The periods and places below are symbolic stages of an interior journey he made in search of the Absolute. We follow in the footsteps of the pilgrim (as he referred to himself) known in history as Iñigo Lopez de Loyola, founder of the Society of Jesus.[1]

The human person is a pilgrim (*homo viator*), passing through the land. The word "pilgrimage" comes from the Latin word *peregrinus*, which means a person wandering the earth in exile, in search of a spiritual homeland. The true purpose of pilgrimage is to be alert, attentive, awake to the holy hidden in the prairies, primroses, and proverbial thornbushes.

---

1. See the app by Ballacer, *Jesuit Pilgrimage*, which I draw on here.

A pilgrimage puts us in the direction of spiritual desire. Sacred sites and spaces greet us; we begin to see the world through sacramental senses, Easter eyes, in childlike wonder and innocence.

GLOSSARY

Along the way, Ignatius incorporates certain terms with which we must become acquainted in order to understand his spirituality better. Here are some of them:

- Attachments or affections (*afecciones*): Refers to feelings of liking/disliking that well up in the heart and can impede objective judgment, altering our perception of reality
- Application of the senses (*traer los sentidos*): This process of bringing the senses to bear is a method wherein one tries to imagine a Gospel scene with all the sensual details (sounds and colors, etc.), to feel part of it and emotionally engaged.
- Colloquy (*coloquio*): Indicates a familiar conversation (with Jesus, for example), which usually occurs at the culmination of an exercise
- Composition (*composición*): A preliminary prayer whereby one "composes" oneself by calling to mind the scene being contemplated
- Consolations (*consolaciones*): The gratuitous God-given spiritual state of joy (interior movements of the soul leading to becoming enflamed with love of the Creator; a state of being more than a feeling or emotion, a lens through which we see creation with God's eyes)
- Contemplation: Here imagination unlocks the door and leads to intimate receptive prayer of the heart. Meditation involves pondering (usually) on the divine persons.
- Desolation: (*desolación*): The spiritual state of torpor and tepidity; darkness of soul; inner disturbance (from the Latin *desolatus*, meaning "to leave alone")
- Examen of consciousness: A method of mindful self-reflection and practice of noticing and self-correction
- Exercises: Ignatius intended the full form for a restricted number of individuals, usually over a month's period, residentially. The

Spiritual Exercises can also be done in daily life (the nineteenth annotated version).[2]
- Feel (*sentir*): A favorite word of Ignatius's, meant to accentuate being aware of
- Spirits (*espíritus*): A term dating back to the Desert Fathers that refers to various psychological phenomena, roughly to good and bad inner movements, motions, or moods

IGNATIUS'S AUTOBIOGRAPHY

Ignatius's reminiscences, or the autobiography (which they are also known as), were dictated to and written down by Luis Gonçalves Câmara, SJ (1519–75), a faithful Portuguese scribe of the memoirs. Mention must be made here also of Jerónimo Nadal, SJ (1507–80), a close collaborator of Ignatius who more than anyone was responsible for institutionalizing the Society of Jesus, which at the time was seen as an innovative, even revolutionary, radical order of religious life.[3] The autobiography was written while Ignatius, who was initially reticent about the project, was still alive. The most compelling way to read it is as sapiential literature, as the matrix of a spiritual process. It will be useful to compare the experience of Ignatius with our own experience and spiritual autobiography that we can begin to write.

It was on August 4, on a Friday morning in the year 1553, when Ignatius gave an account of his soul, highlighting one particular feature/defect: the voice of vainglory, which had troubled him for two years. Ignatius's autobiography would be the story of a pilgrim soul of which he would give an account—a long examen, if you like. Written in the third person, it was begun in August of 1553 and completed on October 20, 1555. All commentators point to Manresa as being the time of intense self-reflection in Ignatius's life.

MY PILGRIMAGE

My own Ignatian pilgrimage began in the summer of 2022 when I arrived in Bilbao Airport before departing for Loyola and staying in the Centro

2. Center for Ignatian Spirituality, "19th Annotation."
3. See Ignatius, *Personal Writings*.

Arrupe on Wednesday, July 27, just a few days before my birthday. Our group visited the Santa Casa (house of Loyola) the following day for a tour and attended Mass in the Chapel of Conversion; later that day, we walked to Azpeitia via the house of Mara de Garín. On Friday, we went for a walk along the river to Azkoitia to visit the house of Brother Garate and the hermitage of Olatz. On Saturday, we traveled by coach to Montserrat via Pamplona and arrived in the evening at Hotel Abat Cisneros where the Eucharist was celebrated. On Sunday, July 31, on the Feast of St. Ignatius, we went to Mass in the Basilica, and Vespers took place in the evening. The following day, we did a tour of Ignatian Barcelona and on Tuesday left for Manresa, visiting a number of sacred sites, including the river Cardoner, the Mystics' Monument viewpoint, and the famous cave (Santa Cova). Let's start our journey and journaling with Ignatius, one of life's most famous pilgrims, beginning in Loyola—the birthplace of the future saint. On the way, we can mull over the series of existential questions Pope Francis addresses in his 2024 encyclical letter of August 24, "*Dilexit Nos*: On the Human and Divine Love of the Heart of Jesus Christ":

> Instead of running after superficial satisfactions and playing a role for the benefit of others, we would do better to think about the really important questions in life. Who am I, really? What am I looking for? What direction do I want to give my life, my decisions and my actions? Why and for what purpose am I in this world? How do I want to look back on my life once it ends? What meaning do I want to give all my experiences? Who do I want to be for others? What am I for God? All these questions lead us back to the heart.[4]

LOYOLA: 1491

Ignatius was born in Loyola Tower House in 1491—the house is now hidden behind sanctuary walls. Composition of place: see yourself standing in front of the Sanctuary of Loyola, an architectural complex constructed around the tower house of the Loyola family. It looks like a fortress. In this castle Ignatius imagined carrying out great knightly deeds. Born into a noble family, Iñigo was the youngest of thirteen siblings. His mother died when he was very young. His father, Beltrán, was one of the local landlords with good connections in the Spanish court. Two women

---

4. Francis, *Dilexit Nos*, para. 8.

brought him up: Magdalena de Araoz (his brother Martin's wife) and María Garín (the blacksmith's wife).

You will need a notebook/journal to take part in the exercises below, which can be done individually or in a group.

Exercise

Reflect on your own childhood.

- What persons and places shaped you?
- How so?
- What were the most significant events of your early life?

AZPEITIA: 1491

Tradition has it that Ignatius was baptized in the parish church of San Sebastián de Soreasu in 1491.

ARÉVALO: 1507–17

Iñigo lived here from age sixteen to twenty-six, where he grew from a boy into a man. Imagine Iñigo being trained in courtly ways, in the service of Juan Velázquez de Cuéllar, chief accountant of the kingdom of Castille. When the Velázquez family fell out of favor, Iñigo left Arévalo to find his own way. The world was his cloister. "Until the age of twenty-six he was a man given up to the vanities of the world, and his chief delight used to be in the exercise of arms, with a great and vain desire to gain honour."[5]

Exercise

- Ignatius recorded that his main vice was vanity. What's your chief personality fault?
- How did you like to pass the time in your late teenage and early manhood years?

5. Ignatius, *Personal Writings*, 13.

- What stands out for you from this decade in your life? Were you happy?
- What consoled you?
- What, if anything, brought you desolation?

PAMPLONA: THE BATTLE OF PAMPLONA, 1521

Iñigo defended the fortress against the French forces who were fighting for the pro-independence party of Navarre. The Spaniards, who were outnumbered, were on the point of surrendering, but Iñigo urged them to fight on, for honor rather than victory. It was at this moment that a cannonball struck his leg, leaving it shattered. His French adversaries spared his life, as they admired his bravery, and transported him to his birthplace in Loyola.

> And so, being in a stronghold which the French were attacking, and with everyone being of the opinion they should give themselves up and save their lives (for they saw clearly that they should not defend themselves), he gave so many arguments that even then he persuaded him to make a defence, though against the opinion of all the knights. These, however, were taking heart at his spirit and vigour. And, the day having come when the attack was expected, he made his confession with one of those companions of his in arms. And, after the attack had lasted a good time, a shot hit him in one leg, completely shattering it for him; and because the ball passed between both legs, the other was badly wounded too.[6]

Exercise

- What blows of fate have you experienced in life?
- What has been your *cannonball moment*?[7]
- When and how did you turn an obstacle into an opportunity, transform a tragedy into a triumph, and find some meaning in unavoidable suffering?

---

6. Ignatius, *Personal Writings*, 13.
7. See Clayton, *Cannonball Moments*.

LOYOLA, 1521: CONVALESCENCE AND CONVERSION

In your mind's eye, see Ignatius in his thirties wounded in body and soul, given to games of arms and women, cared for by his family. In the midst of boredom and brokenness, and in great pain, with his ambitions squashed, aimless, rudderless in life, in anguish, only that now, he is experiencing an inner combat—a fight with himself. "And because he was much given to reading worldly and false books, which they normally call 'tales of chivalry', he asked, once he was feeling well, that they give him some of these to pass the time. But in that house, none of those books which he normally read could be found, and so they gave him a life of Christ and a book of the lives of the saints."[8] While reading he would stop to think, reasoning with himself: How would it be if I did this which St. Francis did, and this which St. Dominic did? "When he was thinking about that worldly stuff, he would take much delight, but when he left it aside after getting tired, he would find himself dry and discontented. But when going about Jerusalem barefoot . . . and about doing all the other rigours he was seeing the saints had done, not only was he to be consoled while in such thoughts, but he would remain content and happy even having left them aside . . . little by little coming to know the difference in kind of spirits that were stirring: the one from the devil, and the other from God."[9]

Exercise

- Were you ever very sick? If so, what was that like for you?
- Have you experienced any times of trial where you floundered rather than flourished?
- Name *three* books that have helped or healed you in life (bibliotherapy), which had a meaningful or positive impact/influence, which changed you for the better. How did they?

---

8. Ignatius, *Personal Writings*, 14.
9. Ignatius, *Personal Writings*, 15.

ARÁNTZAZU (YEAR UNKNOWN)

A center of Marian devotion after the Virgin appeared in 1468, Iñigo experienced a visitation one night in which he saw a likeness of Our Lady with the child Jesus, "at the sight of which, he received a very extraordinary consolation."[10] He was now on his way to Jerusalem and so he held a prayer vigil before the image of Our Lady. "Praying that night so as to draw new strength for his journey, he left his brother in Oñate at the house of a sister whom he was going to visit, and he himself went off to Navarrete."[11]

Exercise

- Do you recall a time when you set out on a new path/adventure?
- How did you fare?
- What became of it and you?

MONTSERRAT: 1522

Ignatius mounts his mule and engages a Moor in dialogue that touched on the topic of Our Lady. The Moor doubted Mary had remained a virgin. This aroused anger in Ignatius, who wished to go after him and stab him for what he had said. He decided "to let the mule go on a loose rein up to the points where the roads divided. And if the mule went along the town road, he would look for the Moor and stab him; and if it didn't go towards the town but went along the main road, he'd leave him be.... The mule took the main road."[12]

Exercise

- How do you make decisions? Arbitrarily, by chance and the toss of a coin, or by consideration—thinking things through and listing your options and choices, the pros and cons?

---

10. Ignatius, *Personal Writings*, 16.
11. Ignatius, *Personal Writings*, 18.
12. Ignatius, *Personal Writings*, 19.

You are surrounded by a majestic mountain range in the heart of Catalonia, near Barcelona. Its rugged ridges, which are visible from a great distance, explain the name—Montserrat means "serrated." It is well known as the site of the Benedictine monastery that hosts the Black Madonna statue in the sanctuary. Its caves have been there since prehistoric times and have attracted over the centuries Christian hermits seeking silent spaces for contemplation as well as pilgrims and tourists. Black Monks (Benedictines) have lived there since 1025. Ignatius arrives there in March 1522. He makes a confession here that lasts three days. Then "stripping himself of all clothes, he gave them to this poor man."[13]

Exercise

Ignatius divested himself of power and possessions.

- What have you left behind in life to begin again?
- What former aspect of your life has been lodged in the past?
- Has it exerted a price?

MANRESA: 1522–23

Arriving in Manresa in March 1522, Ignatius stayed eleven months, leaving in February of 1523 in order to arrive in Rome by Easter Sunday, when permission is given every year to travel to the Holy Land. He worked in the Hospital Santa Lucia, attending the poor and the sick, and going to Mass in the Church of La Seu. He let his hair and nails grow. He saw a serpent, and the more he saw it, the more his consolation grew. Up to this point he had persisted in one identical interior state—that of unwavering happiness and serenity. During this time he suffered from scruples; he persisted in praying seven hours a day in a little room that the Dominicans had lent him. He was tempted to kill himself. Later, these thoughts and scruples would leave him. He was slowly discerning the difference between the good spirit and bad spirit. "At this time God was dealing with him in the same way as a school-teacher deals with a child, teaching him." One day while praying, "he was seeing the Most Holy Trinity in the form

---

13. Ignatius, *Personal Writings*, 20.

of three keys on a keyboard."[14] The impression remained with him for the rest of his life. Second, he experienced the way in which God had created the world, which "was represented in his understanding, with great spiritual joy: it seemed to him he was seeing a white thing, from which rays were coming out, and that God was making light out of it."[15] He stayed in Manresa a year and began to cut his hair and nails regularly. Third incident: at Mass during the consecration, Ignatius saw with interior eyes white rays that were coming from above. With his understanding he saw "how Jesus Christ Our Lord was present in that most holy sacrament."[16] Fourth, with interior eyes he saw the humanity of Christ, which was "like a white body, not very big nor very small, but he did not see any distinction of limbs."[17] He sees Our Lady too in similar form. He spends days and nights in prayer in the famous cave (in great spiritual combat and close to suicide) as well as in the Well of Light, an elevated place with a view over Manresa and at the Cardoner river. Fifth, here, a mile from Manresa, Ignatius sat down by the river, where the eyes of his understanding were opened, "not that he saw some vision, but understanding and knowing many things, spiritual things just as much as matters of faith and learning, and this with an enlightenment so strong that all things seemed new to him."[18] He reported that during his life he had never attained so much as on that single occasion. From then on, it seemed as if he were a different person. (Afterwards, he has another vision of the serpent, but this time realizes that it is the devil.) Three times, Ignatius was near death: "He clearly judged that his soul was due very soon to depart."[19] The second episode was when he was on a ship during a storm; the third time was when in 1550 he was very sick. Thinking about death gave him great joy. (It was at this time that Ignatius started to compose *The Spiritual Exercises* to help others encounter the God of all consolation.)

---

14. Ignatius, *Personal Writings*, 25.
15. Ignatius, *Personal Writings*, 26.
16. Ignatius, *Personal Writings*, 26.
17. Ignatius, *Personal Writings*, 26.
18. Ignatius, *Personal Writings*, 27.
19. Ignatius, *Personal Writings*, 27.

Exercise

- Have you ever had dramatic or subtle experiences of God that led you to being certain of his existence?
- Have you ever struggled with faith, oscillating between belief and doubt, or experienced suicidal ideation? If so, what helped? How did it get resolved?
- Have you ever had a near-death experience?
- How do you view death? Does the prospect of dying scare you?

JERUSALEM: 1523

On July 14, 1523, Ignatius embarks on his way to the Holy Land. Jerusalem was a dangerous place, controlled by the Muslims. Filled with joy, he travels to several places mentioned in the Gospels. After spending twenty days here, Ignatius asks the Franciscans (with whom he was staying) to allow him to remain there indefinitely, but they refuse his request. Ignatius wonders what to do. He decides not to cling to the Jesus of history but to the Christ of faith and the future in his desire to help souls. He proposes a new course of action—study.

Exercise

- What have you done or do to *help souls*?
- How did you react when your requests for various things were turned down, when you didn't get your way?
- Have you committed yourself to making a study of anything?

BARCELONA: 1524

Ignatius knows he needs more study, especially in grammar and Latin, and so he arrives in Barcelona in his thirties, humbly learning as a mature student among schoolboys who make fun of him. Imagine him begging for alms in front of the Church of Santa María del Mar, where there is a statue commemorating him today. He stays two years, where he is helped by two benefactors: Roser and Inés Pascual. Here, he also gives the Spiritual Exercises as a layman, predominantly to other laymen and -women. Eventually, he gathers four companions to himself.

Exercise

Think of the many people you have met through life who have become close companions and friends. Recall what you have shared and learned together.

- Who are they?
- What binds you together?

ALCALÁ DE HENARES: SALAMANCA, 1526

Ignatius walks to the University of Alcalá de Henares, thirty-five km from Madrid, arriving there in March 1526, to continue to study and serve. He stays to study here for a year and a half. He attends courses in logic, physics, and theology and begs and continues to give the Spiritual Exercises and communicates the faith to children. He and his companions arouse the suspicion of the ecclesiastical authorities, as Ignatius is not a cleric. He is taken prisoner for investigation. The inquisitors suspect Ignatius is an *alumbrado* (illuminist), but he is soon released. The first time, Ignatius spends seventeen days in prison. A second time sees him imprisoned for forty-two days. In Salamanca, Ignatius is chained up on suspicion of heresy while his *Spiritual Exercises* handbook is thoroughly examined. Finding no doctrinal error, he is declared innocent of all charges and released after twenty-two days but asked to abstain from any theological discussions until he has studied for four years. Ignatius complies but continues to the prestigious University of Paris.

Exercise

- Have you ever gotten into trouble with the authorities?
- If so, what happened?

- What did you learn from the experience?

PARIS: 1528

Imagine Ignatius traveling in France, which was at war with his country, not knowing the language, making his way to the University of Paris. Informed that Spaniards are put on spits, he moves forward with fearless faith. Here the Society of Jesus would be born. Ignatius enrolls as an external student at the Montaigu College (site of the current Saint Geneviève Library of the Sorbonne) and adopts the Latin for his name—*Ignatius*. Later, he settles at the Saint Barbara College where he completes his theological studies under the direction of John Pena. He develops the Ignatian pedagogy for which the order is famous and comes to know Francis Xavier and Peter Faber (two future saints) who together form the nucleus of the Society of Jesus.

Exercise

- Have you got a good work-life balance between *ora* and *labora*?
- Do you integrate study/work and leisure?
- What are your hobbies and pastimes?

ANTWERP (YEAR UNKNOWN)

Ignatius had received financial support for his studies in Paris from a merchant in Barcelona, but Ignatius was robbed when he left Antwerp, so he had to beg and live temporarily in a hospital. Ignatius makes his way to Bruges and Antwerp and to London, where he raises funds to finance his studies.

Exercise

- Were you ever robbed, either literally or figuratively in the sense of something being stolen from you? How did you respond? What did you do?

- How do you cope with setbacks?
- What's your attitude to having your plans changed or derailed by others?
- Do you support any causes or people, either financially or with your time?

ROUEN (YEAR UNKNOWN)

Shortly after arriving in Paris, Ignatius receives a letter from the Spaniard who stole his money, informing Ignatius that he is seriously ill and sojourning in Rouen. Ignatius visits the man who wronged him, seeking only to help him in any way he can. The desire to walk those eighty-four miles from Paris to Rouen on foot, without shoes, neither eating nor drinking, came upon him; and praying about it, he felt very fearful. In Rouen he comforted the sick man and helped to put him on a ship to Spain; and he gave him letters, directing him to his companions who were in Salamanca.

Exercise

- Do you know anyone who has harmed you? Do you still hold a grudge against them, or have you forgiven them?
- Has anyone ever betrayed you?
- Have you ever reconciled with a former enemy?

MONTMARTRE: 1534

On August 15, 1534, on the Feast of the Bodily Assumption, Ignatius, Francis Xavier, and other companions climb the hill of Montmartre on the outskirts of Paris. Imagine them in the Chapel of the Martyrdom of Saint Denis preparing themselves for service to the Divine Majesty and putting themselves in God's hands. Here they celebrate Mass and take vows of poverty and chastity. Due to the war with the Turks, they know a pilgrimage to Jerusalem may not prove possible, so they offer themselves to the pope so he can send them to serve wherever the church needs them for the greater glory of God. They are united as friends but dispose themselves to be scattered across the globe.

Exercise

- Where can you go to help with the greatest need?
- What needs to be done?
- How can you contribute or make a difference?

AZPEITIA: 1535

Ignatius develops a fever, and his stomach pains worsen. He travels back to Azpeitia in 1535, returning to the village he left thirteen years ago after his convalescence and conversion, riding on a small horse. He refuses his brother's invitation to stay in the family castle, settling in the hospital of La Magdalena instead. This once–local nobleman continues to serve the poor and beg for alms. In the hospital he begins to speak to many who visit him about the things of God. As soon as he arrives, he determines to teach the children Christian doctrine every day; but his brother is very much opposed to this, assuring him that no one will come. But after he begins to teach, many come to hear him, including his own brother. A couple of months later with improved health Ignatius travels to Venice to attend to the affairs of some of his companions. He leaves his homeland, never to return.

Exercise

- Have you been forced into emigration or exile?
- Have you spent any time abroad, away from your native land?
- What was that experience like for you?

VENICE: 1536

Ignatius arrives in Venice at the beginning of 1536 to wait there for his companions who are finishing their studies in Paris, in the hope of setting sail for Jerusalem. Ignatius undergoes another persecution and trial here and spends one year alone before he is joined on January 8, 1537, by the other nine companions, including Xavier. There, on June 24, 1537, Ignatius and five others who are not yet priests are ordained. The companions serve in various hospitals and preach the word of God. After several months, and faced with the impossibility of going to Jerusalem, the companions meet again in Vicenza (in the northeast of Italy) and after several weeks of prayer and deliberations decide to go to Rome instead and place themselves at the disposal of the pope. Ignatius continues to give the exercises and engages in spiritual conversations with all and sundry.

Exercise

- Where do you feel life is taking you?
- Have you a support system?
- How have you navigated plans, projects, and failures?
- What do you see yourself doing in the future?

ROME: 1544–56

Ignatius works in Rome as general of the society from 1544 to July 31, 1556, the day he dies in bed. He writes the *Constitutions* to guide the nascent society and more than seven thousand letters. Ignatius "was very specially visited by God."[20] Every day, he used to write down what passed through his soul.

Exercise

- What has been your main life apostolate/activity?
- What would you say you have achieved/accomplished?
- Imagine being at the end of your days, on your deathbed; looking back on your life, ask yourself, "What would I like to be remembered for?"

20. Ignatius, *Personal Writings*, 60.

- Do you keep a journal, committing to it all those things that pass through your psyche/soul?

Ignatius spent nearly twenty years in the Eternal City. Below are some of the places associated with his legacy.

THE CHURCH OF THE GESÙ

You are now standing in front of the mother church of the Society of Jesus, which in 1551 was commissioned by Ignatius. Its unique style combines Renaissance with Baroque features. Churches at this historical time were meant to overwhelm the senses. What do you see, hear, feel? The church is dedicated to Jesus, whose monogram is composed of three Greek letters: *IHS*. The term "Jesuits" was originally a derogatory one, but Ignatius gladly adopted this appellation in order to be like Jesus.

CHURCH OF SAINT IGNATIUS

Stand and admire this magnificent church vault built by Andrea Pozzo (1642–1709). Step inside this space designed by the Jesuit artist, which blurs the boundaries between heaven and earth, its architecture opening to an encounter with the divine.

CHURCH OF SAINT ANDREW ON THE QUIRINAL

You are standing in the place that housed the first novitiate of the Society of Jesus. The third superior general of the Jesuits, St. Francis Borgia, later acquired the property. The chapel was replaced in 1638 by the famous Bernini. The novitiate remained in operation from 1566 to 1773 and again from 1814 to 1870.

SANTA MARTA HOUSE

This building was the site of one of the social ministries of Ignatius. The Casa Santa Marta (1543) was a mission to help prostitutes. Isabel Roser—a benefactress in Barcelona—oversaw the institution. Later, Ignatius would found the Confraternity of the Vulnerable Virgins, dedicated to giving shelter to girls, from ten years of age and older, at risk. Ignatius also promoted the creation of homes for orphaned children. In 1552, Juan de Polanco, secretary of the society, estimated that there were three hundred women who had been freed from their former life.

PALAZZO VENEZIA

Located in a beautiful garden, this palace served as a residence for the popes. Ignatius visited it with his companions. Two times were especially important: when they received the bull of approval of the society in 1540 (*Regimini Militantis Ecclesiae*) and the official approval of *The Spiritual Exercises* in 1548 (*Pastoralis Officii*). Ignatius's religious congregation had been approved by Pope Paul III. Part of Ignatius's work was spent in drafting the *Constitutions* for members of his order.

CONVENT OF SAN PIETRO IN MONTORIO

San Pietro is located on the Gianicolo Hill near St. Peter's Basilica. It was a former (Spanish) Franciscan convent built on the site where it is thought St. Peter was crucified. It now houses the Spanish Academy. See St. Ignatius celebrating Mass here, resisting his election as general, assailed by scruples, wanting at all costs to avoid any temptation to power or prestige. Despite his best intentions, on April 8, 1541, Ignatius was elected as general of the society. He asked that the election be repeated, which it duly was five days later but with the same result. Ignatius withdrew to make the Easter Triduum and decide. His confessor told him that if he resisted, he would be opposing the desire of the Holy Spirit. Finally, Ignatius accepted the decision.

LA STORTA CHAPEL

On the journey to Rome, Ignatius was specially visited by the Lord. He had determined, after he had become a priest, to go a year without saying Mass, preparing himself and praying to the Virgin that she would place him with her Son. It was in La Storta in Rome that Ignatius "sensed such a change in his soul, and he saw so clearly that God the Father was putting him with

Christ, his Son."[21] This profound mystical experience took place in November of 1537. The La Storta episode marked the definitive configuration of Ignatius with the Crucified Christ. Ignatius was ordained in Venice in June 1537—he waited a whole year before presiding at his first Mass.

BASILICA OF ST. PETER

In his spiritual diary, Ignatius gives an account of visiting the Basilica of St. Peter, built over the tomb of the apostle Peter, commissioned by Julius I. At the beginning of 1574, the work was entrusted to Michelangelo. Ignatius visited St. Peter's in March–April 1523, his first companions visited in March–April 1537, and finally all of them arrived there on the day of their profession, April 22, 1541, as part of the pilgrimage of the seven churches.

BASILICA OF SAINT MARY MAJOR

It was here that Ignatius celebrated his first Mass as general of the Jesuits in 1538.

BASILICA OF SAINT PAUL

On April 22, 1541, Ignatius and the first companions met in Rome. When they arrived at St. Paul's, the six went to confession; then it was decided that all the others would receive the Blessed Sacrament from the hands of Ignatius, pronouncing their vows. Ignatius celebrated Mass and at the time of communion held a sheet of paper on which was written the formula of vows, addressed his kneeling companions, and pronounced the words of their profession.

HEROIC LEADERSHIP

In the words of former Jesuit Chris Lowney, this 450-year-old company (referring to the Society of Jesus) changed the world down the centuries with its heroic leadership.[22] Its professed members were innovators who prized and prioritized self-awareness, ingenuity, love, and heroism. They

---

21. Ignatius, *Personal Writings*, 60.
22. See Lowney, *Heroic Leadership*.

never stood still. Ignatius traveled on foot and on horseback across Europe: Spain, the Holy Land, Belgium, England, France, Italy.[23] He and his companions were always on the road.

INTERSECTIONS

In his book *At a Journal Workshop*, psychologist Ira Progoff has a section entitled "Intersections: Roads Taken and Not Taken." Our life is like a road that passes through many environments and shifts directions, taking unplanned detours, just like Ignatius. Along the way we sometimes get lost. See your life as a road, recognize the intersections, the paths taken and those not taken, the choices you've made and the consequences they've had. Make an open-ended list. See what comes up for you and how you feel about it.

IGNATIUS'S SPIRITUAL DIARY

Ignatius's spiritual diary has survived in its original hand-written form. Its style is elliptic and idiosyncratic; its content are the Spanish saint's mystical experiences, which cover the period of a year. The diary begins in February 1544, though it is not a diary in the traditional sense. It's more of a discernment logbook. It introduces one to the highest levels of Ignatius's spirituality, enabling a better and deeper understanding of the characteristics and charism of Ignatian mysticism.[24]

Ignatius begins with a list of pros and cons related to the poverty or otherwise of his society. He writes down the advantages and disadvantages in having a fixed income for churches of the Society of Jesus. The diary proper that follows contains entries under dates and various Masses that follow a pattern. For example, on February 5, 1544, Ignatius sees a vision of the Mother and Son. A few days later at Mass he experiences a burning of every part of his body. He makes a colloquy with the Holy Spirit, who confirms him in his election (decision). Again and again, he writes of his "devotion and tears," of his "great tranquillity and security of soul," of his interior warmth and consolation.[25] On Friday, February 15, at the consecration, Our Lady shows Ignatius "that her flesh was in that of her

---

23. Comerford, *Pilgrim's Story*; Grogan, *Alone and on Foot*.
24. Costello, *Ignatian Mysticism*.
25. *Spiritual Diary*, in Ignatius, *Personal Writings*, 77.

Son."[26] Often, tears stream down his face. Despite these occurrences, he continues to perform his various spiritual exercises including the examination of conscience and begs for pardon. "*I had very many intuitions about the Blessed Trinity, my understanding being enlightened with them to such an extent that it seemed to me that with hard study I would not have known so much.*"[27] He informs us that any time he sees three creatures together he immediately thinks of the three divine persons and experiences interior joy.[28] All the persons are in the Trinity by their essence—like a knot. He prays that his will may be conformed to the divine one.[29] During Mass on the first day of Lent, Ignatius sees the Blessed Trinity and Jesus, who places Ignatius before the Trinity, and his love only grows stronger. He experiences Jesus in his humanity and also in his divinity. "*Jesus was disclosed to me.*"[30] Once, Ignatius catches sight of the homeland of heaven. These divine visitations bring him great peace. Another time, Ignatius sees in a full bright light "the very Being or Essence of God, appearing as a sphere, a little larger than the sun."[31] However, Ignatius also experiences the tempter, who suggests thoughts against the divine persons. Aside from experiencing God as a sphere, Ignatius also experiences the Divine Being as a circle.[32] There are many more entries. The diary breaks off on February 17, 1545.

Exercise

- How do you experience God?
- What do you feel while praying?
- Do you experience any emotions?

Keep an account to share with your spiritual director.

---

26. *Spiritual Diary*, in Ignatius, *Personal Writings*, 78.
27. *Spiritual Diary*, in Ignatius, *Personal Writings*, 82; emphasis in original.
28. *Spiritual Diary*, in Ignatius, *Personal Writings*, 83.
29. *Spiritual Diary*, in Ignatius, *Personal Writings*, 87.
30. *Spiritual Diary*, in Ignatius, *Personal Writings*, 88; emphasis in original.
31. *Spiritual Diary*, in Ignatius, *Personal Writings*, 93.
32. *Spiritual Diary*, in Ignatius, *Personal Writings*, 103.

IGNATIAN PRAYING

We might conclude this chapter with a few words on Ignatian praying. Ignatius is structured when it comes to praying. To pray the Ignatian way, first choose a Bible text. It could be from one of the biblical readings from the church's multiyear cycle schedule. The focus on Ignatius's prayer pedagogy is quality rather than quantity. It's more about inner relish than knowing. As prayer is encounter, relationship, it is more about heart (the seat of love) than head as we become present to ourselves and to the divine persons. Contemplation is the most typical Ignatian prayer wherein we participate in the story through the imagination. Our senses allow the scene to become audible, visible, and tangible. We hear what is being said as we listen attentively; we smell the scents of the meal; we see the facial expressions of the main characters. We focus our attention on what moves us, on what gives us joy or peace. What expressions in the text evoke something of gladness in us? Prayer is active passivity. We might like to read the full text, then limit ourselves to one paragraph, then one verse or even one word. We conclude the prayer with a short confidential conversation in the silence of our hearts, which is called a *colloquy* in Ignatian spirituality. We may choose to follow this with the Lord's Prayer and the sign of the cross. Afterwards, we can review the experience and see what helped or hindered us, what images caught our attention, what events engaged us. This will help us to discern. As Nikolaas Sintobin describes it in his book *Praying with the Bible: An Ignatian Guide*: "In the Ignatian way of praying with the Bible, the stories about Jesus occupy a preferential place."[33] Biblical praying is not the only way of praying, of course. One might also practice the examen, which involves prayerfully reflecting over the day, using words like "thanks," "sorry," and "please."[34] *Lectio divina* is similar to Ignatian contemplation as we listen, feel, and look at the word, but Ignatian *lectio* favors narrative texts, especially those about Jesus.[35]

---

33. Sintobin, *Praying with the Bible*, 52.

34. Sintobin, *Praying with the Bible*, 54.

35. For a wonderful example of an Ignatian way of contemplating the Gospel story beginning at Matt 14:22, see Sintobin, *Praying with the Bible*, 60–63.

CHAPTER TWO

Considering the *Spiritual Exercises*
The Perspective of Five Jesuit Thinkers

> Saint Ignatius Loyola was a mystic, but his mysticism made him assuredly one of the most powerfully practical human engines that ever lived.
>
> WILLIAM JAMES, THE VARIETIES OF RELIGIOUS EXPERIENCE

WE CAN CONSIDER IGNATIUS'S text of the *Spiritual Exercises* as a mystagogy, in other words, as a path of spiritual transformation, in which every "week" is a step wherein the whole person is introduced to a new understanding of him/herself, of God, and the world, in an interconnected way that has at its heart the objective of *finding God in everything*.

The correspondence of Ignatius is voluminous, far outnumbering the letters of such sixteenth-century contemporaries as Calvin, Erasmus, Luther, and Teresa of Ávila. This letter-writing prowess was aided by Juan Polanco, who was secretary to the society for over twenty-five years (1547–73). Again here we see Ignatius referring to himself when he signs off as "the poor pilgrim."[1] In a letter to Fr. Manuel Miona, dated November 16, 1536, and sent from Venice, Ignatius, referring to the exercises, describes and praises them in his own words thus: "The Spiritual Exercises are all the best that I have been able to think out, experience and understand in this

---

1. *Select Letters*, in Ignatius, *Personal Writings*, 117.

life, both for helping somebody to make the most of themselves, as also for being able to bring advantage, help, and profit to many others."[2]

In *Counsels of the Holy Spirit: A Reading of Saint Ignatius' Letters*, Patrick Goujon, SJ, makes the point that the letters, which aim to help souls, have three aims—to give consolation, advice, and exhortation.[3] We can see a "spiritual pedagogy at work."[4] Goujon notes that the early Jesuits extended the space where preaching might take place, beyond the confines of church buildings, which was radical for its time. Moreover, the Spiritual Exercises (the heart of which was to create an *experience*) were not to be given in their entirety except to the few.[5]

More than a decade ago, I discussed the Ignatian exercises in chapter 7 ("Discerning Divine Desire") of my book *Philosophy and the Flow of Presence* before, in 2024, devoting a whole book to them in my *Ignatian Mysticism*. In this present chapter, I wish to revisit the exercises but this time from the perspective of five seminal Ignatian thinkers (the particular order has no special significance): (1) Anthony de Mello, (2) Karl Rahner, (3) Bernard Lonergan (more centrally), (4) Teilhard de Chardin, and (5) Gerard Manley Hopkins. They all add something unique and different to our understanding and appreciation of the exercises.

DE MELLO

Anthony de Mello, SJ (1931–87), was an Indian Jesuit who became known as a popular spiritual writer. His spirituality can be outlined in four steps:

1. Happiness is the goal (telos) of life. Aristotle was of the same mind. But, instead, many people experience only suffering (as diagnosed by the Buddha and Schopenhauer, among others).
2. The cause of suffering is attachment; that is, happiness sought through conditions.
3. There is a way out: detachment through discernment (Ignatius).
4. Happiness is freedom (liberation/salvation).[6]

---

2. *Select Letters*, in Ignatius, *Personal Writings*, 139.
3. Goujon, *Counsels of the Holy Spirit*, 7.
4. Goujon, *Counsels of the Holy Spirit*, 9.
5. Goujon, *Counsels of the Holy Spirit*, 13.
6. Nayak, *Anthony de Mello*, 59.

Happiness is the motivating factor, the fulfillment of desire. There is acquired happiness and true happiness that is not acquired (or external). Acquired happiness is sought through pleasure, profit, or power. It is transitory. True happiness is here, in the present, and is eternal. It is the experience of joy and gratitude and peace. Attachment (cleaving) is usually to persons or possessions; it is an act of appropriation. However, putting conditions on happiness renders happiness impossible, as happiness is an inner state of being. It is not achieved but awakened to. Attachment causes much misery, the antidote/answer to which is Ignatian *indifference*, which is interior freedom. Detachment happens when one is no longer determined by objects of desire. The detached person doesn't seek happiness; he experiences it in all conditions. Spotting one's attachments is central to discernment; it is the ongoing process of becoming aware. Discernment (*viveka*) is an awakening of the heart. We discern through awareness (*vipassana*), which brings consolation. The spiritual goal is liberty/liberation (*moksha* or *nirvana*). Happiness is seen by de Mello in terms of freedom.

In 1973, de Mello founded the Sadhana Institute, a center for training spiritual directors, near Pune in India. From July to November 1975, he began the course for that group who attended by lecturing on Ignatius's Spiritual Exercises; several members typed up his talks, and thirty years later one of the participants, Albert Menezes, SJ, made his copy available. The pages were eventually published as *Seek God Everywhere: Reflections in the Spiritual Exercises of St. Ignatius*.

De Mello begins by stating that we need to fall in love, in solitude and the silence of the cell, with the Absolute, as "silence is God."[7] Ignatius's First Principle and Foundation, which reads, "Man is created to praise, reverence, and serve God our Lord, and by this means to save his soul," is the touchstone to test the retreatants. If there is an Absolute, then all else is shadow. Our reality is only relative. Thus, for de Mello, "the ultimate meaning of human life is to get in touch with the Absolute, to discover the Absolute, to achieve fusion, union with the Absolute."[8] This is the meaning of the Principle and Foundation; all the mystics say the same thing. The Absolute is to become the ultimate object of adoration and attraction. This attitude should be our starting point. The absolute

---

7. de Mello, *Seek God Everywhere*, 3.
8. de Mello, *Seek God Everywhere*, 7.

reality is God. The formula to follow, therefore, is this one: to love everyone in God.

The following are the Scripture texts to read and pray over for the First Principle and Foundation, according to de Mello:[9]

- Luke 14:25–33
- Matt 13:44–46
- Phil 3:3–9
- Rom 8:35–39

De Mello speaks of the *desire* for God. If we desire God, we repent, in other words, we change our attitude because the kingdom has come. We confront our shadow side. All suffering in the world comes from sin and selfishness. Sin is the refusal to love and become committed/concerned about creation. So the first step is to become conscious of our sinfulness. Sloth is sin; untruthfulness is sin; unproductiveness is sin (see the cursed fig tree parable in Mark 11:12–14). "This consciousness of sin, much like on the psychological level the awareness of one's blocks and, in some cases, of one's neuroses, is of great value."[10] Joy is the result of the grace of repentance; it is "homecoming happiness."[11] St. Paul tells us where sin abounds, grace superabounds (Rom 5:20). Talk of hell is "a mythological way of showing the seriousness of sin."[12] Suffering is a consequence of sin. Sin has a social and not just personal dimension. To deploy an analogy from Teilhard de Chardin, SJ: if we strike a bronze gong in one place, the whole gong reverberates.[13] One of the fruits of the first week of the exercises is sorrow for sin, which is not the same as sadness, as sorrow contains joy. (*Felix culpa!*) The false ego is washed away. The practice commended is the daily particular examination of conscience, in other words, finding out what needs improvement. "It is a kind of exercise in self-awareness."[14] Look and observe. As de Mello summarizes the examen: Ignatius "begins by telling us to thank God for all the graces, ask

---

9. de Mello, *Seek God Everywhere*, 15–16.
10. de Mello, *Seek God Everywhere*, 28.
11. de Mello, *Seek God Everywhere*, 28.
12. de Mello, *Seek God Everywhere*, 29.
13. Cited by de Mello, *Seek God Everywhere*, 34.
14. de Mello, *Seek God Everywhere*, 44.

for light, review the day, and then he recommends an act of contrition and a purpose of amendment."[15]

Exercise

- Go over the day.
- Write down the main events of the day—just two or three are sufficient.
- What was the best thing I did today?
- What was the worst?

This meditative period should last no more than thirty minutes. *The examen is the means for the discernment of spirits.* What spirits are moving me? What is the (spiritual) state I am in now? Consolation? Desolation? Follow this Ignatian principle: do everything as if it all depended on you, and pray as if everything depended on God. Practice *lectio divina*, the Benedictine method of prayer. This involves reading, rereading, and relishing the words of the Psalms and other Scripture passages. Or one can make a colloquy, that is to say, converse with Christ as one friend speaks to another. Then spend some time in complete silence. Sin is forgiven through love (John 21:15–19; 1 Tim 1:15). The (spiritual) dangers of the first week, for de Mello, are:

- False guilt
- Refusal to forgive oneself
- The desire to have a clean slate[16]

To ask for God's grace is to ask for his divine consolation. For de Mello, the greatest work we can do for Christ (when we ask ourselves, What am I doing for Christ? as Ignatius instructs) is to believe in his love (John 6:29). The goal of the first week of the Spiritual Exercises is a complete change of mind and heart. Jesus himself began his public ministry with the words "repent and believe the gospel" (Mark 1:15). This involves a turning to him. Repentance is not renunciation; it is freedom.

---

15. de Mello, *Seek God Everywhere*, 45.
16. de Mello, *Seek God Everywhere*, 49.

Ignatius's application of the senses involves imagination. Ignatius suggests that we imagine the crib in Bethlehem. He gives us three points as a way of fleshing out the scene. Consider those present. Ask:

- Where are they?
- What are they saying?
- What are they doing?

We participate in those scenes. People have objections to this particular practice, as de Mello recognizes. But many mystics have gone in for it; we may mention St. Anthony of Padua (imagining holding the child Jesus), St. Francis of Assisi (imagining taking Christ down from the cross), and St. Teresa of Ávila (consoling Christ in his agony in the garden). They understood the truth of mystery rather than the truth of history. Deep reality abides in such a mystery. The application of the senses is a "very mysterious and very important exercise."[17] It goes further than the contemplation; here, we are invited to smell the infinite fragrance and taste the infinite sweetness of the divinity. It is letting go of oneself in love—this is how de Mello puts it. To repeat: it is *mystical* reality that is being talked about here. God is spoken of in terms of light, sound, sweetness, etc. Ignatius stresses that the Creator deals directly with the creature, and the creature with the Creator: God as the real spiritual director of the exercises.

The point of the thirty-day retreat is to rid oneself of inordinate attachments. Then one will be in a better position to seek the will of God, which happens toward the end of the second week with Ignatius's exercise on the three classes of men, which is about being interiorly free (affective indifference). For an attachment to be ordered, the center of gravity has to be God; all else is relativized to that end. The aim here is to change attachments, with peace being the result. The disposition of freedom is required before any real decision can be made. An *election* is the name given by Ignatius to making a life decision. The two standards and the three degrees of humility are all election meditations.[18] There are moments when I am in consolation, and there are moments when I am in desolation—this is when I start discerning. I never make a decision in desolation. In the *Constitutions*, Ignatius asks us to seek the will of God not only in the choice of life but in all particulars, even in trifles. The question becomes: Where in the ebb and flow of these movements of the

---

17. de Mello, *Seek God Everywhere*, 66.
18. de Mello, *Seek God Everywhere*, 86.

spirits can I find the will of God for myself? The heart of the exercises is the discernment of spirits. We are led by the spirit. The more we grow in spiritual maturation, the more we are aware of these movements within us. We become sensitized to them and learn to distinguish them. We can notice a seeming consolation and yet feel uneasy about it. These spiritual movements are not feelings even if they have repercussions in our emotions. They are beyond the emotions. Spirit has no form or feeling. De Mello poses the pertinent question: "How do we distinguish, for instance, euphoria from spiritual consolation, depression from spiritual desolation? Discernment is learned in the depths of one's heart, in silence, in long exposure to prayer and to the Bible and in suffering."[19] The rules Ignatius gives us are to help with this process. A feeling of deep sadness can be the work of the good spirit. Knowledge of depth psychology is paramount. There is a difference between psychological depression and spiritual desolation. When someone comes to de Mello for direction, his first question tends to be: "What are you feeling, right now?"[20] De Mello clarifies: "When St John of the Cross is speaking of the dark night, he is really speaking about painful consolation."[21] Consolation is the intensity of love that leads to indifference (interior freedom), which is a gift from God. Grace is consolation, as are tears when one weeps over one's sins. Any increase in faith, hope, and love is consolation, as is devotion to heavenly, that is to say the highest, things. De Mello distinguishes between:

1. *Sensible* consolation (referring to the senses)

2. *Spiritual* consolation (which cannot be directly perceived by the senses)

De Mello's advice: "Read St. John of the Cross on the dark night of the senses; namely, when the senses have nothing and sensible consolation has disappeared." This is the time to abide in the dark, loving awareness of God. There is nothing to do save be present. "After a while we will experience a deep peace, a quietness of the heart, and a holy union."[22] The senses and feelings are limited, too drowned in the world of matter.

Desolation, by contrast, is the opposite of consolation. It is darkness of soul, inner turmoil, restlessness, attraction to earthly things, a

---

19. de Mello, *Seek God Everywhere*, 102.
20. de Mello, *Seek God Everywhere*, 111.
21. de Mello, *Seek God Everywhere*, 112.
22. de Mello, *Seek God Everywhere*, 116.

decrease in faith, hope, and love. Desolation is temptation. Desolation is permitted though not caused by God. In desolation, it's as if the animal in the human has taken over. Just as consolation need not be delightful, desolation can be pleasant. A person can think they're blissfully happy and yet be in a state of spiritual desolation. Happy, yes, but not at the level of spirit. When we are tempted to pray less, we should aim to pray more. This is *agere contra*: to go or act against one's inclinations, which is sound psychological advice from Ignatius. There are three reasons we may suffer from desolation:

1. We have become slothful in our spiritual exercises.
2. God is testing our mettle/worth.
3. God may be wishing to give us a true knowledge/understanding of ourselves.

De Mello's recommendation: "Be on alert, be aware of what is going on, be attuned to the movements of these spirits. The price of freedom is eternal vigilance."[23] As consolation can be caused by the evil spirit, we must be wary. Ignatius's *consolation without cause* refers to nothing in the created order being the cause of the consolation; so it comes directly from the Creator as pure gift/grace when he acts in the center of the soul where no phantasms/mental forms are involved, following the thought here of Thomas Aquinas. The Ignatian analogy to help distinguish the actions of the good and bad spirits runs thus:

- Sponge: The actions of the good spirit are delicate and delightful and may be compared to a drop of water penetrating a sponge.
- Stone: The actions of the evil spirit are disturbing and noisy and may be compared to water falling upon a stone.

Throughout the day, we are being solicited/assailed by two camps. "The whole of the interior life consists above all in this fidelity to interior inspirations."[24] If the evil spirit brings excess and commotion, the Holy Spirit brings measure, balance, harmony, and clarity.

After reflecting on profound personal freedom (the practice of unselfing the self), de Mello shows next how prayer brings us to encounter the Crucified Christ in the third week of the exercises, and the Risen

---

23. de Mello, *Seek God Everywhere*, 128.
24. de Mello, *Seek God Everywhere*, 135.

Christ in the fourth week (which is the most important week). "When we come to the crowning glory of the Exercises[,] the 'Contemplation to Attain the Love of God,' there is no mention of Christ at all."[25] Everything is the Father, as the identification is so total. We look at creation through the eyes of Christ, who is the way, not the goal. We come to resurrection through crucifixion.

At the end of the exercises, we are led to become contemplatives in action—the phrase is from Jerome Nadal, SJ (1507–80). We are ready to love (which is manifested more in deeds than words) and serve. To serve means to carry out God's will—God as lover and laborer par excellence. We act or, rather, make action a prayer—selfless action as the purest prayer (*nishkam karma*). As Dag Hammarskjöld (1905–61) expressed it: the path to holiness passes through the world of action, even if what comes first is union with God.[26] The Ignatian injunction is to find God in *all* things, as we have been saying. It is, perhaps, worth noting that Ignatius says contemplation to attain love of God and not contemplation for attaining service. Service is *only* for God; we do it *entirely* for him. Such is mystical grace, which cannot be produced or pursued; we can, however, dispose ourselves for it by loving God.

RAHNER

Karl Rahner, SJ (1904–84), begins his reflections on Ignatius's Spiritual Exercises by reminding us that they are not a theological system.[27] Their Archimedean point is: What does God want from me now? He avers that the most important thing in an Ignatian retreat is the personal election.[28] *Other things* include everything between my ego and God. God's will is the goal. The question we need to ask ourselves, according to Rahner, is whether we're living according to the Suscipe, a prayer of self-giving. By doing so, our life becomes a prayer for *the more*. The whole meaning of the Principle and Foundation is the necessity of indifference and of the choice of those things that are more conducive to the end for which we are created. Active indifference is existential distance—a kind of removal from things that make this vision impossible. It is the work of infinite

---

25. de Mello, *Seek God Everywhere*, 144.
26. de Mello, *Seek God Everywhere*, 168.
27. Rahner, *Spiritual Exercises*, 11.
28. Rahner, *Spiritual Exercises*, 15.

love "preserving our human existence from meaninglessness."[29] We free ourselves from our own prejudices and projections. "The true essence of indifference is its 'elevation' into the decision to do 'more.'"[30] We say yes to that which is and become Christians by *choice* rather than cradle Christians by birth (chance).

The first week of the exercises is a meditation on sin, judgment, and hell. Our eternal salvation is threatened at every turn. There are shadows everywhere, darkness we mistake for the light. Of course, an all-pervading understanding would forgive everything, but God does not forgive everything, Rahner tells us.[31] We need to look into ourselves. We enter eternity with ourselves. Ignatius build his meditations not on speculation but on salvation history. Ignatius wasn't a philosopher or a theologian; he was a holy man, a mystic. He gives first place to human freedom. Such is his anthropology. He determines man (as it were) from his freedom. Sin is a personal act. Our existence is a dialectical unity of sin and grace, darkness and light. "Every moment of my life can be a saving-moment or a damning-moment for my human existence."[32] There is the presence of death in me; I am the person I have become by what Rahner calls my "sin-history," so "take a good look" at your life.[33] Sin is serious. Ongoing work on oneself is required, that is to say, asceticism (Christian *askesis*). "No person should dare to say that he has sufficiently penetrated the meaning of his own self."[34] Rahner mentions Mass, private prayer, the Rosary, visits to the Blessed Sacrament, the sacrament of penance, etc.[35] Thus, the whole point of the first week of the exercises is "to stir up *metanoia*."[36]

Our death is the culmination of the unrepeatable uniqueness and oneness of our personal human existence—death is absolute finality, the end from within myself, my final act. It is also a participation in the kenosis or self-divestment of Christ that was never so great as it was in Christ's death on the cross for the sins of the world. The loneliness of death is

---

29. Rahner, *Spiritual Exercises*, 24.
30. Rahner, *Spiritual Exercises*, 25.
31. Rahner, *Spiritual Exercises*, 29.
32. Rahner, *Spiritual Exercises*, 50.
33. Rahner, *Spiritual Exercises*, 53.
34. Rahner, *Spiritual Exercises*, 61.
35. Rahner, *Spiritual Exercises*, 79.
36. Rahner, *Spiritual Exercises*, 81.

"being-alone before the hidden, living God."[37] In death, I am at the end of the rope; it is the last decision. My death is, thus, my judgment. As for hell, hell is a closed heart, and God can't reach such a one. Hell is self-incarceration. Hell is the culmination of sin. "The possibility of hell that is involved in man's free act is the logical conclusion of the free rejection of God's mercy. . . . As long as I am a wayfarer on this earth, I can only approximate a full existential realization of the meaning of hell as a possibility for myself."[38] Ignatius's meditation on hell, which is an existential experience in imagination, doesn't cease until I place myself under the cross of Christ, where I see the love of the Lord displayed.

The incarnation of the Word—the enfleshment of God—is the subject of the second week of the exercises. To express this truth is the constant task of Christology in every age. God became man. This is the immanent self-expression of God, before whom we tearfully pray. Grace is assimilation to Christ, a participation in the divine life of the Trinity. The imitation of Christ is a true entering into his life and, through him, entering into the triune life of God himself. The meditation on the kingdom of Christ is the fundamental one of the second week. The important thing here is that we say a decisive yes to Christ with the whole heart. Ignatius sketches this manifest world for us in all its multiplicity—the races of men, the wars, the weeping, the laughing, the sicknesses, the births, the deaths. In my constantly changing condition (I am hungry or full, tired or rested, etc.), I am experiencing a small portion of the problem of existence of all mankind. I am involved in the comings and goings, the ups and downs. In the incarnation meditation, we imagine God looking down on our world—the three divine persons make the decision to send the Son. We meditate on the angel of the annunciation (holy angels as spiritual beings cannot be perceived by the senses). We look at Mary, the virgin who is full of grace; we hear the message ("and the Word became flesh"). He dwelt among us. "God wanted to put Himself in those things so that we find Him in them. The desert wasteland of our human existence, our poverty and weakness, our sickness, our incarceration in darkness, our life in a dead-end street right in the midst of death—these things are now basically filled with the truth of His life. . . . He is looking at us from every point of the compass."[39]

---

37. Rahner, *Spiritual Exercises*, 91.
38. Rahner, *Spiritual Exercises*, 95.
39. Rahner, *Spiritual Exercises*, 143.

Ignatius's two standards are the decision meditation of the exercises. "Our life is a chain of decisions."[40] We must dispose ourselves to choose wisely and well. There is a highly directed criterion of decision-making in the rules for the discernment of spirits. The two camps—Christ and Lucifer, ally and adversary—dominate everything that goes on in the depths of our hearts. "According to St. Ignatius, there are no static front lines between the two, but only swift emissaries who are sent to all parts of the globe."[41] The kingdoms of Christ and Satan embrace the whole world. (And Christ can't be simply identified with the church.) Lucifer's standard operates according to the art of seduction, promising a triple temptation of riches, honor, and pride, which the three vows seek to undo.

The three classes of men exercise is a further decision meditation/parable. The point Ignatius is making here is this one: desire to choose what is for the glory of the Divine Majesty rather than for oneself. Ignatius wants the retreatant to consider the "three degrees of humility" before making his decision. The first attitude is that of a humble love of God, the second is more perfect as done from indifference; the third contains an audacious love of the Crucified One. Such a person "has leaped out of self . . . he remains standing under the cross of Christ."[42] The life of the Christian is a mixture of these three levels of humility. Only God gets to decide which degree must be practiced and when.

We can't downplay the agony in the Garden of Olives in the third week of the exercises even if "it is theologically certain that Jesus always had the immediate vision of God."[43] Each one of us has our own measure of suffering meted out to us. Christ shoulders the greater burden. "We do not have to do very much. We do not have to do more than Jesus did in Gethsemane the night before His death. But if we are able to do that much—and we can only do it with the grace He merited for us in the Garden of Olives—then we are able to do everything."[44] From the garden to the cross and Christ's passion. Jesus betrayed and abandoned. Jesus before the Sanhedrin. Jesus in prison. The scourging and crowning with thorns. This is the story of the one who carried his passion into glory. We meditate on the Lord's death on the cross, which is taken from the third week of the exercises, as he is rejected by his people and repudiated

40. Rahner, *Spiritual Exercises*, 169.
41. Rahner, *Spiritual Exercises*, 171.
42. Rahner, *Spiritual Exercises*, 200.
43. Rahner, *Spiritual Exercises*, 218.
44. Rahner, *Spiritual Exercises*, 226.

by the church. But the ultimate fact is the great love that prompted him, in the midst of his own darkness, to forgive and to utter with a cry of confidence: "Into your hands I commend my spirit"—"words which do away with hell!"[45]

Now we enter into the so-called fourth week of the exercises. We ask for the grace to be glad because of the glory of Christ who rose from the dead: resurrection, redemption, ascension. The immanent Trinity. The Spirit and the church. The church and Mary, in whom everything is present in her fiat, who was immaculately conceived and bodily assumed into heaven. The path we are on, affirms Rahner, is the path built on the poverty of Christ, of his renunciation. It is a life of practice of the Beatitudes—a free life, buried under the wordless weight and wretchedness of the world.

Rahner concludes his work with some remarks on Ignatius's contemplation on love. There is a certain parallelism between the *contemplatio* and the *fundamentum*. Christ is hardly mentioned in either one. Both of these are outside of the body of the exercises but nevertheless present in all the meditations and contain within themselves the whole Spiritual Exercises in their own right. They both reveal the more of the love that has been proposed to us. We are to strive for immediate communion with the Creator. This love is the result of the realization of the divine descent. "What must I do?" is addressed to this God of love: What do you want me to do? This is the discovery of God in all things through detachment and discernment that runs through the entire exercises. Rahner's four final points:

1. God *gives* (creation is a blessing).
2. God *inhabits* (dwells in creatures).
3. God *works* (labors for me).
4. God *descends* (down from above).[46]

The world is charged with divine energy and is a holy place; the profane is revealed as being the sacred.

---

45. Rahner, *Spiritual Exercises*, 239.
46. Rahner, *Spiritual Exercises*, 275–76.

LONERGAN

Both the exercises of St. Ignatius and the philosophy of Bernard Lonergan, SJ (1904–84), belong to the same ancient Greek and Latin tradition that viewed philosophy as the site of spiritual exercises. Pierre Hadot reminds us that the intent of ancient philosophy was to form more than just inform—to transform souls, which entails a change of horizon, outlook, perspective so that it can bring about a metamorphosis of one's personality.[47] Ignatius's Spiritual Exercises (*Exercitia Spiritualia*) are a Christian version of this Greco-Roman tradition. Similarly, the aim of Bernard Lonergan's intentionality analysis, which can also be understood as a spiritual exercise, is the self-appropriation of the human subject. His generalized empirical method is to help the human person achieve authenticity and self-transcendence. Lonergan's method invites the reader to an exercise in intentionality analysis, which is an examination of consciousness. We can outline some of the steps involved.

First, notice that the operations within your consciousness have objects. Your consciousness is thus *intentional*—it in-tends, tends toward, reaches out of itself toward an object. One becomes aware of and present to an object. It is a psychological event. Second, be aware that these intentional operations are those of an operator. You are the *conscious* operator in charge of the operations. You are the subject of the verbs to see, to hear, to touch, etc. You are aware of yourself operating; you are consciously experiencing yourself operating. This is the meaning of conscious intentionality. *Self-appropriation* means being present to and grasping what's going on in consciousness. Ignatius's exercises, too, are exercises in self-appropriation. Lonergan gives four instances of self-transcendence, of going beyond oneself.

1. When you awake, you attend to what is around you; you pay attention to our experience.

2. You go beyond mere sensing to understanding. You ask why and what and how, etc. You live in a universe of meaning.

3. You go beyond understanding to judging whether your understanding is correct. You reflect and ask: Is it so? You go further out of yourself.

---

47. See Hadot, *Philosophy as a Way*.

4. You go beyond judging to deliberating and acting. You go from the cognitional to the volitional level. The top level of consciousness is conscience. And the most deliberate act is love.

Ignatius's examen of consciousness proceeds in the same way as Lonergan's method. We can summarize Lonergan's method thus, beginning with the four levels of consciousness:

1. Empirical
2. Intellectual
3. Rational
4. Responsible

(The set culminates in loving.) Consciousness is self-presence, immanent awareness. Knowing is a compound of:

- Experiencing
- Understanding
- Judging
- Deciding

We thus:

- Experience at the empirical level
- Understand on the intellectual level
- Judge on the rational level
- Decide on the responsible level

We become:

- Attentive in experiencing
- Intelligent in understanding
- Reasonable in judging
- Responsible in deciding

Lonergan sets all this out principally in *Insight: A Study of Human Understanding* (1957). For Ignatius and Lonergan, desire is the natural bent of our being. Again and again in the exercises, Ignatius enjoins us to find what we deeply desire. Indifference is desire in its purest state. As for

God's desire, he desires to give us his very self. Such is the divine design. To embark on a program of self-appropriation is to discover our desires; it is to come to full self-consciousness. The question of God arises naturally within our consciousness, for both Lonergan and Rahner.

Lonergan's transcendental method is a pattern of recurrent and related operations that yields cumulative and progressive results. It underlies the methods of the natural sciences as well as history, sociology, theology, etc. It is self-correcting and blends theory and praxis. This description fits the process of the Spiritual Exercises to a *t*. What Ignatius is doing is having us deal with what existential philosophers call *Existenz*—the becoming aware/becoming oneself; it's a growth in self-consciousness, a heightening of one's self-appropriation. It is the existential moment when we pass from substance to subject. When we dream, we are only minimally subjects; but when we awake and are actively intelligent, reasonable, and free, we are existential subjects. The being of a human subject is a becoming. The existential moment is a *kairos* (burning bush) moment. Ignatius's Principle and Foundation, which is Ignatius's vision or mission statement, performs the same role. We gain insights into the truths of the Christian religion concretely for our daily living.

Where Ignatius speaks of inordinate attachments (distorted desire), Lonergan will speak of bias, which is a flight from understanding and responsibility. A bias is a block in intellectual development. It could be unconscious motivation, personal egoism, group bias, or the bias of common sense. The exercises begin where Lonergan also begins: they start with an exercise in self-awareness, with an examination of consciousness. You ask: "Where am I?" and "What have I been doing with my life?" There are four imperatives Lonergan expounds as a way of dealing with biases and blockages, which we encountered earlier:

- Be attentive.
- Be intelligent.
- Be reasonable.
- Be responsible.

And be more loving. To give a Lonerganian gloss to Ignatius: Ignatius asks and tasks us also to be aware, intelligent, rational, and responsible, albeit from the framework of his Spiritual Exercises, which are a practical manual on a method of cooperating with grace.

CONSIDERING THE SPIRITUAL EXERCISES

As Lonergan specialist Daniel Helminiak puts it: the human spirit has built-in laws of operation, of which there are four, which he renders thus:

1. Being open-minded
2. Being questioning
3. Being honest
4. Being responsible/good-willed[48]

I like to add "being adventuresome in planning."[49] As Helen Keller powerfully remarked and reminded us: "Life is a daring adventure, or it is nothing." These four requirements correspond to the fourfold structure of the human spirit—its capacity for experience, understanding, judgment, and decision. We collect the data, come up with some understanding, base our judgment upon the evidence, check our understanding is correct. These three correspond with the scientific method of observation, hypothesis, and verification. The fourth—be responsible—has to do with what is right, good, and loving. We could reduce these four to two: knowledge and love, intellect and will, or beliefs and morals.

In the first week, Ignatius recalls the sin of the angels, of Adam and Eve, of each individual human being. He has you make a moral inventory of your life in light of the Principle and Foundation. It's a diagnostic tool to see where you stand as a Christian. There is progress, decline, redemption. Where sin violates the four transcendental precepts above, the presence of bias in our psychological lives blocks insight and understanding. Bias causes decline, which is a flight from understanding and responsibility.

Question: What is your individual bias of egoism? Gluttony, sloth, lust, envy, anger, and ambition can skew your quest for truth and goodness. The enemy is the relentless, self-scheming ego. By contrast, group bias is represented by the unholy materialist trinity of eighteenth-century capitalism, nineteenth-century communism, and twentieth-century Nazism. Common sense, for its part, can be erroneous, fallacious, egregious. It can deal with false facts. Authenticity is never some pure, one-for-all-time achievement; rather, it is always in danger of slipping into inauthenticity. This is why we have to examine ourselves, be it through Lonergan's

---

48. Helminiak, *Meditation Without Myth*, 154–58.
49. Costello, "Meaning at the Crossroads."

philosophical-psychological analysis or through the Ignatian examen of consciousness or the long (thirty-day) retreat, which is an exercise in autobiography, or through Enneagram coaching. We want to understand what is going on in our lives. Unconscious bias is the result of misinterpreted experience. Whatever program we are on, the object is the same: to recover the freedom to act without compulsion. The journey is from fixation to liberation.

Not just our thoughts but our feelings are of paramount importance. They give intentional consciousness its mass and momentum. There are positive feelings, such as being in love, and negative feelings, such as resentment. There are repressed feelings that are denied and there are affect-laden images—symbols—which emerge from the nonconscious depths that Carl Jung and Ira Progoff have studied and made central in their psychologies. Some may choose to have a personal analysis or to combine the various methods outlined above. The first requisite is to *pay attention* to the movements of the spirit within, for both Ignatius and Lonergan.

In the two standards exercise we see the battle lines drawn between those who are agents of God's kingdom and those who oppose it. We can describe it thus:

God	Lucifer
Good spirit	Evil spirit
Love	Hate
Progress	Decline

This cosmic battle wages in the human heart. The war is the conflict between positions and counter-positions. Dialectic takes place within consciousness. There are the hermeneutics of suspicion and the hermeneutics of affirmation/recovery. There are the authenticity of a good conscience and the inauthenticity of an unhappy conscience. There is, in other words, within us all the struggle between self-serving positions and self-transcending ones. There are pull and counterpull in the *metaxy* (Plato's word for the in-between). The two standards provide the hermeneutical method that leads to spiritual growth and holiness; they focus on the tension between the pull to poverty and the counterpull to wealth, the pull to humility and the counterpull to pride. For whom are you for, and whom or what are you against? Ignatius and Lonergan would have us decide. "No one can serve two masters" (Matt 6:24). Our being is in process; our existing lies in developing. Conversion is a slow and often painful process of maturation. It is always precarious, never a permanent achievement. "All human development is largely a matter of conflict resolution."[50] The work of dialectic and of the two standards occurs on the fourth level of consciousness, where one evaluates, deliberates, makes a decision, which will be foundational because it's less about what you think and more about whom you love. In a way, the two standards are the Principle and Foundation. They are an effort at threefold self-transcendence: intellectual, moral, and religious.

In Ignatian contemplation, the Christian comes to know, love, and serve Christ by being attentive, intelligent, rational, and responsible. The aim is always the same: the transformation of consciousness. When Ignatius urges us to imagine the place (composition), this is the first step in being attentive to the sense data provided by Scripture. There is a direct correlation between Ignatius's exercises and Lonergan's method. Visualizing the scene—the Gospel story/event—is only a tool that should be brief; it's just a starting point. One mustn't dwell excessively on constructing the representation of the place. For each of the points Ignatius makes are the following steps Lonergan makes:

1. Be attentive: *pay attention.* See the various persons; behold them; listen to them. Attend to the data of the senses presented by the Gospel writers. This is the empirical level on which we sense, perceive, imagine, feel, speak, move. Attention is twofold, involving the operation of seeing, hearing, touching, tasting, smelling, as well as awareness of the effect the data of sensation is having upon one's feelings. One applies the senses.

2. Be intelligent: *explore intelligently.* Ignatius instructs us to observe, consider, contemplate what the persons in question are saying; behold what they are doing. In other words, we should listen carefully and understand what they are saying; watch them and understand what they are doing. To be intelligent means to understand the data that the Gospel writers are presenting in the text. By asking questions (inquiry), we gain insights. An accurate understanding will depend on biblical exegesis and hermeneutics. One mediates and contemplates the meanings of the text. One prays intelligently, reasonably, and responsibly.

---

50. Connor and Fellows of the Woodstock Theological Center, *Dynamism of Desire*, 202.

3. Be reasonable: *judge soundly*. Ignatius asks us to reflect on the persons' words and actions. To be reasonable means to verify the truth of the Gospel writers' understanding of the data for myself. This is the rational level whereby we marshal evidence and pass judgment on the truth or falsity, on the certainty or probability of a statement. We conduct a personal theological reflection, asking: "What is the Lord trying to say to me now through this particular Gospel text?" We deliberate on the existential level.

4. Be responsible: *decide and act responsibly*. Ignatius asks us to reflect and draw profit from these matters and meditations. It is the reminder to become engaged, committed, convinced. To be responsible means to deliberate about what action is called for from me. So, the issue is not just the data, not just the interpretation, not just the question of fact, but decision—the deed. What are we to choose to be, to make of ourselves? It is the moment of an existential crisis. By our choices we have to decide what to make of ourselves.[51]

Exercise

Choose the Gospel reading from the day or any passage from Scripture and slowly read it.

- Did any sentence, phrase, word, or image speak directly/personally to you?
- Did any images or insights accrue? If so, what effect did they have upon you?
- Any consolations?
- Any adverse reactions (dismay, dread, fear, reluctance)?
- Any graces received?

Ignatian spirituality may begin with asceticism, but it culminates in mysticism; one withdraws from the world mediated by meaning into the cloud of unknowing, as we let lapse all images and thoughts so as to allow God's love to permeate, suffuse, and absorb us. This involves silent surrender to the divine initiative.

---

51. Connor and Fellows of the Woodstock Theological Center, *Dynamism of Desire*, 247–57.

For Lonergan, human development is always a struggle, proceeding "through the resolution of conflicts and, within the realm of intentional consciousness, the basic conflicts are defined by the opposition of positions and counter-positions."[52] Ignatius's three classes of men exercise raises the intensity of this struggle. Here a meditation is made on the three classes of persons to aid one embracing what is better. It shows, in relation to money, the presence of attachment. (Ignatius supported himself as a student at the University of Paris on fifty ducats a year, so anyone with ten thousand ducats in the sixteenth century was a millionaire by today's standards.) The first case study is in sheer indecision; the first millionaire has a weak will. There is an inconsistency between knowing and doing—he is rational in his knowing but irresponsible in his doing. There is no shift in the millionaire's horizon. "Refusal of self-transcendence contributes to personal decline."[53] The drifter has not yet discovered his own deed. He doesn't know his own mind. The second case study deals in half measures. He wants to get rid of the attachment but in such a way that he can keep the acquired money. He balks and bargains with God. His knowledge needs to be brought more in harmony with his doing. The third case study demonstrates unrestricted antecedent willingness—this person desires to get rid of the attachment to money but such that there remains no inclination to keep it. The third millionaire is truly indifferent. He has undergone a religious conversion, and so this existential subject has been transformed into a subject grasped by otherworldly love.

In the Lonerganian scheme of things, human development is an ongoing project, a process of self-appropriation. Recall: my being is a becoming. "The Spiritual Exercises assist me to be my true self. Lonergan helps me to appropriate myself in the process. Self-appropriation means that I come to a realisation of what is going on in consciousness when I inquire, understand, judge, deliberate, decide, and act, and in the process fashion myself. Aided by Lonergan's intentionality analysis, I grow in self-awareness and so set up the process of self-appropriation."[54]

Ignatius's three degrees of humility (three ways of being humble), we might call, following Lonergan, three degrees of authenticity and self-transcendence. The three degrees exercise is a reality check in humility:

---

52. Lonergan, *Method in Theology*, 252.

53. Connor and Fellows of the Woodstock Theological Center, *Dynamism of Desire*, 299.

54. Connor and Fellows of the Woodstock Theological Center, *Dynamism of Desire*, 306.

To what extent have I undergone religious conversion, a vocation to holiness, a transformation in living, in my thoughts, feelings, words, deeds, and omissions?—in such a way that I hasten the advent of the kingdom. The first degree is *obedience* to the commandments (moral conversion); the second degree is *indifference* and readiness to do God's will (attitudinal adjustment); the focus in the third degree is on *imitation* of Christ (divine desire).

Ignatius's charism of leadership consisted in his power of discerning the actions/movements (*mociones*) of the spirit within consciousness and directing others in this art. Ignatius discovered the "experience of spiritual consolation and spiritual desolation as the means of finding God's will in all things."[55] Feelings are movements that a subject experiences on the fourth level of intentional consciousness. There is a polyphony of voices in consciousness. The pulls and counterpulls are like a chorus of conflicting and competing voices. The leading voice, the medium, and the low voices are all clamoring for attention. The leading voice may be audible or barely noticeable. We are pushed and pulled from all sides. When Ignatius was thinking of the things of the world, he was filled with delight, but afterwards he felt dry and dissatisfied. The foremost question to ask: Is this life I have chosen worthwhile? Discernment is how we interpret the experiences of the heart's desires. We put our attention on movements within consciousness so as to discover the difference between consolation and desolation, God's will for me and my will for myself. Ignatius gives five practical tips for those in the throes of spiritual desolation:

1. Never change course.
2. Take vigorous action against the desolation.
3. Rise to the challenge, for you have sufficient grace.
4. Be patient; the desolate mood will pass.
5. Plan for future bouts of desolation.[56]

It was Plato who had initially described the pull to light and life and the counterpull to darkness and death. The engendering experience is a movement of spirits within consciousness. Yielding to the light, we

---

55. Connor and Fellows of the Woodstock Theological Center, *Dynamism of Desire*, 322.

56. Connor and Fellows of the Woodstock Theological Center, *Dynamism of Desire*, 331–34.

will experience a movement luminous with truth; experiencing the counterpull is existence in untruth. Both Greek philosophy and the Gospels, according to Lonergan and Eric Voegelin, symbolize existence as a field of tension—of pulls and counterpulls.[57] It is perhaps the difference between information and revelation. We choose the gentle pull of the golden chord, the movement of which draws me up rather than drives me forward or drags me down. We can combine Lonergan and Ignatius in relation to the discernment process via intentionality analysis in three steps, which are:

1. The experience of the data of consciousness
2. The understanding of the data
3. The judgment about the accuracy of our understanding of the data[58]

Our existence in the *metaxy* draws us to the Beyond. The movement is from the mover and in the moved. It is divine in so far as the drawing is from the Father. To discern is to distinguish the pull and counterpull. The motions are empirical presentations within consciousness—the data of sensible consciousness, whereby we become aware of ourselves when we are experiencing something. This is the first level, which, to repeat, is discernment at the level of experience—the data of consciousness. The second level of discernment is at the level of understanding—it is inquiry, insight, formulation. So, in this second step, we understand the meaning of these movements (practical understanding). We ask: What is the meaning of this consolation? Why am I being drawn so powerfully? I experience consolation, for example, in the first level, then I wonder about it, asking questions, and then something clicks—the aha moment: *eureka*. The third level is discernment at the level of judgment of fact. Here, we intelligently receive or expel these spiritually significant motions of the soul. All that glitters is not gold. "Believe not every spirit but try the spirits, to see if they are from God" (1 John 4:1). The criterion for making such judgments lies in the results that follow the movements of the spirits in the way I live my life. A life must change: the focus must be on the transformative effect. Such consolation is a supernaturally bestowed spiritual experience. Finally, I am in a position to offer the contemplation

---

57. Connor and Fellows of the Woodstock Theological Center, *Dynamism of Desire*, 342.

58. Connor and Fellows of the Woodstock Theological Center, *Dynamism of Desire*, 345.

to attain love. "Take Lord, and receive all my liberty, my memory, my understanding, and all my will—all that I have and possess. You, Lord, have given all that to me. I now give it back to you, O Lord. All of it is yours. Dispose of it according to your will. Give me love of yourself along with your grace, for that is enough for me" (the words of the Suscipe, which is a radical prayer of self-giving).[59] Besides the discernment of the sources of the movements of the spirits within consciousness, the question of God's will is expressed by Ignatius in his Principle and Foundation, which states that we are made for the greater glory of God. Discerning God's will is the election which, as an act of choice, is the decision one reaches on the fourth level of consciousness. It is here that we achieve the authenticity inherent in self-transcendence.

There are three times for making a good election; each of them is suitable. The first time can be dramatic and leaves us in no doubt about what to do. Indeed, we are drawn to doing it. This first-time experience occurs at the fourth level of consciousness.

In the second time, sufficient clarity is gained; knowledge is received from the experience and discernment of consolations and desolations. We attend to the data of consolation and desolation. Once we identify the movements, we test them. When we are consoled, to which choices are we drawn? When we experience desolation, to which choices are we drawn? We must keep asking relevant questions before reaching judgment of fact and value that lead to decisions. Here are some questions to ask:

- Are the consolation and desolation truly spiritual?
- Is the spiritual consolation caused by the evil spirit?
- Am I moved to choice A or choice B because God wills it?
- Did the impulse/inclination to a particular act come during the spiritual consolation itself or immediately before or after it?
- To which choice (A or B) does the impulse move me the more (*magis*)?[60]

We pay attention to the movements. *Sentir* is an Ignatian word, meaning to sense or experience in consciousness a divine action that is felt and accepted.

---

59. Ignatius, *Spiritual Exercises* (2021), para. 234.

60. Connor and Fellows of the Woodstock Theological Center, *Dynamism of Desire*, 380–81.

The third time is made in tranquility. Here, I consider the end for which man is made. I am at peace, not moved by many spirits. The Principle and Foundation is the heuristic procedure to discover an unknown X. Feelings, which are apprehensions of values, can be selfish or disinterested; they require discernment. The fruit of self-transcendence is being attentive, intelligent, reasonable, responsible. As we pray, further consolations act as confirmations.

Here is a list of Ignatius's favorite words in the discernment process, which closely coincides with Lonergan's intentional and conscious acts on the four levels of operations: inquiry, understanding, judgment, deliberation. They are to seem, to look at, to feel, to judge:

- *Parecer*: An opinion from observing data
- *Mirar*: Prayerful reflection upon all the available evidence
- *Sentir*: Felt knowledge/sense based on the reaction of feelings to reflection.
- *Juzgar*: The final act of judgment or decision at the end of the discernment process[61]

The drama of life is shaped by three forces/vectors: progress, decline, and redemption, as I already mentioned. Each of us is born with the capacity for growth and self-transcendence. The solution to the problem of egoism and evil is self-sacrificing love. This is the emphasis in the third week. The "Third Week needs the Fourth Week just as the Principle and Foundation needs the Contemplation."[62] The passion of Jesus needs to be joined to the resurrection. The law of the cross is the source of self-surrendering love. "The law of the Cross is the method that is best calculated to move us away from evil and towards what is good."[63] The third week confirms the conversion of the retreatant and creates the condition where the good flourishes.

"Follow me" is Jesus's message. The response on the existential level is deliberation and deed. Resurrection, which is the theme of the fourth week of the exercises, is transformation. We contemplate how Christ

---

61. Connor and Fellows of the Woodstock Theological Center, *Dynamism of Desire*, 397.

62. Connor and Fellows of the Woodstock Theological Center, *Dynamism of Desire*, 401.

63. Connor and Fellows of the Woodstock Theological Center, *Dynamism of Desire*, 410.

appeared to Mary and the apostles. Ignatius's personal confidant and secretary, Juan Polanco, assures that the retreatant who makes the exercises well reaches four objectives:

1. Liberation
2. Illumination
3. Discernment
4. Intense love[64]

The eye of love discerns the presence of the Absolute everywhere. The world is the fruit of God's self-transcendence. The experience of God's love is consolation without cause. In the Ignatian *contemplatio*, we behold God in all things. We come to know that God desires to give his very being. God gives everything existence and conserves all things in existence. St. Paul talks about the love that has been poured into our hearts by the Holy Spirit (Rom 5:5). For Lonergan, there is a trinity in the human psyche that suggests the Trinity in the Godhead. The psychological analogy he develops is based on the operations of the human mind, in the synthesis of intellectual, rational, and moral consciousness, which is the dynamic state of being in love. God is agape love. In the fourth week, I pray to be brought to the peak of enthrallment and to the dynamic state of peace that is the fulfillment of my being and experience the wellspring of joy that can endure despite the sorrow of failures, humiliation, privation, and pain. In the *contemplatio* to enkindle love for God, I pray to be enthralled enough to say, "Take, Lord, receive."[65] For I am nothing without him who is my everything.

A LONERGANIAN PERSPECTIVE ON THE EXAMEN

Simon Wong, SJ, penned an article in 2014 entitled "Bernard Lonergan's Cognitional Theory and the Ignatian Examen of Consciousness," which he kindly emailed to me, which shows the striking similarities between Ignatius's examen and Lonergan's transcendental method. First, let's look

---

64. Connor and Fellows of the Woodstock Theological Center, *Dynamism of Desire*, 435.

65. Connor and Fellows of the Woodstock Theological Center, *Dynamism of Desire*, 464.

at the structure of the examen, according to Ignatius, before grafting Lonergan's insights on to it and around it.

The examen of consciousness, as expounded by Ignatius in the exercises, reveals the nature of the sensory data in consciousness. In the first week of the exercises, Ignatius outlines what he calls a method for making the general examination of conscience in five points:

1. Give thanks to God for the graces (benefits) I have received.
2. Ask for the grace to know my sins and rid myself of them.
3. Seek an account of my soul from the hour of rising until now—hour by hour—first thoughts, then words, then deeds (a review).
4. Petition God for forgiveness (pardon) for my faults.
5. Resolve (with God's grace) to amend them. Close this prayerful period with an Our Father.[66]

There are many ways to put this. In *God Moments*, Andy Otto describes the process of sorting or sifting through consciousness (events, encounters, experiences, feelings, thoughts), *with God*, thus:

1. Presence: Awareness of the divine at work in the world
2. Review: Reflecting back over the happenings of the last twenty-four hours; conversing with God about your day
3. Feelings: Focusing on one's emotions, as they are indicative of how we experience the world
4. One feature selected: What one aspect is calling for your attention? In all your interactions what do you keep going back to? This will usually be accompanied by a high-feeling tone/affect.
5. *Magis*: Looking forward to the next day and asking, "What *more* can I do for God [to make his kingdom come]?"[67]

What the *existential* (as I call it) examen is to Ignatius, cognitional theory is to Lonergan, who, as we have seen, enjoins us to experience (which includes imagining and speaking), to understand (searching for the premises), to judge (reflecting rationally, organizing evidence), and to decide (decision-making, practical choices). The four levels of subjective consciousness are: experiential (empirical), intelligent (inquiry), rational

---

66. *Spiritual Exercises*, in Ignatius, *Personal Writings*, para. 43.
67. Otto, *God Moments*.

(examining our formularies/methods), rational self-consciousness (the self-conscious transcending subject). For Ignatius and Lonergan, we must pay attention to our experience, be wise in our understanding, be reasonable in making judgments, and be responsible with decision-making (consulting one's conscience). This is the core of Lonergan's transcendental method, as we have seen. We're to experience carefully, understand wisely, judge rationally, and choose responsibly. We have to work on becoming aware of and removing cognitive barriers, biases, and blind spots (with which the Enneagram can help). This involves more mindful living, as we shift from being distracted by many things to becoming more concentrated on the one thing needed, from being stupid to being wise, from being irrational to being rational, and from being irresponsible to being responsible. With Lonergan's method, we are better able to carry out Ignatius's injunctions; we have a solid methodology for tracing the origin of our thoughts to their source to see which are from the good spirit and which from the evil spirit. In all endeavors, we attempt to be more present to the meaning of the moment, the sacrament of the present hour. We try to discern the point and purpose of our existence. This is the essence of the discernment of spirits. Focusing on my experience is the starting point. I seek God's will. Conscious reflection, which is at the heart of Lonergan's method and Ignatian spirituality, is a spiritual activity in itself (under the inspiration of the Spirit). We can describe the dialectic thus:

> Good spirit → peace
> Bad spirit → perturbation

We look for empirical evidence and judge whether the understanding is correct, examining the fruits of discrimination, using the principles of judgment. We then put decisions into practice. So, in light of the above, we:

- Pay attention to experience in the review of the day—to my feelings, thoughts, images, sensations
- Seek to understand wisely the content and source of these experiences (seeing their origin/whence they derive)
- Judge reasonably—seek sufficient evidence to discern whether my understanding is right or wrong, correct or incorrect
- Decide responsibly—whether it is in conformity with God's will, in which case I act decisively and with resolve

In short, Lonergan's cognitional theory *is itself an examen of consciousness*, just as Ignatius's examen proceeds in exactly same the way and according to the same transcendental precepts as set out by Lonergan's cognitional theory. These cognitional activities (be attentive to experience, be intelligent in understanding, be reasonable in judging, be responsible in deciding) are presupposed in the examen of consciousness. Wong (correctly and soundly, I would argue) utilizes Lonergan's theory as a philosophical and theological methodology for the Ignatian examen. Each enriches the other.

DE CHARDIN

The Spiritual Exercises were the core of Jesuit paleontologist Pierre Teilhard de Chardin's life. Indeed, the exercises lead to a Christified universe, for Teilhard. The Ignatian Christocentric emphasis received, with Teilhard (1881–1955), a new evolutionary and holistic perspective. Teilhard was a stretcher bearer in the First World War. His commitment and courage to the wounded earned him the War Cross in 1915, the Military Medal in 1917, and the Legion of Honour in 1920. His work in geology centered on the study of human fossils. Between November 1926 and March 1927, he wrote *Le milieu divin* (*The Divine Milieu*). Between June 1947 and 1948, he wrote *Le phénomène humain* (*The Human Phenomenon*). He died in New York on Easter Sunday of 1955. Teilhard's universe was dynamic. He adapted the Ignatian exercises, on which he took notes, in 1952, where he referred to them no longer as THE exercises but "MY Exercises."[68]

Teilhard deploys the term "pleromization" to mean the final realization or fullness (*pleroma*) of the universe and humanity in Omega Christ (the future point in which the entirety of the universe spirals toward unification) in which, according to St. Paul, Christ will be all in all (Col 3:11). Teilhard conceives of the exercises in a new way.

Teilhard's scientific work compelled him to look for the divine in and through matter, in union with matter. Matter and spirit are not opposed. Indeed, the universe has been occupied by divinity itself. Teilhard resists all forms of Manichean and gnostic dualism, which sees matter as evil. After all, matter has been divinized by the incarnation in the body of Christ. Humanity will evolve into the noosphere (sphere of thought),

---

68. Udías, *Spiritual Exercises with Teilhard*, xx; uppercase in original.

according to Teilhard, which is part and parcel of the cosmic evolution converging on the Omega Point of creation (union in God). The unitive force is love just as the line of evolution is the increase in complexity (from the particles of the big bang to atoms, molecules, chemical compounds, living beings). Love is the power present at all levels of the universe—it is the power of unification and spiritualization. It is "the attraction exercised on each unit of consciousness."[69] Love calls us to the great union. Because God is intimately omnipresent, "we should be passionate about the things of the Earth."[70] Whatever has been realized, has been eternalized. Our works are preserved, conserved, as part of the new heavens and the new earth, in some mysterious way. The "divine so thoroughly permeates all our creaturely energies."[71] Our little finger, our smallest tasks all go to the making of the opus Dei—the labor of God in the world. The Christian divinizes the world in Christ. There is nothing, thus, that is profane. Everything is sacred. The entire universe resides within the atom. This is the meaning of the "divine milieu." Teilhard's vision is cosmic, earthy, and mystical all at once. God acts in us despite what he calls "the passivities of diminishment,"[72] such as adversities, infirmities, ageing, suffering, and death—through what affects us negatively. Death is the consummation of our diminishments. Hell is a mystery. Evil is a mystery. We can't know with certainty that anyone has been damned. But neither evil nor hell spoil anything in the divine milieu.

We move from the first week into the second week now with Teilhard, the meditations of which consist of the call of the King, the two standards, the three classes of men, the three degrees of humility. For Teilhard, the cosmogenesis of the universe will become Christogenesis, the Christogenesis of which St. Paul and St. John speak—the world converging on Christ, who occupies its center. Putting this another way, all creation converges on Christ the center. All things have been created by him and for him (Col 1:16). Ignatius's eternal King/Divine Majesty is Teilhard's Cosmic Christ, who is the ultimate purpose of the whole universe. *Omnia in omnibus Christus*—Christ is everything in all (Col 3:11). "The presence of the Incarnate Word penetrates everything, as a universal element," Teilhard writes.[73] Ignatius's God of the above is Teil-

69. Udías, *Spiritual Exercises with Teilhard*, 8.
70. Udías, *Spiritual Exercises with Teilhard*, 13.
71. Udías, *Spiritual Exercises with Teilhard*, 15.
72. Udías, *Spiritual Exercises with Teilhard*, 19.
73. Udías, *Spiritual Exercises with Teilhard*, 30.

hard's God of the ahead, toward whom all creation teleologically tends. Transcendence and immanence together form a single compound. Teilhard uses two terms—transparency and diaphany—to denote how God reveals himself in the created world. The divine surrounds and shapes us. Such is the marvel of the divine milieu. Diaphany is translucency, luminosity. Everything in the universe becomes incorporated into Christ. The mystical Christ is none other than the Christ who was born of Mary and who died on the cross. Things are transfigured from within. Teilhard muses: "They bathe inwardly in light, but, in this incandescence, they retain—this is not strong enough, they exalt—all that is most specific in their attributes"[74]—Christ as both Alpha and Omega.

In *The Divine Milieu*, Teilhard presents three virtues that contribute to the concentration of the divine in our lives: purity, faith, and fidelity. These three are a reflection of the conditions to follow Ignatius's meditations. Purity is rectitude and needed by the person shut up in himself and his own selfish pleasures. Purity acknowledges Christ's primacy. Faith is trust in and knowledge of the divine Being. Through fidelity, we situate ourselves in the hands of God and welcome "the universal and perpetual overtures of the divine milieu."[75] Teilhard makes the whole earth his altar. The aim, and end, is mystical transfiguration.

The third week of the exercises is focused on contemplating the passion. Our Lord suffers in his humanity. For Teilhard, the Eucharist (Last Supper) is a sacramental consecration of the world just as the cross bears all the pain of humanity. Teilhard writes that "the whole of nature vibrates to the radiation of the consecrated Host."[76] In the words of *Hoc est corpus meum* the incarnation of divinity can be seen. God passes through the cosmos as bread. There is only one Mass and one communion. Through the Eucharist, the incarnation is realized in each and every individual. As Teilhard puts it: "As the Host assimilates our humanity, the eucharistic transformation goes beyond and completes the transubstantiation of the bread on the altar. Step by step it irresistibly invades the universe."[77] Teilhard calls the eucharistic consecration "fire in the world."[78] It is not limited to the bread and wine on the altar but is spread across the whole universe. Matter is incarnated. All things in the cosmos converge and are

74. Udías, *Spiritual Exercises with Teilhard*, 37.
75. Udías, *Spiritual Exercises with Teilhard*, 41.
76. Udías, *Spiritual Exercises with Teilhard*, 50.
77. Udías, *Spiritual Exercises with Teilhard*, 51.
78. Udías, *Spiritual Exercises with Teilhard*, 54.

divinized in Christ. Teilhard describes it thus: "The transubstantiation is encircled by a halo of divinization—real, even though less intense—that extends to the whole universe."[79] The whole of nature vibrates to the radiation of the consecrated host; every single atom cooperates in this fulfillment; every particle and every living process participates in the definitive reality of Christ. "The universe assumes the form of Christ."[80] The host, present in the monstrance for worship, extends its presence everywhere across the whole of creation. The host becomes dazzling, illuminates all things, transforming everything in a vast nebula. Once, as Teilhard knelt before the Blessed Sacrament, he experienced a strange impression. He relates it thus:

> I had then the impression as I gazed at the host that its surface was gradually spreading out like a spot of oil but of course much more swiftly and luminously.... Little by little, as the white orb grew and grew in space till it seemed to be drawing quite close to me, I heard a subdued sound, an immeasurable murmur, as when the rising tide extends its silver waves over the world of the algae which tremble and dilate at its approach.... So, through the mysterious expansion of the host, the whole world had become incandescent, had itself become like a single giant host. ... The *white glow was active*; the whiteness was consuming all things from within themselves. It had penetrated, through the channels of matter, into the inmost depths of all hearts.[81]

United with the sufferings of Christ on the cross, we can reach a sympathy with all suffering: cosmic compassion. "On Calvary He is still, and primarily, *the centre on which all earthly sufferings converge*."[82] Without Christ, suffering and sin would be human waste.

St. Ignatius devotes very little space to the fourth week, dedicated to the mysteries of the Risen Christ. For Teilhard, the resurrection has a cosmic character. Christ contributes to the construction of the world. The Cosmic Christ is the Universal Christ—the organic center of the entire universe; the resurrection is a cosmic event of seismic proportions in the divine drama.

Teilhard wished to die on Easter Day—for that he prayed—and it was granted to him. "All of us, inescapably, exist in you, the universal

---

79. Udías, *Spiritual Exercises with Teilhard*, 60.
80. Udías, *Spiritual Exercises with Teilhard*, 61.
81. Udías, *Spiritual Exercises with Teilhard*, 61–62.
82. Udías, *Spiritual Exercises with Teilhard*, 67.

milieu in which and through which all things live and have their being."⁸³ The cosmic body is to be found in all things, for Ignatius as much as for Teilhard de Chardin. Indeed, the Cosmic Christ "is eminently the *mystical Milieu*."⁸⁴ Ignatius's contemplation to attain love, which is the final contemplation of the exercises, is, for Teilhard, the amorization of the universe. Love becomes the ultimate goal of evolution, which consists in nothing less than the ultimate union of the world in Omega Christ. The world itself is "Christified." Mysticism does nothing other than disclose the sacramental consecration of the world: *Erit in omnibus Deus* so that "God may be all in all" (1 Cor 15:28).

HOPKINS

The Jesuit poet Gerard Manley Hopkins (1844–89) penned his "Comments on the Spiritual Exercises of St Ignatius Loyola" between 1878 and 1885.⁸⁵ An entry of August 20, 1880, on Ignatius's Principle and Foundation, reveals that Hopkins was thinking about creation, specifically, that *Homo creatus est*, which guided his own experience of the exercises which he made in Liverpool. Hopkins examines his personality, place, pains, powers, shame, hopes, and fears—what he calls his "selfbeing,"⁸⁶ his being more *selved* (distinct) than other beings (the principle of individuality or *haecceitas*). Nothing can compare to "my being-myself."⁸⁷ Questions arise: Whence did I come? By chance? Did I create myself (self-existent substance), or did some extrinsic power bring me into existence? These were the thoughts preoccupying Hopkins prompted as he was by the Principle and Foundation of the exercises.

Chance is a passive power—pure possibility. "No man can believe that his being is due to chance," Hopkins says.⁸⁸ Am I necessary (as distinct from being contingent)? No, because I am finite and nothing finite can exist of itself/determine its own being, "the inmost self of mine,"⁸⁹ as most highly selved (to use his typical terminology). I find I can't be

---

83. Udías, *Spiritual Exercises with Teilhard*, 76.
84. Udías, *Spiritual Exercises with Teilhard*, 77.
85. Hopkins, *Notebooks and Papers*, 309–420.
86. Hopkins, *Notebooks and Papers*, 309.
87. Hopkins, *Notebooks and Papers*, 310.
88. Hopkins, *Notebooks and Papers*, 311.
89. Hopkins, *Notebooks and Papers*, 312.

self-existent; even if a universal mind created my consciousness; this universal mind would be identified with other minds and not with what is individual in me. As Hopkins puts it: "The universal cannot taste this taste of self as I taste it."⁹⁰ The universal mind would be outside of my inmost self; moreover, it wouldn't share my state or standing. A self, for Hopkins, consists of a center and a circumference (surrounding area)—a point of reference, a field of belonging. There is an "inset" and an "outsetting."⁹¹ There is no universal self that is selved/pitched in every other self, even if there may be in me my true self. Thus, I am due to an extrinsic power, to a necessary self-existent being—the great being, or God who caused me to be, created my being out of nothingness (*creatio ex nihilo*).

In his comments on the *examen conscientiae generale*, Hopkins explores the faculty of the will—its purpose and intention, together with guilt, sin, the act of commission and consent. Hopkins, in accord with classical metaphysics, views the human person as a rational supposit, as the support of a rational nature. A supposit is a self. "Self is the intrinsic oneness of a thing, which is prior to its being." The bare self is zero in the score of existence. Hopkins expounds: "For in the world, besides natures or essences or 'inscapes' and the selves, supposits, hypostases, or, in the core of rational natures/persons which wear or 'fetch' or instance them, there is still something else—fact or fate."⁹² Selves are intrinsically different, but we are all moved by something mysterious. There is, with selves, freedom of pitch and play. The self shows more freedom the higher its nature—it is more selved in angels than men. God, then, can shift the self that lies in one to a higher, that is better, pitch of itself—on the side of good.⁹³ The range of pitch will extend from bad to good, from sinner to saint. The self, as personality, is prior to nature but not prior to pitch. Grace adds to nature; it doesn't negate or annul it.

- Freedom of pitch is self-determination—choice.
- Freedom of play is the execution of choice.
- Freedom of field is the field or objects of choice (there is more than one coin to choose from, to draw on Hopkins's analogy).⁹⁴

90. Hopkins, *Notebooks and Papers*, 313.
91. Hopkins, *Notebooks and Papers*, 315.
92. Hopkins, *Notebooks and Papers*, 322.
93. Hopkins, *Notebooks and Papers*, 324.
94. Hopkins, *Notebooks and Papers*, 326.

There is, so, correspondence with choice and grace. Choice is the instress of my will. *Instress* and *inscape* are complementary concepts relating to identity and uniqueness. Hopkins derives these terms/ideas from the medieval Franciscan philosopher and theologian Duns Scotus. Inscape is the external design, the aesthetic conception, the form of a thing, the individual self, the core of individuality, its distinctive design, which is dynamic, not static. Each being in the universe *selves*, that is to say, enacts its identity—brings it forth. We recognize the *inscape* of other beings through *instress*, which is the apprehension of an object in an intense thrust of energy toward it that enables one to recognize its uniqueness. For Hopkins, the instress of inscape leads one to Christ (as each individual identity is created in the image of the Creator, has the stamp of divine creation on it). If the Creator is a perfect prism, creation is the refraction of this perfect light. (In parenthesis, I would like to make the philosophical point that Blessed Duns Scotus distinguishes between the *concept* of being and the *mode* of being, and this has given rise to some conceptual confusion. The concept [not the reality] of being is univocal for both God and creatures. The mode of being, however, couldn't be more disparate—God is infinite being, creatures are finite beings. Scotus is not saying that the metaphysical reality of being is univocal between God and creatures, which would proximate to heresy, in the Christian tradition.)

Now, where there is but one alternative, there is no alternative. Only in the presence of multiple alternatives does the elective will possess existential freedom. The choice (election) is to be made, according to Ignatius and Hopkins, for Christ. This changes one. With great changes (conversions, for example), there are shifts in perspectives, alterations in attitudes of mind. What is called *transubstantiation* is the conversion of one substance into another whole substance—this due to divine power. Hopkins writes: "For a self is an absolute which stands to the absolute of God as the infinitesimal to the infinite."[95] This shift is grace, that is to say, God acting on a being/creature, bringing them toward salvation, and this work is done by Christ as if Christ was playing at being me; "Christ *being me* and me being Christ,"[96] as Hopkins beautifully describes it.

We pray for such grace. Ignatius commends this throughout the exercises. If prayer is the sigh of desire in the direction of the divine, grace

---

95. Hopkins, *Notebooks and Papers*, 331.
96. Hopkins, *Notebooks and Papers*, 332.

is heaped on grace. It is granted gratis, "this stirring of the spirit towards God."[97] It brings home to us the importance—the everlasting imperative—of making a good choice. As Hopkins explains: "The will is surrounded by the objects of desire as the needle by the points of the compass."[98] It is drawn to A one minute and to B the next minute. We need supernatural grace to aid us to determine the will toward the right object in the field of choice and to lift this particular plane to a higher one (an elevation), which "lifts the receiver from one cleave of being to another."[99] This is God's finger touching the very vein of personality. What gets in the way is sin, which is disobedience, insubordination to God. If disorder is the soil of sin, repentance is the disavowal of sin—its repudiation.

A quick note on composition of place: When we see the persons present at the Last Supper, to take an example, we see the specifications and specifics of the room—how it is furnished; we give the room, to deploy Hopkins's beautiful neologism, its "personallings."[100] We look upon Jesus with adoration, just as we look upon Judas with grief. In this way and by this manner, the Gospel scenes are brought alive, made vivid to the mind (and senses).

Finally, the *contemplatio ad obtinendum amorem*: the last mystery meditated on in the exercises—this is when we "see" the Spirit sent to us and *selving* in us,[101] which takes place in the Eucharist, wherein we are spiritually nourished for eternal life as we partake in divinity itself. Let me bring this chapter to a close with a discussion of the discernment of spirits, so central for St. Ignatius.

DISCERNMENT OF SPIRITS

Often, either circumstance or our unconscious emotions such as fears and desires do our deciding for us. To put it in Ignatian terms: the *evil spirit* pulls us away from God while the *good spirit* pulls us toward God. There is such a thing as self-deception because we are not transparent to ourselves precisely due to the presence of unconscious mental processes. The state of self-deception Ignatius calls *false consolation*.

---

97. Hopkins, *Notebooks and Papers*, 333.
98. Hopkins, *Notebooks and Papers*, 336.
99. Hopkins, *Notebooks and Papers*, 337.
100. Hopkins, *Notebooks and Papers*, 342.
101. Hopkins, *Notebooks and Papers*, 344.

The signs of consolation are being in sync with God and his action in the world, having great desires for faith, hope, and love, experiencing inner peace and deep-down tranquility despite surface stress. Desolation is the opposite: being unaligned with God, experiencing a lack of desire for faith, hope, and love, being in inner turmoil and disquiet. The trickiest state to recognize is to detect false (counterfeit) consolations, because one's inclinations and actions seem loving and full of hope, etc., but they have the serpent's tail. There may be present a subtle rebelliousness or resentment, a lack of transparency (secrecy), a reversal of past good decisions, a false sense of urgency. To give an example: infatuation is one form of false consolation.

Where Ignatius uses the term "evil spirit," Jesuit Mark E. Thibodeaux uses the term "false spirit" to define any movement within myself that leads me away from God, from faith, from hope, from love.[102] For my part, I define *consolation* as the spiritual state of being attuned to the flow of divine presence,[103] and *desolation* as the spiritual state of being estranged and alienated from the divine ground of being. These states can be general, particular, situational; they can be of a brief spell or more long term. We also need to distinguish a spiritual state and an emotional one; not all consolations and desolations are spiritual. For example, as Thibodeaux rightly recognizes, "one might experience emotional desolation in the midst of spiritual consolation."[104] I could experience sadness but still have an acute sense of God's presence. Emotional desolation would be depression. Thibodeaux provides this useful exposition, where the sign ~ stands for "approximately equal."[105]

> Consolation ~ Ignatian indifference ~ spiritual freedom
> Desolation ~ disordered attachments ~ spiritual unfreedom

Neither consolation nor desolation can be reduced to feeling good or bad. They are less psychological emotions than they are ontological moods. To repeat: we can *feel* consoled while unconsciously being in a state of desolation.

> False consolation = desolation

---

102. Thibodeaux, *Ignatian Discernment of Spirits*, 3.
103. Costello, *Philosophy and the Flow*.
104. Thibodeaux, *Ignatian Discernment of Spirits*, 17.
105. Thibodeaux, *Ignatian Discernment of Spirits*, 21.

When it feels like consolation and actually is, Ignatius calls it *consolation*. When it feels like desolation and actually is, Ignatius calls it *desolation*. *False consolation* (what I call *counterfeit consolation*) is the name of the state in which it feels like consolation but actually is desolation. A question invariably/inevitably arises: What might we call the state in which it feels like desolation but actually is consolation? Ignatius has no name for this. Thibodeaux, though, does. He calls it "difficult consolation"[106] and gives the example of Mother Teresa of Calcutta as someone who experienced this spiritual state of being. "The same might be said of St. John of the Cross's experience of the 'dark night of the soul.'"[107]

Dark night of the soul = difficult consolation

To summarize these four states, then:

	Actually is consolation	Actually is desolation
Feels like consolation	Consolation	False consolation
Feels like desolation	Difficult consolation	Desolation

Often the path from desolation to consolation passes through difficult consolation. Thibodeaux distinguishes the following eight states:

1. Dramatic consolation: I am overwhelmed with joy.

2. Placid consolation: I am happy and at peace but not exactly overwhelmed.

3. Dramatic desolation: I am in despair and feel miserable/fearful/hopeless.

4. Placid desolation: I feel lethargic and apathetic, lacking energy and initiative.

5. Dramatic false consolation: Feels like dramatic consolation; I am manic and don't know it.

6. Placid false consolation: I believe I am in placid consolation, but what I am calling peace is really indolence.

7. Dramatic difficult consolation: I am sad/lonely, but I know God stands by me; though I may be tempted to make a dramatic decision, I realize it's the depression talking.

---

106. Thibodeaux, *Ignatian Discernment of Spirits*, 26.
107. Thibodeaux, *Ignatian Discernment of Spirits*, 27.

8. Placid difficult consolation: I am feeling lethargic, but I force myself to get up and go to work—*agere contra*.[108]

Our primary focus should be on the discernment of *spirts* rather than the discernment of choices. Bad decisions are the result of bad discernment. We can discern not just consciously but through synchronicity, dreams, etc. Finally here, what Ignatius in rule 2 of the second week calls "consolation without previous cause" is not an unmediated experience of the divine, for Thibodeaux—impossible this side of heaven, he argues—but rather a spiritual experience wherein the *intensity* of the consolation is far out of proportion to the preceding cause.[109] The pertinent questions to ask are: What state of being am I in—desolation, consolation, false consolation, or difficult consolation? What am I feeling? What am I thinking? What are the voices in my head telling me? Journaling is a crucial exercise in this regard. For example, here are some questions we might ask if we are experiencing a desolation:

- When did the desolation begin? When did it end?
- What were the external events and internal thoughts and feelings that preceded the desolation?
- In the midst of the desolation, what things did I do or say or think that helped me feel better?
- What kinds of things made the experience worse?
- What were the twisted truths being proposed to me by the false spirit?
- What brought me into consolation?

We need to track and trace the causes and cures. This involves paying attention to both psyche (soul) and polis (society) to discern not only *that* God is present but *how* God is present in the pots and pans (as it were), in people as well as places.

---

108. Thibodeaux, *Ignatian Discernment of Spirits*, 37–42.
109. Thibodeaux, *Ignatian Discernment of Spirits*, 53–55.

CHAPTER THREE

Conversion in Charles Taylor and Bernard Lonergan

I have come that they may have life and have it to the full.
(John 10:10)

AGAIN AND AGAIN IN Christianity, and not just in Ignatian spirituality, we are reminded that Christianity is all about *fullness* of life. This is made possible by spiritual conversion (*metanoia*)—the process of changing one's beliefs, which is a matter of the heart. Such a turning (*periagoge*) emerges from our love (*eros*) of truth. But what exactly is fullness, and what is conversion? My aim in this chapter is to unpack and describe the notion of fullness as it features in Canadian philosopher Charles Taylor's *Secular Age* before delineating the dynamics of conversion, according to another Canadian philosopher-theologian, Bernard Lonergan, whom we have already encountered, which will help us appreciate and better understand, in retrospect, not only Ignatius's own religious conversion but many others who have undergone such a significant metamorphosis.

Philosopher David Walsh's criticism of Charles Taylor (b. 1931), in a footnote in *The Third Millennium: Reflections on Faith and Reason*, makes the point that in *Sources of the Self*, Taylor "has drawn our attention to the centrality of ordinary life within the modern worldview, but he fails to exhibit the capacity for transcendence that renders it worthy of celebration."[1] Taylor's *Secular Age* answers this criticism. In the last chapter of this work, Taylor calls the experiences of fullness "conversions," a notion extensively explored by Lonergan in his *Method in Theology*, and whose reflections on the subject will be highlighted here to fill in the gaps of Taylor's account of the subject. This philosophical exposition will seek to make sense of what a conversion actually/exactly is.

TAYLOR ON FULLNESS

For Taylor, fullness takes us beyond mere human flourishing and relates us to the realm of the transcendent. Of course the notion of flourishing was given full voice by Aristotle in his *Nicomachean Ethics*; the word he employs is *eudaimonia*, which is usually translated as "happiness," but which can also be rendered as "flourishing." Taylor is thus critiquing this eudaimonistic ethic.[2]

Taylor diagnoses this shift to secularity, where belief in God is no longer axiomatic despite the undoubted search for the spiritual that also abounds. Aristotelian flourishing is understood as leading an ethical life, by cultivating the moral and intellectual virtues, in the polis. Flourishing in the city-state or society needn't have any reference, though, to ultimate reality. Flourishing is a secular symbol. *Secularism* may be defined as the space emptied of God or of any reference to transcendent reality. Fullness, by contrast, explicitly relates us to the transcendent, however that is conceived. Before we define what Taylor means by fullness and in keeping with Eric Voegelin's injunction that we return to the engendering *experiences* to which subsequent symbols give rise, let me begin with an experiential epiphany enjoyed by Bede Griffiths, the British Benedictine monk, which he reports in his autobiography and which Taylor cites in his introduction to *A Secular Age*:

> One day during my last term at school I walked out alone in the evening and heard the birds singing in that full chorus of song, which can only be heard at that time of the year at dawn or at sunset. I remember now the shock of surprise with which the sound broke on my ears. It seemed to me that I had never

---

1. Walsh, *Third Millennium*, 232n13.
2. See Costello, *Ethics of Happiness*.

heard the birds singing before and I wondered whether they sang like this all year round and I had never noticed it. As I walked, I came upon some hawthorn trees in full bloom and again I thought I had never seen such a sight or experienced such sweetness before. If I had been brought suddenly among the trees of the Garden of Paradise and heard a choir of angels singing, I could not have been more surprised. I came then to where the sun was setting over the playing fields. A lark rose suddenly from the ground beside the trees where I was standing and poured out its song above my head, and then sank still singing to rest. Everything then grew still as the sunset faded and the veil of dusk began to cover the earth. I remember now the feeling of awe which came over me. I felt inclined to kneel on the ground, as though I had been standing in the presence of an angel; and I hardly dared to look on the face of the sky, because it seemed as though it was but a veil before the face of God.[3]

Following Taylor, we can describe this conversion experience as one of fullness; Bernard Lonergan and Viktor Frankl would call it self-transcendence. The space in which we live has a certain moral and spiritual shape, and somewhere, in some condition or activity, there lies a fullness or richness. There, "life is fuller, richer, deeper, and more worthwhile, more admirable, more what it should be," as Taylor puts it. We often experience it as "deeply moving, as inspiring. Perhaps this sense of fullness is something we just catch glimpses of from afar off; we have the powerful intuition of what fullness would be, were we to be in that condition, e.g., of peace or wholeness . . . of integrity or generosity or abandonment or self-forgetfulness."[4] These experienced moments bring joy and fulfillment; they are referred to by some as *transpersonal experiences*. In such cases, it seems that ordinary reality is abolished or obliterated; they are experiences that unsettle and break through our feelings of familiarity and our tried and tested ways of being in the world. Something other shines through our consciousness and leaves us with a sense of the uncanny. However, it is important to note, as Taylor does, that the experience of fullness may not always be identified with such limit or peak experiences, be they uplifting and edifying, or frightening and traumatic. They may be moments when "the deep divisions, [Pascalian] distractions, worries, sadnesses that seem to drag us down are somehow dissolved, or brought into alignment, so that we feel united, moving forward, suddenly

3. Cited by Taylor, *Secular Age*, 5.
4. Taylor, *Secular Age*, 5.

capable and full of energy."[5] These experiences touch on our highest capabilities and aspirations. They transform us. They situate us morally and spiritually.

> They can orient us because they offer some sense of what they are of: the presence of God, or the voice of nature, or the force which flows through everything, or the alignment in us of desire and the drive to form. But they are also often unsettling and enigmatic. Our sense of where they come from may also be unclear, confused. . . . We are deeply moved, but also puzzled and shaken. We struggle to articulate what we have been through.[6]

We think of Aquinas's reverential silence before the mystery. So often instead of fullness we experience ennui or melancholic acedia, when fullness fails. Between these two extremes of fullness and forlornness lies ordinary human happiness, which fulfills us in various ways, even permitting us to flourish and to contribute to what we conceive of as the good. It is essential, Taylor opines, that we have continuing contact with the place of fullness. For the theist, of course, this place of fullness will be faith, but it need not be so theistically construed. Such faith-filled fullness brings peace and joy, a sense of satisfaction and completeness. The unbeliever may experience satisfaction with his lot or a sense of achievement, but so long as his life is not ordered to God as the divine flow of presence in it, "he still has some way to go."[7] Perhaps he hasn't conquered his nostalgia for something really transcendent, Taylor contends.

For the theist, "the account of the place of fullness requires reference to God."[8] For the atheist, fullness may be interpreted naturalistically in terms of human potential and possibility. Experiences of fullness vary, but believers often say that it comes to them as a gratuitous gift, as grace; that it is dependent on a relationship of love; that it involves practices of prayer, of charity; often such people feel very far from such conditions of caritas and experience themselves instead as preoccupied with lesser, mortal things, that what is needed or required is a (Christian) conversion or opening out, a Heideggerian clearing (*Lichtung*), a Platonic *periagoge* or Rilkean turning, a Murdochian unselfing or Weilian *décreation*, whereby the ego is transmogrified. Such experiences of fullness seem to

---

5. Taylor, *Secular Age*, 6.
6. Taylor, *Secular Age*, 6.
7. Taylor, *Secular Age*, 7.
8. Taylor, *Secular Age*, 8.

come from a power beyond me. What does this mean? Taylor answers thus: "The best sense I can make of my conflicting and moral experience is captured by a theological view of this kind. That is, in my own experience, in prayer, in moments of fullness, in experiences of exile overcome, in what I seem to observe around me in other people's lives—lives of exceptional spiritual fullness, or lives of maximum self-enclosedness, lives of demonic evil, etc.—this seems to be the picture that emerges."[9] To repeat, such experiences may be construed differently, nontheistically. It seems to me, though, that God is the best explanation of them. Like Lonergan's, Taylor's hermeneutic is avowedly a Christian construal. Of course, Taylor is aware of the postmodern problems associated with a word such as "fullness." We have just to think of Derrida's critique of the metaphysics of *presence*. Taylor describes Derridean deconstruction as a "non-religious anti-humanism"[10] or of Levinas's stress on the *trace*. Taylor observes:

> "Fullness" has come to be my shorthand term for the condition we aspire to, but I am acutely aware how inadequate all words are here. Every possible designation has something wrong with it. The glaring one in the case of "fullness" is that according to one very plausible spiritual path, visible clearly in Buddhism, for instance, the highest aspiration is to a kind of emptiness (*sunyata*); or to put it more paradoxically, real fullness only comes through emptiness. But there is no perfect terminological solution here, and so with all these reservations I let the word stand.[11]

These considerations of what constitutes fullness contrast with conceptualizations about flourishing. We all have some conceptions of what human flourishing is, of what constitutes a fulfilled life, of what makes life worth living. These may be codified in moral codes or philosophical or religious practices. The question Taylor poses is: Does the highest or best life involve seeking or acknowledging a good that is beyond, in the sense of independent of, human flourishing? The highest human flourishing could include our aiming at something other than human flourishing. Taylor calls these final goals.[12] Of course, in the Judeo-Christian tradition the answer to the question just posited is affirmative. "Loving, worshipping God is the ultimate end. Of course, in this tradition God is seen as

---

9. Taylor, *Secular Age*, 10.
10. Taylor, *Secular Age*, 19.
11. Taylor, *Secular Age*, 780n8.
12. Taylor, *Secular Age*, 16.

willing human flourishing, but devotion to God is not seen as contingent on this. The injunction 'Thy will be done' isn't equivalent to 'Let humans flourish', even though we know that God wills human flourishing."[13] Many people on different religious paths detach themselves, or try to do so, from their own flourishing to the point of the extinction of the self. Flourishing is good or a good, but seeking it is not our ultimate goal, for Taylor.[14] But secular humanism does not accept any final goals beyond human flourishing or ordinary human happiness. By contrast, Taylor defines religion in terms of transcendence, of that something that is higher than or beyond mere human flourishing. Christianity calls this agape. *Fullness*, construed theistically, is "a condition in which our highest spiritual and moral aspirations point us inescapably to God, one might say, make no sense without God."[15] Fullness, so, as a gift from God—fullness as the felt presence of God even in our secular society, our disenchanted world.

St. Augustine had held that all times are present to God. "His now contains all time," as Taylor puts it—a *nunc stans*.[16] So God's presence is the intersection of timelessness with time, as T. S. Eliot describes it. Rising to eternity is participating in God's instant. All times are present to him. This is the beyond of (ordinary) human flourishing which is so crucial to Christianity.[17] But in a world "shorn of the sacred"[18] many people, Taylor contends, are happy living for purely immanent goals; "they live in a way that takes no account of the transcendent."[19] The secular age is not only that age that is not tied to religion, but the original sense of the secular was that which pertained to profane rather than sacred time; it posited time as purely profane. Of course Taylor realizes that our moral and spiritual resources can be experienced as purely immanent; fullness may be formulated with an exclusively human reference—to human time. The move to immanentization is a rejection of the Christian aspiration to transcend flourishing. Nontheistic Romantics could interpret Bede Griffiths's experience and description of a moment of fullness pantheistically as a worship of nature, or panentheistically. It will all depend

13. Taylor, *Secular Age*, 17.
14. Taylor, *Secular Age*, 18.
15. Taylor, *Secular Age*, 26.
16. Taylor, *Secular Age*, 57.
17. Taylor, *Secular Age*, 67.
18. Taylor, *Secular Age*, 80.
19. Taylor, *Secular Age*, 143.

on one's hermeneutic reading. So if flourishing pertains to our human or profane time (*chronos*), fullness belongs to God's time (*kairos*) or eternity. The secular, so, points or refers to the affairs of the world, to temporality, as distinct from the city of God. Communism and Fascism, as modes of anti-religion, attempt to capture something of a higher purpose but in purely immanentistic terms.[20] Modernity is marked by this anthropocentrism in the same way that the medieval period was characterized, in the main, by theocentrism. Our contemporary culture attests to "the eclipse of the transcendent"[21]—Buber had called it the "eclipse of God" in his book of the same title.

The question is: Can we find meaning in the malaise of modernity, in the "malaise of immanence"[22]? The sense of emptiness and meaninglessness, of absurdity and nausea, well documented by Sartre and Camus, is ubiquitous. We seem to have lost a sense of the sacred, of truth and goodness and beauty and depth and sense, in our quotidian, dry, flat, banal, mundane modern lives, of the *one thing necessary*/needful, in our crass, cardboard culture. Taylor distinguishes *three* modes of these malaises of immanence: (1) the fragility of meaning, the loosening of a sense of or search for an overarching significance; (2) the felt flatness of attempts to solemnize important moments of our lives; and (3) the emptiness of the ordinary.[23] Transcendence is the answer for some—a return to or deepening relationship with the transcendent; for others who don't share such faith, they will seek their solutions in their own ways, perhaps in working for greater prosperity or peace or justice in a world no longer full of gods/God. For the theist, God's existence is felt and flows through all creation. As Schiller writes in *The Gods of Greece*: "Life's fullness flowed through creation / And there felt what never more will feel / . . . Everything to the initiate's eye / Showed the trace of a God."[24] William Wordsworth, too, speaks of this presence we are identifying, with Taylor, Bernard Lonergan, and Eric Voegelin, too, as God where, in *Tintern Abbey*, Wordsworth writes the following:

> A presence that disturbs me with the joy
> Of elevated thoughts; a sense sublime

---

20. Taylor, *Secular Age*, 267.
21. Taylor, *Secular Age*, 307.
22. Taylor, *Secular Age*, 308.
23. Taylor, *Secular Age*, 309.
24. Cited by Taylor, *Secular Age*, 316.

> Of something far more deeply interfused,
> Whose dwelling is the light of setting suns,
> And the round ocean and the living air,
> And the blue sky, and the mind of man;
> A motion and a spirit, that impels
> All thinking things, all objects of all thought,
> And rolls through all things.[25]

This is an epiphanic experience of the flow, of "the fullness of joy."[26] It is the fulfillment that goes beyond flourishing and even morality, and which is the real "point of our existence."[27] This entails, for the Christian, participating in agape love, which calls us to go beyond flourishing and to transform our purely immanentistic perspectives and frameworks, supported as they are by a materialist mentality. Ultimately, it will mean more than pursuing our own happiness. The pursuit of happiness in our contemporary commercial culture means the pursuit of private pleasure and self-satisfaction; the modern turn to the self/subject, as in realizing my so-called higher or *true self* is a turn to hedonism where the stress is predominantly on personal development and individual self-expression. Self-cultivation represents the higher selfishness involving not mindless accumulation but engaging in tasks that are seen to be socially constructive and emotionally enriching or edifying. Taylor calls this the *horizontal* focus and form of the modern worldview; this libertarian *Zeitgeist* lacks the vertical dimension—the irruption of the Wholly/Holy Other. The question is: Can a life encased in a purely immanentistic order provide ultimate purpose, or *is this all there is*? Many seekers searching for the self rather than salvation say they are interested in spirituality rather than religion or institutionalized forms of expression. But this so-called spirituality can be saccharine and subjectivistic, focused, as it is, on the self and its concerns. This kind of spiritual quest is often New Age in its immanentistic understandings and frames of reference,[28] as wholeness is emphasized and cultivated rather than holiness, and sickness replaces sin in "the triumph of the therapeutic," as Rieff called it in a book of the same name in 1966. This age of (alleged) authenticity signifies the retreat

---

25. William Wordsworth, *Tintern Abbey* 2.94–102; cited by Taylor, *Secular Age*, 357–58.
26. Taylor, *Secular Age*, 358.
27. Taylor, *Secular Age*, 358.
28. Taylor, *Secular Age*, 508–9.

of Christendom.[29] It is this hegemony that Taylor is challenging. He calls such a secularist spin a "closed world structure,"[30] reminiscent of Bergson's notion of the closed soul, wherein capitalism has replaced Christianity and where the entertainment media and advertising encourage egomania, self-satisfaction, the pursuit of pleasure, and personal fulfillment. "We feel called to happiness," says Taylor;[31] we *demand* to be happy. But alongside this is a longing for clarity or ultimate meaning, for God, if you like, whose call echoes in the human heart. Can we make sense of life without invoking something transcendent? Does the "immanent frame," as Taylor calls it, and which Voegelin famously and felicitously calls the immanentization of the eschaton, suffice with its relegation of the religious sense of life? Can materialism or Marxism answer our questions about meaning? How do we make sense of our ethical actions or artistic experiences without speaking in terms of a transcendent being who "interpellates us"[32]? The absence of a life of fullness would leave us, according to Taylor, "in abject, unbearable despair."[33] Taylor points out that Nietzsche had poured scorn on ordinary happiness, describing it as a pitiable comfort; and Camus's Dr. Rieux, in *La peste*, insisted too on aiming for something higher and engaged in ethical acts despite Sisyphean senselessness and the feeling of futility.[34] There are rival notions of fullness, but for the theist they will probably be mirages, (Baudrillardian) simulacra, merely naturalistic ontologies. The theist will want, therefore, to include Bede Griffiths's experience or any epiphanic experience we enjoy in our encounter with great music or art within the religious register, what Taylor is calling the fullness beyond flourishing. Commenting on happiness, Taylor has this to say:

> The belief in untroubled happiness is not only a childish illusion, but also involves a truncation of human nature, turning our backs on much of what we are.... Hasn't Christian preaching always repeated that it is impossible to be fully happy as a sinful agent in a sinful world? Certainly this illusion can't be laid at the foot of the Christian faith, however much contemporary

---

29. Taylor, *Secular Age*, 514.
30. Taylor, *Secular Age*, 551.
31. Taylor, *Secular Age*, 583.
32. Taylor, *Secular Age*, 597.
33. Taylor, *Secular Age*, 600.
34. Taylor, *Secular Age*, 582–86.

> Christians may be sucked into this common view of the "pursuit of happiness" today.[35]

Humanistic happiness is not what transcendent happiness is ultimately about. Taylor opines: "If the transcendental view is right, then human beings have an ineradicable bent to respond to something beyond life."[36] Conversion. Self-transcendence. Transformation. Attunement or orientation of the soul to God, to the flow of divine Presence. For the Christian consciousness, so, human flourishing, which is the aim of an exclusive humanism, is not the final goal. Christianity needn't and shouldn't crush human flourishing but point beyond it to the fullness of redemption, to the "richness which transcends the ordinary,"[37] to the eschatological banquet promised in paradise. This eschatological emphasis lifts us beyond a teleological tending toward attaining *my* happiness in this historical here and now. Taylor notes: "Human happiness can only inspire us when we have to fight against the forces which are destroying it; but once realized, it will inspire nothing but ennui, a cosmic yawn."[38]

Taylor speaks of a desire for eternity in human beings, of "a desire to gather the scattered moments of meaning into some kind of whole."[39] Doesn't love call for eternity, as Nietzsche rightly recognized? Doesn't joy strive for it? By contrast, "the collapse of a sense of the eternal brings on a void, a kind of crisis."[40] Mallarmé gives voice to this feeling of *le rien, le néant*: "Sprawled in the happiness in which only his appetites / Feed."[41] Taylor observes:

> The individual pursuit of happiness as defined by consumer culture still absorbs much of our time and energy, or else the threat of being shut out of this pursuit through poverty, unemployment, incapacity galvanizes all our efforts. All this is true, and yet the sense that there is something more presses in. Great numbers of people feel it: in moments of reflection about their life; in moments of relaxation in nature; in moments of bereavement and loss; and quite wildly and unpredictably. Our age is very far from settling into a comfortable unbelief. Although

35. Taylor, *Secular Age*, 635–36.
36. Taylor, *Secular Age*, 638.
37. Taylor, *Secular Age*, 677.
38. Taylor, *Secular Age*, 717.
39. Taylor, *Secular Age*, 720.
40. Taylor, *Secular Age*, 722.
41. Cited by Taylor, *Secular Age*, 724.

many individuals do so, and more still seem to on the outside, the unrest continues to surface. Could it ever be otherwise?[42]

In the concluding chapter of *A Secular Age*, entitled "Conversions," Taylor relates another epiphanic experience, that of Václav Havel—like Bede Griffiths's one, it is an experience of what Taylor calls conversion. Griffiths's and Havel's and St. Ignatius's experiences/conversions broke them out of the immanent frame of focus. In *Letters to Olga* Havel recounts:

> Again, I call to mind that distant moment in [the prison at] Hermanice when on a hot, cloudless summer day, I sat on a pile of rusty iron and gazed into the crown of an enormous tree that stretched, with dignified repose, up and over all the fences, wires, bars, and watchtowers that separated me from it. As I watched the imperceptible trembling of its leaves against an endless sky, I was overcome by a sensation that is difficult to describe: all at once, I seemed to rise above all the coordinates of my momentary existence in the world into a kind of state outside time in which all beautiful things I have ever seen and experienced existed in a total "co-present"; I felt a sense of reconciliation, indeed of an almost gentle assent to the inevitable course of events as revealed to me now, and this combined with a carefree determination to face what had to be faced. A profound amazement at the sovereignty of Being became a dizzy sensation of tumbling endlessly into the abyss of its mystery; an unbounded joy at being alive, at having been given the chance to live through all I have lived through, and at the fact that everything has a deep and obvious meaning—this joy formed a strange alliance in me with a vague horror at the . . . unattainability of everything I was so close to in that moment, standing at the very "edge of the infinite"; I was flooded with a sense of ultimate happiness and harmony with the world and myself, with that moment, with all the moments I could call up, and with everything invisible that lies behind it and has meaning. I would even say that I was somehow "struck by love," though I don't know precisely for whom or what.[43]

Men like Griffiths and Havel as well as sages and saints such as Francis of Assisi, Bonaventure, Teresa of Ávila, John of the Cross, and Ignatius of Loyola, the mystics and the prophets of all time, have radiated a sense of

---

42. Taylor, *Secular Age*, 727.
43. Cited by Taylor, *Secular Age*, 728–29.

direct contact with transcendent reality. They have articulated fullness. Taylor writes: "We need to enlarge our palette of such points of contact with fullness, because we are too prone in our age to think of this contact in terms of 'experience'; and to think of experience as something subjective distinct from the object experienced; and as something to do with our feelings, distinct from changes in our being: dispositions, orientations."[44] But they are experiences as well as events—heart transforming, life changing. There are those like Griffiths and Havel and St. Ignatius who have contemplatively grasped this fullness; they have left us their records and reflections. They have wrought paradigm shifts that signaled a move from an immanent therapeutic perspective and framework to a spiritual one. "The internal economy of the immanent theory, say a Freudian one, in which the various forces which count are purely intra-psychic, and are rooted in the patient's desires and fears, is now disrupted. The genesis of guilt, alienation, internal division is now found at least in part in the aspiration to something transcendent."[45] In so doing, they upset the parameters of our time and raise up human life to the divine (theosis). They take us beyond immanent realities and challenge mainstream materialism as well as the nature/supernature distinction. But as St. Thomas reminds us, grace builds on nature; it doesn't abolish it. They are responding to transcendent reality. Others may respond to it too but may misrecognize it such as in the exclusive humanisms. Griffiths initially interpreted his experience in the light of a Wordsworthian Romanticism; only later did he come to see it in the light of Christian revelation. Rilke, commenting on his poem "Turning," which he penned between June 18 and 20, 1914, to Lou Andreas-Salomé, wrote: "May this gazing out of myself, which consumes me to emptiness, be rid of through a loving preoccupation with interior fullness."[46] For Taylor, our sense of this fullness "is a reflection of transcendent reality (which for me is the God of Abraham)."[47] To find fullness is to find God, ultimately, for Taylor. It is to be converted. Taylor writes: "The convert's insights break beyond the limits of the regnant versions of immanent order . . . to a larger, more encompassing one, which includes it while disrupting it."[48] While Taylor calls these experiences conversions, it is Bernard Lonergan who details the dynamics

44. Taylor, *Secular Age*, 729–30.
45. Taylor, *Secular Age*, 731.
46. Cited by Hederman, *Manikon Eros*, 92.
47. Taylor, *Secular Age*, 769.
48. Taylor, *Secular Age*, 732.

of such conversions in *Method in Theology*, and so it will prove instructive to consider his thoughts on the subject. Taylor defines conversion as "breaking out into the broader field,"[49] but it is Fr. Lonergan, whom Taylor interestingly doesn't cite, who distinguishes between three types of conversion and who offers a more systematic and nuanced account than Taylor, one that can fill in some of the caveats in Taylor's considerations of the subject and theoretically add to Ignatius's experiences.

LONERGAN ON CONVERSION

For Bernard Lonergan, by a differentiation of consciousness, we are engaged in a moral pursuit of goodness, a philosophic pursuit of truth, a scientific pursuit of understanding, and an artistic pursuit of beauty in our attempt to be attentive, intelligent, reasonable, and responsible, as we experience, understand, judge, and decide; this is the crux of his transcendental method, as we have seen, and as set by him in *Insight* and *Method in Theology*. It is to this latter work that we will now look for his insights into the nature and dynamics of conversion. Like Taylor, Lonergan holds that being in love with God is "the basic fulfilment of our conscious intentionality,"[50] one that brings a "deep-set joy."[51] In Ignatian terms, such spiritual happiness is consolation without a cause.

A conversion ushers in a change in the direction of development, a change for the better as one grows in authenticity. Values are apprehended, scales of preference shift. Conversion may issue in a violent change that disrupts psychological continuity, but it may be preceded by transient dispositions. More commonly, conversion is a slow process of maturation as one finds out what it is to be intelligent, reasonable, responsible, and loving. Conversion doesn't rest on this once-and-for-all dynamic of change; "conversion is life-long."[52] The objectification of conversion provides Christianity with its foundations. Lonergan defines *conversion* thus: "By conversion is understood a transformation of the subject and his world." Normally it is a prolonged process that results in a change of the course of direction of one's life. "It is as if one's eyes were opened, and one's former world faded and fell away.... Conversion is

---

49. Taylor, *Secular Age*, 769.
50. Lonergan, *Method in Theology*, 105.
51. Lonergan, *Method in Theology*, 105.
52. Lonergan, *Method in Theology*, 118.

existential, intensely personal, utterly intimate. But it is not so private as to be solitary."[53] Conversion affects all of man's conscious and intentional operations. "It directs his gaze, pervades his imagination, releases the symbols that penetrate to the depths of his psyche. It enriches his understanding, guides his judgments, reinforces his decisions."[54] Conversion is the basic step; after it comes the labor of thinking out everything from the profounder perspective. Conversion heralds in the transition from inauthenticity to authenticity. It is the work of (a good) conscience. The dark decreases, and the light increases. Conversion occurs when man discovers what is inauthentic in himself and turns away from it and embraces instead the fullness of authenticity. It is cognate with the Christic edict: "Repent, the kingdom of God is at hand!" Conversion manifests itself in deeds and words; it is radical revision.

According to Lonergan, there are three types of conversion (Robert Doran, SJ, adds a fourth: psychic conversion). They are modalities or fundamental forms of self-transcendence. "Conversion may be intellectual or moral or religious. While each of the three is connected with the other two, still each is a different type of event and has to be considered in itself before being related to the others."[55] Lonergan elucidates the three types thus: "Moral conversion changes the criterion of one's decisions and choices from satisfactions to values." Moral conversion, thus, consists in opting for or choosing the truly good. "Religious conversion is being grasped by ultimate concern. It is other-worldly falling in love. It is total and permanent self-surrender without conditions." It is "fated acceptance of a vocation to holiness."[56] For Christians it is God's love flooding our hearts through the Holy Spirit given in the gift of (operative) grace. *Operative grace* is religious conversion, whereas *cooperative grace* is the effectiveness of such a conversion; it is "the gradual movement towards a full and complete transformation of the whole of one's living and feeling, one's thoughts, words, deeds, and omissions." Intellectual conversion "is to truth attained by cognitional self-transcendence."[57] When all three occur within a single consciousness their relations can be conceived in terms of sublation in Karl Rahner's sense rather than Hegel's. When religious conversion occurs, desire turns to joy, and the subject is

---

53. Lonergan, *Method in Theology*, 130.
54. Lonergan, *Method in Theology*, 131.
55. Lonergan, *Method in Theology*, 238.
56. Lonergan, *Method in Theology*, 240.
57. Lonergan, *Method in Theology*, 241.

held, grasped, arrested, possessed, owned by an otherworldly love; it involves loving with one's whole heart, soul, mind, and strength. "Holiness abounds in truth and moral goodness, but it has a distinct dimension of its own. It is other-worldly fulfilment, joy, peace, bliss."[58] The absence of such fulfillment, in contradistinction, reveals itself as despairing unrest, the absence of joy, what St. Ignatius calls desolation.

In relation to the ordering of these three types of conversion, Lonergan delineates their interrelationships thus: "Though religious conversion sublates moral, and moral conversion sublates intellectual, one is not to infer that intellectual comes first and then moral and finally religious."[59] By contrast, in terms of the causal viewpoint, there is first God's love, and the eye of this love reveals values in their luminosity and splendor, while the strength of this love brings about moral conversion. Finally, one discerns in the light of this love the truths taught by the religious tradition; the seeds are thus sown for intellectual conversion. The religious conversion grounds both the moral and intellectual conversion; "it provides the real criterion by which all else is to be judged."[60] Religious conversion is the experiential event that gives the name God its fundamental meaning. The word penetrates to all four levels of intentional consciousness: experience, understanding, judging, and deciding. The whole man is thus evoked. And aside from conversions one has breakdowns or derailments, distortions.[61] In any single consciousness all three types of conversion may be present or lacking; any one may be present, or two or all three of them. Conversion manifests itself in deeds and words. Conversion consists in a radical revision of formerly held opinions, beliefs, or positions and "transforms the concrete individual" completely.[62]

Fullness takes us beyond flourishing (ordinary happiness), and conversion issues in joy. For Taylor, Lonergan, and Voegelin, the fullness of joy is found in an encounter with the divine ground of being, who reveals himself as ground and goal, origin and end. In this alone is man's (final) fulfillment. Taylor uses this term "fulfillment" in a broader sense than the ordinary word, which is usually used to describe whatever fulfills my own personal needs or self-satisfactions. He explains: "I want to extend it to whatever realizes (what we see as) the highest and fullest form of

---

58. Lonergan, *Method in Theology*, 242.
59. Lonergan, *Method in Theology*, 243.
60. Lonergan, *Method in Theology*, 283.
61. Lonergan, *Method in Theology*, 243–71.
62. Lonergan, *Method in Theology*, 338.

life, even if this demands the sacrifice of personal 'fulfilment.'"[63] Fullness is the overflow of presence, the radiance of being—the splendor of form (*splendor formae*).

St. Ignatius's Spiritual Exercises function as a program for what Lonergan calls religious conversion, resulting in a change in the meaning system of the exercitant, the capstone of which is the contemplation to attain love. The *imitatio Christi* is the mimetic desire that so many mystics encourage. The exercises are made precisely to move toward a greater and more glorious fullness of existence as followers of Christ.

---

63. Taylor, *Secular Age*, 838n9.

CHAPTER FOUR

Consolation in Boethius

JUST AS WE SAW how *conversion* operated through an attitudinal alteration illustrated by Lonergan and Taylor, so too we will come to a better comprehension of how Ignatian *consolation* functions by reference to a classic text on the subject: Boethius's *Consolation of Philosophy*, where it is evidenced with penetrating clarity. The nurse who appears in Boethius's cell is described as Lady Philosophy. We could also consider her as perhaps the first female logotherapist or as an anima figure or as a symbol of the senex/self—the immanent Absolute, as the archetype of Christ, to put it in Jungian terms, or as the good spirit, in Ignatian terms. Whosoever she is, she certainly succeeds in bringing Boethius's soul into the spiritual consolation of faith, hope, and love, as he prepares for the end of his earthly existence and entrance into the next.

BOETHIUS

Anicias Boethius (477–524) was a prominent Roman philosopher, public figure, and exceptional Greek scholar under the Gothic emperor Theodoric. Born in Rome, he was a member of an ancient and aristocratic family who fell from favor and was imprisoned in Pavia. His father had attained to the consulship, as would Boethius's two sons. His family exerted huge influence. He married Rusticiana, daughter of Symmachus, prefect of Rome and head of the senate. Boethius himself was a senator by the age of twenty-five but was imprisoned by King Theodoric the Great, who thought he was conspiring with the Eastern Roman Empire. He was executed in 524.

While waiting for his brutal execution, he penned *The Consolation of Philosophy*, a philosophical treatise on fortune, death, happiness, and attitude. It is a dialogue of alternating prose and poetry (thirty-nine poems, to be exact) between the ailing prisoner and his "nurse" Philosophy, whose instruction in the nature of fortune and happiness brings him to health and enlightenment. From time to time it reads like a logotherapeutic session, but one could also read it as an exercise in Jungian active imagination. Boethius regards the hour of his greatest happiness as being when he was in prison and heard that his two sons were appointed consuls together. But though actively engaged in politics, Boethius considered philosophy to be his *summum vitae solamen*. He was also a Christian who wrote a number of treatises and tracts in theology and may be seen as a forerunner of the Scholastics.

THE CONSOLATION OF PHILOSOPHY

The Consolation of Philosophy is, as the title says, a type of consolation—a moral meditation and medication. The book talks a lot about illness, remedy, and cure. It was a hugely popular work in medieval Europe, and Boethius's ideas suffuse the thought of both Chaucer and Dante, with Dante setting Boethius among the twelve lights in the heaven of the sun. Dante tells us that the words of Boethius provided him with his greatest consolation after the death of Beatrice. *The Consolation of Philosophy* combines poetic intensity with brilliant philosophical insight in a light and lyrical manner. While drawing on medical metaphor, it is primarily a meditation and moral medication that is being offered by Boethius's therapist, as he is bid to reconsider his conception of happiness.

Boethius stands at the crossroads of the classical and medieval worlds. The title of his work says it all; it is less about argument than it is about the consolation that philosophy can bring generally and in the face of death particularly. Boethius's book restores and celebrates a Platonic tradition of dialoguing. It is somewhat akin to Plato's *Last Days of Socrates*, which similarly discusses Socrates's final hours before his own execution by hemlock in 399. Boethius's book tells of Philosophy, personified throughout, as descending to Boethius from on high and leading him by various paths to God himself. The schema is Platonic and mirrors Plato's description in book 7 of the *Republic* of the soul's ascent in the famous allegory of the cave—from seeing shadows to seeing the sun as a metaphor for the Form of the Good. We may also compare the book to Sir Thomas Moore's *Dialogue of Comfort Against Tribulation*, which was also written in prison and under the threat of execution. Boethius's bitter experiences led him, in the work we are here considering, into a redescription and reexamination of the nature of happiness. In its conversational commentary and tone it is akin to the writings of Pseudo-Dionysius and St. Augustine. It is a philosophical rather than theological consolation, so there is no talk of the Trinity or paradise or the incarnation, etc. Boethius draws a distinction between faith and reason. The Boethian doctrine of salvation is the ascent of the individual by means of philosophical introspection to the knowledge of God; it is close to Neoplatonic philosophy and post-Augustinian Christianity.

The method of Boethius's execution varies in the sources; he was perhaps killed with an axe or a sword or bludgeoned to death. According to another version a rope was attached round his head and tightened till his eyes bulged out, then his skull was cracked.

Boethius is recognized as a martyr for the Catholic faith by the Roman martyrology, his feast day being October 23. He was declared a saint by the Sacred Congregation of Rites in 1883, and I once heard Benedict XVI explain the relevance of Boethius to contemporary Catholics by linking his teachings to an understanding of divine Providence.

THE TEXT

Turning now to the text itself. We see Boethius in a state of much distress and deep despair—from happy youth to hapless age. As the first poem opens: "Foolish the friends who called me happy then / Whose fall shows how my foothold was unsure."[1] As Boethius is giving vent to his sorrow and anger, he becomes aware of a woman standing over him, with an awe-inspiring appearance and burning eyes. On the bottom of her gown there are embroidered two Greek letters, *pi* and *theta*, which correspond to the two kinds of philosophy: practical (*pi*) and contemplative (*theta*). *Pi* is praxis; *theta* is theory (*teoria*). The former includes moral philosophy and ethics; the latter, metaphysics, theology, and physics. Philosophy

---

1. Boethius, *Consolation of Philosophy*, 35.

is defined, so, as both theory and practice on her gown. This nurse, who comforts the imprisoned Boethius, helps her noetically depressed patient change his attitude toward his suffering and thus his life. Boethius is describing and drawing on the ancient philosophical practice of Platonic *therapeia* or ethics. It is this ethical dimension, which is also a moral and spiritual conversion, of Boethius's *Consolation* that we are treating here.

Lady Logotherapist (one might call her) consoles Boethius by discussing the ultimate superiority of things of the mind, which she calls the "one true good" and which Frankl throughout his works labels the noetic core of the spiritual person. She contends that happiness comes from within and that one's virtue is all that one truly has, because it is not imperiled by the vicissitudes of fortune—blows of fate. In *The Consolation*, Boethius answered religious questions without reference to Christianity, relying solely on natural philosophy and the classical Greek tradition. He believed in the correspondence between faith and reason. The truths found in Christianity would be no different from the truths found in philosophy. It is, thus, a work written by a Platonist who happens also to be a Christian; it is not a Christian work per se. The philosophical message of the book fits in rather well, however, with the religious piety of the Middle Ages. Readers were encouraged not to seek worldly goods such as money and power, but to seek internalized virtues instead. Evil had a purpose, to provide a lesson to help change for good. Because God ruled the universe through Love, prayer to God and the application of Love would lead to true happiness. The book is heavily influenced by Plato and his dialogues. Found within *The Consolation* are themes that have echoed throughout the Western canon: the female figure of wisdom that informs Dante (a kind of archetype of the wise old woman), the ascent through the layered universe that is shared with Milton, the reconciliation of opposing forces that find their way into Chaucer's *Knight's Tale*, and the wheel of fortune so popular and prevalent throughout the Middle Ages. It is a fusion of allegorical tale, Platonic dialogue, and lyrical poetry.

Lady Philosophy, as Logotherapist, tells her patient that it is a time for healing not lamenting. When he turns to look at his physician (the piece is replete with medical metaphors, as we said) he discovers it was his nurse in whose house he has been cared for since childhood—Philosophy.

He gains some consolation from knowing that many illustrious philosophers suffered similar fates: Anaxagoras was banished from Athens, Zeno was tortured, Socrates was put to death. While Boethius displays his grief, Philosophy remains unperturbed, stoic-like in silence, and says that Boethius is full of grief and alternating between fits of rage, wrath, anguish, and disturbing passions and so in need of a cure. The cause of his illness is that he has forgotten his true nature, and Philosophy, as analyst, attempts to restore his health so that treacherous passions become dispelled in the resplendent light of truth. He is told to banish grief, as his mind is clouded and bound in chains. Frankl would similarly suggest we need to move from reacting to responding. At the level of the instincts we are driven, but at the level of spirit we are drawn. We are pushed by the past but pulled by the future. Through free choice and responsibility we are ultimately deciding beings, suffering and acting persons. Lady Logotherapist tells him she prefers "gentler medicines" but no less potent.[2] She tells him that in "discovering his state of mind," she can cure him.[3] She bids him let go of his emotional distractions and concentrate on the meaning of the moment and the "purpose of things" in true logotherapeutic fashion.[4] The best hope of restoring her patient to health is to help him attune his life to the divine Logos and order his life to the mysterious meaning of his present suffering. The mind is clouded where grief holds sway.

In book 2 (there are five in all), Lady Philosophy who, we are told, falls silent for a while like an analyst to let her patient speak, says that she has discovered and diagnosed the nature of his condition—that he has been pining for his former good fortune, and this has catapulted him into the slough of despondency. She puts some maieutic questions to Boethius: What type of happiness is it that is destined to pass away? Philosophy reveals that change and inconstancy are Fortune's normal behaviors, and that Fortune has lured and enticed him with a false happiness that is ephemeral. Just as a farmer entrusts his seed to the fields, balancing the bad years against the good, so should he have done. Things change quickly on the wheel of chance, and in one short hour one can see "happiness from utter desolation grows."[5] Wealth, honors, fame, and power are all under Fortune's jurisdiction. In life there are both fruit and flowers, cloud and cold—inconstancy is Fortune's very essence, and sometimes "the overthrow of happy realms" is carried out "by the random strokes of Fortune"[6] and the mind of man is plummeted in a "deep

---

2. Boethius, *Consolation of Philosophy*, 49.
3. Boethius, *Consolation of Philosophy*, 50.
4. Boethius, *Consolation of Philosophy*, 51.
5. Boethius, *Consolation of Philosophy*, 56.
6. Boethius, *Consolation of Philosophy*, 58.

seated melancholy."[7] Philosophy says that this is not a cure for Boethius's condition but an application to help soothe his grief and console his heart. Philosophy reminds him of how fortunate he has been in so many ways, having enjoyed the blessings of a wife and two consular sons, etc. Lady Logotherapist bids him "not dwell on it."[8] It is sound therapeutic advice: bow to the past, but don't be bound by it. If we can't change our situation, we are challenged to change ourselves. Boethius is suffering because of his "misguided belief,"[9] and it is his beliefs or attitudes that Lady Logotherapist is seeking to change in Boethius's existential analytic session. She admonishes him gently thus:

> You are a happy man, then, if you know where your true happiness lies, since when the chief concern of mortal men is to keep their hold on life, you even now possess blessings which no one can doubt are more precious than life itself. So dry your tears. Fortune has not yet turned her hatred against all your blessings.[10]

Philosophy continues:

> But I can't put up with your dilly-dallying and the dramatization of your care-worn grief-stricken complaints that something is lacking from your happiness. No man is so completely happy that something somewhere does not clash with his condition. It is the nature of human affairs to be fraught with anxiety. . . . Some men are blessed with both wealth and noble birth but are unhappy because they have no wife. Some are happily married but without children. . . . Some again have been blessed with children only to weep over their misdeeds. No one finds it easy to accept the lot Fortune has sent them. . . . Remember, too, that all the happiest men are over-sensitive. They have never experienced adversity and so unless everything obeys their slightest whim they are prostrated by every minor upset, so trifling are the things that can detract from the complete happiness of a man at the summit of fortune. . . . No one is so happy that he would not want to change his lot if he gives in to impatience. Such is the bittersweetness of human happiness. . . . It is evident, therefore, how miserable the happiness of human life is; it does

---

7. Boethius, *Consolation of Philosophy*, 59.
8. Boethius, *Consolation of Philosophy*, 59.
9. Boethius, *Consolation of Philosophy*, 61.
10. Boethius, *Consolation of Philosophy*, 62.

not remain long with those who are patient and doesn't satisfy those who are troubled.[11]

Philosophy reveals the secret of happiness: that it lies *within*. She observes:

> Why then do you mortal men seek after happiness outside yourselves, when it lies within you? . . . I will briefly show you what complete happiness hinges upon. If I ask you whether there is anything more precious to you than your own self, you will say no. So if you are not in possession of yourself you will possess something you would never wish to lose and something Fortune could never take away. In order to see that happiness can't consist in things governed by chance, look at it this way. If happiness is the highest good of rational nature and everything that can be taken away is not the highest good—since it is surpassed by what can't be taken away—Fortune by her very mutability can't hope to lead to happiness.[12]

Such a happiness, based on chance and which comes to an end at death, is unreliable, as Fortune changes all the time. This is a false happiness, but Philosophy says to Boethius she knows he is convinced that the human mind cannot die, and so others have sought happiness actually through death and even suffering. She proclaims: "It seems that the happiness which cannot make men unhappy by its cessation, cannot either make them happy by its presence."[13]

Philosophy then proceeds to show up how barren and poor riches really are: from precious stones to the beauty of the countryside, the sea, the sun, the stars and sky and moon, flowers and fine clothes, etc., none of which belong to man. Life is full of plenty as well as poverty, pearls as well as perils. And he who has much, wants much. Philosophy poetically exclaims: "O happy was that long lost age / Content with nature's faithful fruits."[14]

Like riches, power, fame, and high office, Fortune is not worth pursuing either and is of no intrinsic good or value. However long a life of fame and fortune is, "when compared with unending eternity it is shown to be not just little, but nothing at all."[15] A philosopher (someone who actually deserves the title) practices virtue and seeks out heaven in

11. Boethius, *Consolation of Philosophy*, 62–63.
12. Boethius, *Consolation of Philosophy*, 63.
13. Boethius, *Consolation of Philosophy*, 64.
14. Boethius, *Consolation of Philosophy*, 68.
15. Boethius, *Consolation of Philosophy*, 74.

freedom and despises earthly affairs. Fortune may seem to bring happiness but deceives man with her smiles. As Fortune is capricious, wayward, and inconstant, so also is human happiness—"how fragile a thing happiness is."[16] Boethius is encouraged to attend to the beauty of the countryside in his mind's eye—to look upon the sea, the stars, the sky, the sun and practice virtue and ethical values as he prepares to leave the existential vacuum.

Here he is told to get in touch with the profound unity of his being, which is the integration of psyche and soma but more: to unify also the noetic part of his personality structure. This will produce the harmony and wholeness for which he is unconsciously seeking and lead to ultimate health. Book 2 ends with Philosophy crying:

> Love promulgates the laws
> For friendship's faithful bond.
> O happy race of men
> If Love who rules the sky
> Could rule your hearts as well![17]

Book 3 begins by Philosophy telling Boethius that she is trying to bring him to his true destination, which is true happiness. She criticizes him thus: "Your mind dreams of it . . . but your sight is clouded by shadows of happiness, and [you] cannot see reality."[18] Boethius begs her to show him the nature of true happiness, which Philosophy promises to do. She tells him that "all are striving to reach one and the same goal, namely, happiness, which is a good which once obtained leaves nothing more to be desired. It is the perfection of all good things and contains in itself all that is good."[19] She asserts that perfect good does not, as some suppose, reside in wealth or respect, fame, enjoyment, power, position, popularity, whose "acquisition is fortuitous and its retention continuously uncertain,"[20] or pleasure. All men desire happiness and are looking for it in all these pursuits, but they will not find it in these, though some people, through the possession of these, snatch at a false appearance of happiness. But nothing satisfies greed—it is insatiable, and once dead, "his fickle fortunes

---

16. Boethius, *Consolation of Philosophy*, 76.
17. Boethius, *Consolation of Philosophy*, 77.
18. Boethius, *Consolation of Philosophy*, 78.
19. Boethius, *Consolation of Philosophy*, 79.
20. Boethius, *Consolation of Philosophy*, 89.

him forsake."[21] Philosophy says of the pursuit of bodily pleasure that it is "full of anxiety and its fulfilment full of remorse,"[22] and if bodily pleasure can produce happiness, why then the animals are very happy because their whole life is directed to the fulfillment of their bodily needs and requirements. All these paths to happiness are sidetracks. The distinction between pleasure and happiness here accords with the logotherapeutic perspective in that Frankl views pleasure as somatic and happiness as psychical. Joy, as spiritual happiness, would be noetic.[23] If you want to hoard money, you have to take it by force; if you want high office, you will have to grovel to those who bestow it; if you want to outdo others in honor, you will have to humiliate yourself by begging; if you want power, you will have to expose yourself to risks and plots; if you want fame, you will find yourself on a hard road and worn with care; if you decide to lead a life of pleasure, some others will pour scorn on you and see you as a slave of the body. All these things are puny as is man himself when compared to an elephant in size, a bull in strength, a tiger in speed. "Look up at the vault of heaven . . . and stop admiring things that are worthless."[24] Beauty is ephemeral too. The point here is that the mind should concentrate more on the eternal than the evanescent.

> The sleek looks of beauty are fleeting and transitory, more ephemeral than the blossom in spring. If, as Aristotle said, we had the piercing eyesight of the mythical Lynceus [one of the Argonauts who could see in the dark and discover hidden treasure] and could see right through things, even the body of an Alcibiades [an Athenian military leader of the fifth century, whom we will encounter later on; he was famous for his wealth and beauty and notorious of the use he made of them, as the footnote tells us], so fair on the surface, would look thoroughly ugly once we had seen the bowels inside.[25]

These things "are not the way to happiness and cannot by themselves make people happy."[26] The supreme good is happiness, but it is not, as Eudoxus or Epicurus believed, to be found in pleasure. Man is a drunkard who

---

21. Boethius, *Consolation of Philosophy*, 84.
22. Boethius, *Consolation of Philosophy*, 90.
23. For fuller treatments of the subject, see Costello, *Ethics of Happiness*; and *Beyond Hope*.
24. Boethius, *Consolation of Philosophy*, 90.
25. Boethius, *Consolation of Philosophy*, 92.
26. Boethius, *Consolation of Philosophy*, 93.

cannot find his way home. Happiness is, rather, a state of self-sufficiency with no wants. True "and perfect happiness is that which makes a man self-sufficient, strong, worthy of respect, glorious and joyful."[27] Nothing in the mortal state of things can furnish such a state of complete happiness—things are only shadows of the truly good. Only an imperfect happiness exists in perishable goods, which means "that there can be no doubt that a true and perfect happiness exists."[28] God is filled with supreme and perfect goodness. And the perfect good is true happiness, so it follows that true happiness is to be found in God. This is Philosophy's conclusion. "God is the essence of happiness."[29] And "supreme happiness is identical with supreme divinity," a position Aquinas will adopt. Through the possession of happiness, people become happy; and since happiness is divinity, it is through the possession of divinity that a person becomes happy. "Each happy individual is therefore divine."[30] Heaven is man's true homeland, and "God is happiness itself."[31] Boethius's tragic melody and tearful melancholy are over, and he addresses Philosophy thus: "The conclusion of this highest of arguments has made me very happy, and I am even more happy because of the words you used. I am now ashamed of the stupidity of all my railing."[32] This is the ultimate attitudinal change.

But in book 4, Boethius admits that the greatest cause of his sadness is the realization that evil exists and the wicked go unpunished and virtue unrewarded. Philosophy, as nurse/logotherapist/doctor of the soul, answers thus: All men desire the good, and happiness is the good itself, and both good and bad men strive to reach the good, and men become good by acquiring goodness, so they obtain what they are looking for. But if the wicked obtained what they wanted—that is, goodness—they could not be wicked. Both groups want it, but only one attains it, so this demonstrates the power of the good and the weakness of the bad. They desire good through the things that give them pleasure, but they don't obtain it, "because evil things cannot reach happiness."[33] Philosophy says simply: "Goodness is happiness,"[34] and the punishment of the wicked is their very

27. Boethius, *Consolation of Philosophy*, 96.
28. Boethius, *Consolation of Philosophy*, 99.
29. Boethius, *Consolation of Philosophy*, 101.
30. Boethius, *Consolation of Philosophy*, 102.
31. Boethius, *Consolation of Philosophy*, 110.
32. Boethius, *Consolation of Philosophy*, 111–12.
33. Boethius, *Consolation of Philosophy*, 123.
34. Boethius, *Consolation of Philosophy*, 124.

wickedness. Someone who "robs with violence and burns with greed" is like a wolf; someone who is wild and restless and is forever engaged with lawsuits is like a dog yapping; the person who lies in ambush in order to steal is like a fox; the person of quick temper is like a lion; the timid coward is like a hind; the lazy person is like an ass; the fickle person is like a bird with ever-changing interests; the person wallowing in impure lusts and filth is like a sow. "So what happens is that when a man abandons goodness and ceases to be human, being unable to rise to a divine condition, he sinks to the level of being an animal."[35]

So, the good are happy while the bad are unhappy, and they are more unhappy, according to Philosophy, if they go unpunished. When the wicked receive their punishment, they receive something good, since the punishment itself is good because of its justice. "So the wicked are much more unhappy when they are unjustly allowed to go scot free, than when a just punishment is imposed on them."[36] Punishment must alternate between a penal severity and a purifying mercy. The wicked are used to the dark and haven't yet come into the light. Further, Philosophy opines that those who commit an injustice are more unhappy than those who suffer it. Plato had said that it was better to suffer injustice than to do it. The guilt of the wicked could be cut back by punishment "like a malignant growth,"[37] and wickedness is compared to "a disease of the mind."[38] Health means goodness; and wickedness, sickness (a Platonic motif).

Philosophy (and Boethius too) brings this dialogue to an end by saying that evil is necessary for some good. We think of the sufferings of Job. Philosophy/Logotherapy addresses Boethius thus: "Providence stings some people to avoid giving them happiness for too long, and others she allows to be vexed by hard fortune to strengthen their virtues of mind by the use and exercise of patience."[39]

The Consolation of Philosophy concludes with this advice of Lady Logotherapy's: "Avoid vice, therefore, and cultivate virtue; lift up your mind to the right kind of hope and put forth humble prayers on high."[40] The logotherapeutic session has ended with words of hope and meaning that motivate and strengthen Boethius's inner resolve and noetic

35. Boethius, *Consolation of Philosophy*, 125.
36. Boethius, *Consolation of Philosophy*, 129.
37. Boethius, *Consolation of Philosophy*, 131.
38. Boethius, *Consolation of Philosophy*, 132.
39. Boethius, *Consolation of Philosophy*, 139.
40. Boethius, *Consolation of Philosophy*, 169.

resilience and help him face his fate without flinching (spiritual resilience). As Viktor Frankl remarks in *Man's Search for Meaning*: "Man is that being who invented the gas chambers of Auschwitz; however, he is also that being who entered those gas chambers upright, with the Lord's Prayer or the *Shema Yisrael* on his lips."[41] This is the real meaning of universal humanity as *imago Dei*.

---

41. Frankl, *Man's Search for Meaning*, 136.

CHAPTER FIVE

Desolation, Dark Night, and Depression in Guardini, John of the Cross, and Hopkins

> In the middle of the journey of our life I came to myself
> within a dark wood where the straight way was lost.
>
> DANTE, *THE DIVINE COMEDY*

INTRODUCTION

IN "ROMANCE DE LA Guardia Civil Española," Federico García Lorca relates the story of a police raid on a gypsy community. Lorca puts it beautifully: "En la noche platinoche / noche, que noche nochera" (In the night, the silver night, night that darkened night [my translation]).[1] The drama and danger unfold in the darkness. Fear is in the air. Night symbolizes spiritual darkness and ignorance (*avidya*). A related theme to "night" is "negation" (mystical apophasis). This is expressed by T. S. Eliot, who was much influenced by St. John of the Cross (who makes

---

1. Lorca, *Romancero gitano*, 82.

this concept/symbol central in his theology), in *East Coker*. Compare this to John of the Cross's *Ascent of Mount Carmel*:

> To reach satisfaction in all
> Desire its possession in nothing,
> To come to the knowledge of all
> Desire the knowledge of nothing.
> To come to possess all
> Desire the possession of nothing.
> To arrive at being all
> Desire to be nothing.
> To come to the pleasure you have not
> You must go by a way in which you enjoy not.
> To come to the knowledge you have not
> You must go by a way in which you know not.
> To come to the possession you have not
> You must go by a way in which you possess not.
> To come to be what you are not
> You must go by a way in which you are not.
> When you turn toward something
> You cease to cast yourself upon the all,
> For to go from the all to the all
> You must possess it without wanting anything.
> In this nakedness the spirit finds its rest,
> for when it covets nothing
> nothing raises it up and nothing weighs it down,
> because it stands in the centre of its humility.[2]

In the third division of *East Coker*, Eliot embarks upon a journey (*the journey*) into the dark (the cloud of unknowing), which is initially equated with death. However, at the end of the section Eliot suggests a different kind of darkness—another type of death—which can be wrought only as we proceed along the dark way (*via negativa*), the dark night of the soul. It is dark because ego must die; false images of the self must be surrendered in the light of the divine Logos, which appears as (divine) darkness to those not equipped to perceive or receive it. Death *to* self is not death *of* self. To die is to live more fully. Disidentification. Detachment. Paradise succeeds purgatory. It is a gentle growth into new being, spiritual stepping stones to the foothills that lead to Mount Carmel. The steep ascent up this mountain involves a shedding of the self along the way.

---

2. John of the Cross, *Ascent of Mount Carmel* 1.13.11.

My aim in this chapter is to show the similarities (convergences) as well as differences (divergences) between Ignatian *desolation*, psychological *depression*, and the San Juanist *dark nights*, as we travel this pathless path in the hope of not only shedding some light on these states but also disentangling the conceptual confusion that still surrounds them. By so doing, I bring Ignatian and Carmelite, especially Teresian, spirituality into creative dialogue with each other. These two traditions are complementary to one another rather than being in conflict. They both emerge from the spiritual soil of sixteenth-century Spain. They differ in emphasis, but both strands and dimensions are surely needed in any understanding or appreciation of mystical theology. I will also consider Evagrian acedia, melancholy as it prefigures in Romano Guardini, and Carl Jung's night sea journey (very briefly), as well as Gerard Manley Hopkins's so-called desolate poems.

In *The Story of a Soul*, which is the autobiography of "the little flower," St. Thérèse of Lisieux admits: "There was only night, utter desolation, like death itself."[3] Of course, there are crossovers and connections between desolation, dark night, and depression.

ST. IGNATIUS ON DESOLATION AND CONSOLATION

In his Spiritual Exercises, St. Ignatius of Loyola defines what he means by spiritual desolation. In rules for the discernment of spirits, Ignatius describes desolation as "obtuseness of soul, turmoil within it, or disquiet from various agitations and temptations. These move one toward lack of faith and leave one without hope and without love. One is completely listless, tepid, and unhappy, and feels separated from our Creator and Lord."[4] The opposite of desolation is spiritual consolation, which occurs "when some interior motion is caused within the soul through which it becomes inflamed with love [St. John of the Cross will use a similar phrase—"the living flame of love"] of its Creator and Lord. . . . Under the word consolation I include every increase in hope, faith, and charity, and every interior joy which calls and attracts one toward heavenly things and to the salvation of one's soul, by bringing tranquillity and peace in its Creator and Lord."[5]

---

3. Thérèse of Lisieux, *Story of a Soul*, 62.
4. Ignatius, *Spiritual Exercises* (2021), para. 317.
5. Ignatius, *Spiritual Exercises* (2021), para. 316.

The dialectic of consolation and desolation is the means of discerning the movements of the spirits within one's life, according to St. Ignatius, as we have seen. This is the reason the examen is primarily practiced. To repeat: *Consolation* is the spiritual state of the soul when it is infused with love of its Creator. *Desolation* is the spiritual state of the soul that is without faith and hope and love; it is inner agitation and turmoil, the experience of a tepid and sad soul separated from its Creator. Consolation and desolation are all to do with relationship. Consolation is that feeling of being connected to the content of the Ignatian Principle and Foundation, which stipulates that we should love and serve the Lord above all else. Desolation is resistance to the Principle and Foundation. Of course, sometimes an experience of profound sadness or loneliness can lead to consolation and conversion. One may experience dryness (in one's prayer life) without depression, just as one may experience darkness without disbelief. Darkness, of course, can lead to doubt (the example of Mother Teresa or Thérèse of Lisieux, albeit differently) just as depression can lead to despair. Many mystics have spoken of divine darkness—the *via negativa*, such as St. Gregory of Nyssa in the fourth century and, more famously, St. John of the Cross in the sixteenth century. Indeed, when John was writing of the dark night in his canticles, Ignatius was writing of desolation in his exercises. Let's give a concrete case to highlight the dynamics of desolation and consolation.

HOPKINS'S SONNETS OF DESOLATION

The Jesuit poet Fr. Gerald Manley Hopkins, SJ, was born in 1844. He boarded at Highgate School, read classics in Balliol at Oxford, became a prolific poet, forged many friendships that would last a lifetime, especially with Robert Bridges (later poet laureate of the United Kingdom), and converted from Anglicanism to Catholicism; he was received into the church by Cardinal John Henry Newman on October 21, 1866. Later, he felt the call to enter the priesthood and decided to become a Jesuit. He was appointed professor of Greek at University College Dublin in 1884. He experiences melancholia during the spring and summer of 1885 and makes a retreat in the Jesuit-run Clongowes Wood College (boarding school) in Co. Kildare in Ireland on August 21. His poetry employs sprung rhythm and establishes him as an innovator. His vivid use of imagery, especially in describing nature and praising God, is particularly distinctive. He dies in Dublin in 1889 and is buried in Glasnevin Cemetery. By 1930 his work is seen as one of the most original literary advances of the century.

He penned what became known as the Terrible Sonnets (referring not to their content but to his experiences of melancholy). They detailed his experiences of desolation. The sonnets of desolation refers to a group of untitled poems (known by their first line) written during 1885–86, of which there are six. Their opening words begin thus: "To Seem the Stranger," "I Wake and Feel," "No Worst," "Carrion Comfort," "Patience, Hard Thing," and "My Own Heart." They certainly suggest Hopkins was suffering from depression at this time of his life. In the first poem, he writes: "My heart breeds dark heaven's baffling ban / Bars or hell's spell thwarts. This to hoard unheard, / Heard unheeded, leaves me a lonely began."[6] The second one begins "I wake and feel the fell of dark, not day / What hours, O what black hours we have spent / This night / . . . I am gall, I am heartburn."[7]

Hopkins had a heavy workload; he disliked Dublin, suffered from scrupulosity in religious life and insomnia, felt alienated politically and socially; his health was poor, as was his eyesight; and he generally felt dejected. The general of the Jesuits in Hopkins's time was Jan Philip Roothaan, who was known for his legalistic interpretation of the exercises, which, no doubt, exerted an influence on how Jesuits gave them. This ascetic tradition superseded the more mystical tradition and was prevalent until the early 1960s when, thankfully, things reverted to the older form of spirituality.[8] After several years of ill health, Hopkins died of typhoid fever. His funeral took place in St. Francis Xavier Church in Gardiner Street in Dublin.

How are we to make sense of this apparent contradiction in Hopkins's character, between the melancholic poet and the Jesuit priest? Norman White writes: "For most of 1885 depression was a usual part of Hopkins' life."[9] The question is: Was Hopkins's depression constitutionally or chemically or clinically present within him, with pessimism being a permanent state of his soul, or was his melancholia experienced fleetingly or perhaps as recurrent bouts throughout his life? White cites Hopkins's own words on the subject: "The melancholy I have all my life

6. Hopkins, *Selected Poems*, 59.
7. Hopkins, *Selected Poems*, 59–60.
8. See Costello, *Ignatian Mysticism*; H. Egan, *Ignatius Loyola the Mystic*; O'Leary, *Ignatius Loyola*.
9. White, *Hopkins in Ireland*, 62.

been subject to has become of late years not indeed more intense in its fits but rather more distributed, constant, and crippling. . . . The lightest and but a very inconvenient form of it, is daily anxiety about work to be done. . . . When I am at the worst . . . my state is much like madness."[10] In a letter to Bridges, Hopkins writes, in capitals, all of a sudden: "AND WHAT DOES ANYTHING AT ALL MATTER?"[11] But there were also positive aspects to those eight months. Hopkins indulged in pleasures, conversations with friends, artistic endeavors. He stole joy in all that toil. The beauty of nature uplifted and inspired him. In one of his journal entries Hopkins muses: "There is a happiness, hope, the anticipation of happiness hereafter. . . . It is as if one were dazzled by a spark or star, seeing it but not seeing by it: we want a light shed on our way and a happiness spread over our life."[12] It seems that within him, perhaps competing and vying, were alternating moods, but as a poet he felt deeply and accessed these affective ontological states when he was writing poetry, which doesn't mean that melancholy was a permanent lodger in his heart—the always-solemn song. He was a committed Catholic, a believer in redemptive suffering.

In *Hopeful Hopkins*, Desmond Egan argues, by contrast, that the sad Hopkins has been overemphasized, sometimes at the expense of the other Hopkins, who was playful, fun, enjoyed a pun, and popular with his confrères. This side of Hopkins's personality has been overlooked, excluded even from scholarly exegesis and commentary. We might legitimately inquire as to whether Hopkins was completely happy anywhere. He was, after all, "physically frail," "hyper-sensitive," "nervous," and "thought-haunted," as Egan puts it.[13] Was Hopkins *essentially* melancholic? He did write some twenty-eight poems while in Dublin for those five years, in the so-called funk of depressive disorder, which constitute a third of his overall output and are among his finest written oeuvre.[14] Egan calls the so-called sonnets of desolation, which Hopkins wrote in Dublin, the "sonnets of hope."[15] Not a single one of them declines into hopelessness. The writing is fresh, exciting, inventive, energized by life. Hopkins never

---

10. White, *Hopkins in Ireland*, 64–65.
11. White, *Hopkins in Ireland*, 76.
12. White, *Hopkins in Ireland*, 187.
13. D. Egan, *Hopeful Hopkins*, 17.
14. See D. Egan, *Hopeful Hopkins*, 18.
15. D. Egan, *Hopeful Hopkins*, 19.

waned or wavered in his vocation; he committed himself wholeheartedly to Ignatius's Spiritual Exercises, which were the bedrock of his life.

I have mentioned some social factors that undoubtedly contributed to his melancholy, but a question, which can only remain unanswered as it pertains to speculation, arises: perhaps Hopkins was experiencing anemia or chronic fatigue syndrome. These certainly can contribute to and induce a low-level depression, as can seasonal affective disorder—but one mustn't confuse these with somatogenic depression. I think we can rule out despair in Hopkins, as despair does not admit of hope. Hopkins himself recognized he had been "a little ill and am a little pulled down; however I am in good spirits."[16] Happy Hopkins, so.

Hopkins is a complex character, and any attempt to reduce him to a single drive or description shows at best myopic misunderstanding. Again to quote Hopkins: "I am ill today, but no matter for that as my spirits are good." His letters suggest hope in Christ, show an optimistic person. After all, his last words from his deathbed were "I am so happy, I am so happy."[17] We have to bear in mind that the artistic temperament is deep, sensitive, probing, possesses an unusual capacity to feel, marking the artist out as an outsider by society's norms, and this is what makes the creative person especially vulnerable to the vicissitudes of fate.

In a chapter on Hopkins in *A More Beautiful Question: The Spiritual in Poetry and Art*, philosopher Glenn Hughes introduces Bernard Lonergan's concept of elemental meaning and applies it to Hopkins's poetry.[18] Elemental meaning is bound to the level of experience. It is concrete, embodied meaning. An example would be music, where the meaning it mediates is nonconceptual. Of course, just because it is bound to the level of experience does not mean that other aspects of cognition are not involved, such as understanding, judging, deciding. Elemental meaning is symbolic—it pertains to the deep psyche that operates below conscious objectification. Art, in general, is the experience and expression of elemental meaning. This is the case with Hopkins's experimentalism in poetry which was a precursor to modernism. Hughes observes: "From the *Spiritual Exercises* of St. Ignatius, Hopkins drew the crucial message that the created world in all its particularity is the gift and expression of God through His Word, the Logos who is Christ."[19] All of nature thus becomes

16. D. Egan, *Hopeful Hopkins*, 23.
17. D. Egan, *Hopeful Hopkins*, 32.
18. See Hughes, *More Beautiful Question*, 38–61.
19. Hughes, *More Beautiful Question*, 45.

Christified. This is the Ignatian personality of Gerard Manley Hopkins that is evident everywhere in his poetry. The world's purpose and purport are God so, as Hopkins puts it in the first line of "Pied Beauty": "Glory be to God for dappled things"; he concludes with "Praise him" in the last line.[20] This is Ignatian through and through. Famously, in "God's Grandeur," Hopkins opens with and opines that "the world is charged with the grandeur of God."[21] Everything in nature is the incarnated instress of God's boundless beauty. Poetry, for Hopkins, is spiritual epiphany. Hopkins wanted to convey to readers his own experiences of inscape and instress of an object or person that he considered and contemplated. Hughes sees Hopkins's desolation as a mode of sharing in Christ's suffering. In "No Worst," Hopkins avers: "No worst, there is none. Pitched past pitch of grief, / More pangs will, schooled at forepangs, wilder wring. / Comforter, where, where is your comforting?"[22] This is the description of feeling the absence of meaning, separation from God. Still, "Of now done darkness I wretch lay wrestling with (my God!) / my God," which is the last line of "Carrion Comfort."[23] All things pass to ash, but despite death, there is the promise of the resurrection. Man may be "mortal trash" as Hopkins says in "That Nature Is a Heraclitean Fire and of the Comfort of the Resurrection," but "this Jack, joke, poor potsherd, / patch, matchwood, immortal diamond, / Is immortal diamond."[24] Mortal things refine into their true essence, participate in a world of transcendence. Creation is a constant *selving* of the eternal Logos, a continual Christing.

We might say that consolation and desolation are both at play in the poetry and life of Gerard Manley Hopkins, but *the desolation he experienced was one of painful consolation*, despite his depression. He praised God with his poetry and, therefore, can be regarded as an Ignatian knight of faith. As Karl Rahner put it in his epigraph: "Darkness can only be perceived by an eye which was created for light."[25]

---

20. Hopkins, *Selected Poems*, 24.
21. Hopkins, *Selected Poems*, 20.
22. Hopkins, *Selected Poems*, 54.
23. Hopkins, *Selected Poems*, 54.
24. Hopkins, *Selected Poems*, 63.
25. Rahner, *Practice of Faith*, 43.

DARK NIGHTS

Darkness, as a symbol, features explicitly in the writings of Spanish Carmelite St. John of the Cross. John distinguishes between two types of dark nights:

- The dark night of the *senses* (here there is a removal of attachment to the consolations felt in prayer)
- The dark night of the *soul* (a crisis of faith)[26]

If the first is a passive process of purgation that occurs as one grows closer to God; the second is an *experience* of no consolations being present. In the darkness, one can encounter God in the nada—the nothingness. Zen speaks of an emptiness (*sunjata*) which is, in fact, a fullness as well as an openness.

Dryness, by contrast to darkness, is an experience of emptiness or aridity during periods of prayer; it's a dullness where there is little by way of sensible consolations. Doubt is the intellectual uncertainty, indecision about the existence of God. Disbelief is the assent to God's nonexistence— it is nonacceptance, refusal to admit. Desolation is more than a feeling of dejection. It is existential estrangement, isolation. *Ignatian desolation is distinct from the Juanist dark night of the soul.* In desolation, there is no hope or faith or love present. *The dark night is the opposite; the dark night is actually painful or difficult consolation.* Depression is profound sadness. In the dark night, there is seldom the experience of acute or morbid guilt, self-loathing, or suicidal ideation that characterizes clinical depression. In the dark night, one still experiences God's presence or illumination, albeit obscurely.

Below I adumbrate the phenomenology of acedia (a state of torpor or listlessness), which is not exactly identical to depression, before returning to discuss melancholy some more.

ACEDIA

Acedia has been commonly called the *noonday demon*, as it strikes in the tedium of the afternoon. It has received some attention in early monastic literature. We have this insight from Evagrius of Ponticus, a fourth-century Egyptian monk, who describes the demon as causing the monk

---

26. John of the Cross, *Dark Night of Soul*.

continuously to look out the window and to step out of his cell, encouraging him to hate the place (the enclosure) and the work of his hands.[27] Acedia is sloth, but it is spiritual sloth as in frustration and disgust at life rather than mere laziness as such. It is withdrawal into self. It is the mood of purposelessness and pointlessness. This experience of emptiness, of the existential vacuum, is, I would argue, following Viktor Frankl's theorizing, a noögenic, that is to say, spiritual, despair, which is distinct from both a psychogenic (reactive) depression, which is psychological, and a somatogenic (psychotic) or endogenous depression, which is biological.[28]

The Benedictine motto is *ora et labora*: work and pray. Acedia makes both problematic if not impossible. Acedia is the encounter with the unbearable heaviness of being—the weightiness of the world. It transmogrifies into boredom (meaninglessness) and nihilism, the main symptoms of which are addictions, inner restlessness, floating from one task to another, dissatisfaction, agitation, the desire to leave one's cell in search of conversation, stimulation, distraction. It is internal instability. Thomas Aquinas identifies two characteristics of it: a sadness at the divine good (*tristitia de bono divino*) and an aversion to acting (*taedium operandi*).[29] Spiritual sloth is sadness and sorrow about one's own happiness, directed at the divine ground of reality. With acedia, the meaning of desire is lost. Sloth "enervates the meaning of desire and the point of action."[30] Acedia ushers in the law of diminishing returns; it is ontological boredom where even goodness no longer delights. As such, acedia is a heresy. God saw that the world was good, very good, indeed. By contrast to the sin of sloth, Catholic minds like St. Thomas's and Chesterton's were positioned positively, were filled with meaning and mirth, soaked with sunshine, with the warmth of wonder. As Hilaire Belloc (1870–1953) proudly and poetically proclaimed:

> Wherever the Catholic sun doth shine,
> There's always laughter and good red wine.
> At least I've always found it so.
> Benedicamus Domino.[31]

---

27. Snell, *Acedia and Its Discontents*, 10.
28. Frankl, *On Mental Disorders*, xviii.
29. Snell, *Acedia and Its Discontents*, 64.
30. Snell, *Acedia and Its Discontents*, 70.
31. Cited by Snell, *Acedia and Its Discontents*, 77.

The Catholic cast of mind sees the dearest freshness deep down things (Hopkins), can sacramentally see into the still-sad music of humanity and within the mundane glimpse the mystical and majestic. The Catholic glances around and experiences fullness and freshness, recalls that at the core of being is radiance, the (over)flow of divine presence, superabundance, splendor. What is the opposite of sloth? Snell maintains it is *celebration*.[32] Acedia's opposite is affirmation, acceptance, love—the will to act (service, social justice). Only lovers sing. The attitude of celebration is contemplation—contemplation understood, though, not as prime passivity but as active receptivity, as recognition of creation's goodness, as recalibration to reality. We might say that this attitude involves a sort of Sabbath living—Sabbath seen as the end of the creation of heaven and earth. And Sabbath work is worship, which serves an ultimate rather than an ulterior purpose. Like a festival, it is good in itself. Snell summarizes thus:

> Against sloth we have Sabbath work, work such as God did on the seventh day. Of course there is a call to rest on the Sabbath, but that command elevates and sanctifies all good work, even unpleasant and toilsome drudgery (*bonum arduum*), offered as worship by those with festive hearts.[33]

Sloth/acedia is, thus, an aversion to being, a failure to love. Staying in the cell (of one's heart) can be difficult. Simple things can seem like trifles. However, Christ plays even in oranges and onions. Sloth's cure? Remaining yoked to the work God has given us. Snell sets out the nontrivial tasks thus:

> We stay in the cell in very concrete ways—keeping the prayers, finishing the report, paying our bills on time, wiping away childish tears, doing the dishes, cleaning the car, caring for our tools—through staying in the quotidian, the mundane ordinary work.[34]

This is the true meaning of the Ignatian injunction of finding God in all things. Our ordinary load in life. An ordinary Lord who, in his hidden life, carried out carpentry with hammers, held wood and tools in those holy human hands that would be hoisted on another piece of wood, at the end of the world, as host for all humanity.

---

32. Snell, *Acedia and Its Discontents*, 96.
33. Snell, *Acedia and Its Discontents*, 108.
34. Snell, *Acedia and Its Discontents*, 118.

MELANCHOLY IN GUARDINI

Melancholy is a kind of pensive sadness, a depression, of sorts. Romano Guardini (1885–1968), the Italian priest, philosopher, and theologian who influenced Josef Pieper, Luigi Giussani, Pope Benedict XVI, and Pope Francis, among others, wrote a beautifully Kierkegaard-inspired essay on "The Meaning of Melancholy." Guardini draws on many passages from the writings and journals of Søren Kierkegaard, the founder of modern existentialism, who probed in his soul the depths of melancholy. Kierkegaard writes of the "black hole" that is melancholy, of the "agony of pain" he experienced in "the deepest suffering of melancholy."[35]

Kierkegaard movingly describes and depicts the mood of manic depression, as he seesawed from "the self-contented silence of the night, like the quiet monologue of midday" where he was at his "highest peak" to plummeting to a "bit of dust"[36] and toppling down "into the abyss of despair,"[37] "alone in anguish unto death."[38] But when Kierkegaard is not left to his own devices, as the saying goes, but rather sees aright and finds repose in God, "blessedness returns again."[39] Loathing of life is replaced by longing for life. Kierkegaard, cited by Guardini throughout the essay, admits that, since childhood, he was "under the sway of a prodigious melancholy," which he hid with an apparent gaiety and joie de vivre.[40] If his father made him unhappy (even though out of love), God's love was a marvel to Kierkegaard, who writes that he was "blessedly *consoled* by the knowledge that he [God] cared for me—and thereby he gave this life of pain a meaning that almost overwhelmed me."[41] Kierkegaard realizes that his affliction was more madness (somatogenic depression/bipolar disorder) than melancholy. Guardini finds in Kierkegaard a kindred soul; his line of thought on the subject matter of melancholy follows a similar spiritual trajectory to Kierkegaard, rather than adopting a medical or psychological approach emphasized by so many writers on melancholy.

Etymologically, *melancholy* means "black bile," conveying the idea of a heaviness of spirit. Melancholy is a demon. The melancholic person

---

35. Guardini, "Meaning of Melancholy," 39.
36. Guardini, "Meaning of Melancholy," 41.
37. Guardini, "Meaning of Melancholy," 42.
38. Guardini, "Meaning of Melancholy," 45.
39. Guardini, "Meaning of Melancholy," 46.
40. Guardini, "Meaning of Melancholy," 47.
41. Guardini, "Meaning of Melancholy," 50; emphasis added.

perceives his problems to be insurmountable—indeed, they mount before him like a mountain. The metaphysical emptiness of melancholy bears down on him. Guardini puts it thus: "At this point melancholy teams up with tedium."[42] Things are finite; finitude is a defect; this defect disappoints for hearts that yearn for the absolute. This is melancholy's logic. This disappointment spreads and creates the feeling of a void, that nothing worthwhile exists. "Existence by and in itself becomes a source of pain to him."[43] The mood of melancholy mixes freely with self-destructive tendencies and feelings of inferiority. Guardini maintains that the real roots of melancholy "lie in the spiritual realm."[44] Melancholic being is an existence of masks; what lurks behind the wit is often dark despair and deep misery.

However, it is also true to say that *la grande tristeza* can bear precious fruit. Clarity and mental penetration are often the results of melancholic moments. There is the "inner gravitation of the soul towards the great center, the impulse to seek interiority and depth, the yearning for that region where life passes from a fortuitous jumble to a protected haven."[45] In fact, the melancholic person "has a most profound feeling for the fullness of existence."[46] Melancholy, at bottom, according to Guardini, is a yearning for love and desire for beauty.[47] The melancholic nature experiences the pain of transience; they realize beauty passes, youth fades, and life is haunted by death. What the melancholic yearns for is the absolutely perfect, for transforming union, for contact with being. Their natures feel more than most the "insufficiency of the finite."[48] Bitterness and sweetness are mixed into everything.

What is the meaning of melancholy, so? It is a sign that the absolute exists. Melancholy may be described as "the birth pangs of the eternal in man."[49] Melancholy is, thus, both menace and blessedness simultaneously, on which only the mystery of Gethsemane can shine and shed a light. Guardini concludes his reflections thus: "Only in the Cross of Christ do

42. Guardini, "Meaning of Melancholy," 53.
43. Guardini, "Meaning of Melancholy," 54.
44. Guardini, "Meaning of Melancholy," 60.
45. Guardini, "Meaning of Melancholy," 67.
46. Guardini, "Meaning of Melancholy," 68.
47. Guardini, "Meaning of Melancholy," 69.
48. Guardini, "Meaning of Melancholy," 70.
49. Guardini, "Meaning of Melancholy," 72.

we find the solution for the distress caused by melancholy,"[50] for it is true to say that no solution to it exists on earth. After having highlighted some aspects of acedia and melancholy, let's look in more detail at the notion of dark night in John of the Cross.

JOHN OF THE CROSS'S DARK NIGHT

John's poem "Dark Night of the Soul," which was likely written between 1577 and 1579, consists of eight stanzas of five lines each, which narrates the journey of the soul to mystical union with God. The darkness in question symbolizes the fact that the destination is unknowable, as in the fourteenth-century classic *The Cloud of Unknowing*, derived as it is from the sixth-century Pseudo-Dionysius the Areopagite. "En una noche oscura, / con ansias en amores inflamada" (On a dark night, inflamed with yearning love). This pilgrim ventures forth, without being observed and disguised, while the house was at rest. "En la noche dichosa, / en secreto, / cuando nadie me veía, / no vi nada / salvo la que / ardía en / mi corazón" (In the happy night, in secret, when nobody saw me, and I saw no one, save that which burned in my heart). The light guided our pilgrim more securely than the light of noonday. "O noche que / me guiaste! / o noche amable mas / que aurora!, o noche que / juntaste / amado con / amada, / amada en el / amado / transformada!" (Oh night that guided me, oh night lovelier than the dawn, oh night that joined lover with beloved, lover transformed in the beloved).[51]

The dark night of the soul is a final purification and marked by a helplessness, a sense of the withdrawal of God's presence—surrender. The final stage is union with the Absolute, where the self is now established on the transcendental level. The dark night precedes rebirth, revelation. The darkest night of the soul's crucible is followed by the most radiant of dawns. The dark night is akin to kenosis (self-emptying) and *nigredo* in alchemy.

The dark night of the soul is not negative even if it can be experienced in a less-than-positive light. It is an ongoing process of being liberated from disordered desires, compulsions, fixations, attachments. The darkness of the dark night does not imply or infer anything sinister, only that the light is fading fast. It is dusk more than black darkness.

---

50. Guardini, "Meaning of Melancholy," 80.
51. John of the Cross, *Dark Night of Soul*, 33–34.

In *The Science of the Cross*, Edith Stein (1891–1942), the Carmelite philosopher-saint, writing about John's dark night and God, understood as the archetype of all spiritual being, suggests that one might reach a crossroad when one previously had been employing "an Ignatian method,"[52] drawing on the senses, imagination, and the will, but now they won't work. These spiritual exercises have now become intolerably dull. We are shocked interiorly by night itself, which has a psycho-spiritual significance. This dark night is uncanny and other than "the moonlit magic night, which is flooded by a mild, soft light."[53] John was sensitive to the cosmic night, spending entire nights gazing over wide landscapes from a window. But, says Stein, the mystical night should not be confused with the cosmic night. The former has its origin in the interior of the soul; the latter comes from without. Such a dark night "casts the soul into loneliness, desolation, and emptiness."[54] It is something shapeless whose "fullness of meaning can only be indicated but not exhausted."[55] One hears in it the echo of the message emanating from the cross. It is the nocturnal and narrow way of faith understood as "dark knowledge" in which God remains hidden from us even in the bliss of transforming union.[56]

The dark night of the soul gives meaning to life—the meaning of not knowing. Swedish former secretary-general of the United Nations Dag Hammarskjöld (1905–61), in his book *Markings*, in an entry made on Whitsunday, 1961, described this experience of not-knowing but of trust, nonetheless, thus:

> I don't know Who—or what—put the question. I don't know when it was put. I don't even remember answering. But at some moment I did answer *Yes* to Someone—or Something—and from that hour I was certain that existence is meaningful and that, therefore, my life, in self-surrender, had a goal.[57]

He was led by Ariadne's thread through the labyrinth of life to a source of ultimate meaning, a journey that paralleled Viktor Frankl's:

> The dawn was grey around us; grey was the sky above; grey the snow in which my fellow prisoners were clad, and grey their

---

52. Stein, *Science of the Cross*, 39.
53. Stein, *Science of the Cross*, 40.
54. Stein, *Science of the Cross*, 41.
55. Stein, *Science of the Cross*, 42.
56. Stein, *Science of the Cross*, 46.
57. Hammarskjöld, *Markings*, 205.

faces.... I was struggling to find the reason for my sufferings, my slow dying. In a last violent protest against the hopelessness of imminent death, I sensed my spirit piercing through the enveloping gloom. I felt it transcend that hopeless, meaningless world, and from somewhere heard a victorious "Yes" in answer to my question of the existence of an ultimate purpose.[58]

TERESA OF ÁVILA

One cannot comprehend the incomprehensible God. Our ways are not his ways; knowledge of God is always, in part, a matter of unknowing and non-saying. Praying is always done in the dark. Like Jung, John of the Cross (schooled by the Jesuits) and St. Teresa of Ávila (counseled by the Jesuits) plumbed the depths and dynamics of the psyche, spiritually. Commenting on Teresa of Ávila, psychiatrist Gerald May observes, "Teresa's psychological insights compare favourably with those of Freud and his twentieth-century followers. John's descriptions of attachment brilliantly enhance modern addiction theory."[59] I would add that they also compare to Jung's. There are a number of works that have dealt with Jungian parallels to and interpretations of both Teresa and John.[60]

Teresa of Ávila, for her part, penned this beautiful poem precisely about *la nada*:

> Nada te turbe;
> nada te espante;
> todo se pasa;
> Dios no se muda,
> la paciencia
> todo lo alcanza.
> Quien a Dios tiene,
> nada le falta.
> Solo Dios basta.
>
> Let nothing disturb you,
> nothing make you afraid;
> All things pass;
> God does not change,

---

58. Frankl, *Man's Search for Meaning*, 51.
59. May, *Dark Night of Soul*, 38.
60. See, for example, Welch, *Spiritual Pilgrims*; Arraj, *Christian Mysticism*; McLean, *Diamond Heart*.

> Patience
> achieves everything.
> The one who has God
> lacks nothing.
> God alone suffices. (My translation)

Together, these two Spaniards—Teresa of Ávila and John of the Cross—began and collaborated on the great Carmelite reform. It's important to stress from the outset that in Spanish *la noche oscura* (the dark night) has more of a connotation of *obscure* than darkness per se. *Oscura* does mean darkness, yes (figuratively), but it also means incomprehensible—that which is obscure. For both John and Teresa, the images of the soul take the shape of circles or mandalas, which, for Jung, symbolize wholeness. To our senses, God is nada—no-thing, in other words, not an object. For these two Spanish mystics, the life of the soul (*alma*) goes on beneath our conscious awareness. It is to this unconscious dimension that Teresa and John are referring when they deploy the term "dark." *La noche oscura* is something unknown, unconscious, something more mysterious than macabre. The more sinister kind of devilish darkness would be *tinieblas* in Spanish. "In *oscuras* things are hidden; in *tinieblas* one is blind,"[61] that is to say, one is attached. The journey to union is the freeing of love from attachment; such transformation requires more freedom *for* desire than freedom *from* desire.

THE DARK NIGHT OF THE SENSES AND THE DARK NIGHT OF THE SPIRIT: ACTIVE AND PASSIVE

For John, each aspect of the soul undergoes its own liberation. There is the dark night of the senses and the dark night of the spirit, both of which are dark nights of the soul. During the dark night of the senses, the soul finds freedom from attachments to particular sensory gratifications, while the dark night of the spirit releases attachments to rigid beliefs, compulsive choices, etc. Our minds/hearts need to be darkened, emptied of false idols. If the dark night of the senses is like dusk, the night of the spirit is more like midnight. The coming of the dawn is the third part of the night. There are also passive and active dimensions to both nights:

---

61. May, *Dark Night of Soul*, 68.

- Active nights: Here people are aware of participating in their spiritual journey. The *active* night involves prayers and practices, exercises, retreats, journaling, spiritual direction. Memory, will, and imagination are all deployed, as is work on the virtues. The movement involved is one of subtraction rather than addition, simplification rather than complication, and relinquishment rather than accumulation (in both the active and passive nights).

We can cite this excerpt from John's *Ascent of Mount Carmel*:

> To achieve satisfaction in everything,
> Desire it in nothing.
> To possess everything,
> Desire to have nothing.
> To be everything,
> Desire to be nothing.
> To know everything,
> Desire to know nothing.[62]

- Passive nights: We experience the pain and loss that cause the dark night to be associated with suffering. We are being freed from our possessions, relationships, feelings, etc. It is an act of kenosis (emptying). Prayer that used to console may now seem dry. The spiritual faculties are being freed up. One's relationship with the divine changes as a result. We become more willing to accept God's being as God's will.

Of course, these nights overlap and interpenetrate. The point John is making is this: God is working obscurely within our very souls. The dark night is an inflow of God into the soul. "El centro del alma *es* Dios" (The center of the soul *is* God), as he puts it in *The Living Flame of Love*.[63] Or, as May puts it: "God in me, I in God, God as me."[64] The dark night is experienced by me as something difficult, as desolation but it is a time of grace. May writes: "The dark night liberates desire by diminishing attachment."[65] This opens up the space for contemplation, which is the sheer gift of grace. (The word "contemplation" derives from the Latin roots *com* and *templum*,

---

62. John of the Cross, *Ascent of Mount Carmel* 1.13; cited by May, *Dark Night of Soul*, 84.
63. Cited by May, *Dark Night of Soul*, 39.
64. May, *Dark Night of Soul*, 76.
65. May, *Dark Night of Soul*, 98.

meaning "with" and "temple.") The dawn after the night is the pinnacle, the point of blissful union, which is the fullness of agape love.

We can depict four main points in John diagrammatically as four quadrants thus:[66]

Active Night of the Senses	Passive Night of the Senses
Our efforts to detach ourselves from those things that obstruct our relationship with God (Teresa's "reptiles") (*Ascent of Mount Carmel*, bk. 1)	God seems hidden. A sign to move from meditation to contemplation (*Dark Night of Soul*, bk. 1)
Active Night of the Spirit	Passive Night of the Spirit
Our response to God's seeming absence; persevering in contemplative prayer (*Ascent of Mount Carmel*, bks. 2–3)	God seems radically absent. Experience of powerlessness; persevering in dark contemplation (*Dark Night of Soul*, bk. 2)

MEDITATION AND CONTEMPLATION IN TERESA OF ÁVILA

For Teresa, there are two forms of active prayer: vocal prayer (rote recitation) and mental prayer (meditation). She considers three types of meditation:

- Reflection: Visualization
- Active recollection: Attentiveness to the divine presence, like centering prayer, Christian meditation, Zen, and Vipassana
- Passive recollection: The first step toward contemplation[67]

Meditation is something we do, such as reading Scripture, repeating a holy word or mantra, journaling; contemplation is done to us (it's gifted). Meditation includes all acts and exercises; contemplation, by contrast, cannot be practiced. It's the difference between effort and grace. There are two psychological qualities present in contemplation singled out in classical descriptions:

1. Open awareness, as distinct from the focused awareness in meditation
2. Centeredness in the present moment (eternal now)

66. McColman, "Praying with Spanish Mystics."
67. May, *Dark Night of Soul*, 105.

We can say with the Carmelite mystics, indeed, with all the mystics, that contemplation is loving. Both John and Teresa rely on metaphor to convey its mysteries; indeed, they have created some of the most compelling imagery of mystical literature ever written. Teresa likens the soul to an interior garden (also to a castle) with God dwelling in the center. The water is prayer, and prayer is loving attentiveness (didn't Simone Weil tell us that pure attention is prayer?).

There are four ways or degrees of watering the soul garden with prayer (*grados de oración*), for Teresa, the first of which is meditation, with the other three requiring deepening dimensions of contemplation:

1. The first way of watering the garden is by hauling the water from a well in a bucket (this great labor is meditation).
2. The second way is by means of a waterwheel, which is less work but gives more water. Such is the prayer of quiet, which is the beginning of contemplation.
3. In the third way, a nearby stream or spring does most of the watering naturally, the gardener needing to supplement it only occasionally.
4. In the fourth way, rain waters the garden. This is the prayer of union.[68]

The progression is from meditation through contemplation to the prayer of union. These phases are cyclical rather than linear, fluid rather than fixed. They are experiences more than steady states or chronological stages. Now, consolations (*contentos*) come in meditation during moments Teresa calls *active recollection*, when the work of meditation quiets the mind and brings one into awareness of the present moment. For Teresa, contemplative experience brings *gustos* or delights—a type of consolation. Gerald May describes the dark night as "nothing other than our ongoing relationship with the Divine."[69] The darkness is holy unknowing. What are the signs of the "night"? St. John describes three such signs to help differentiate an authentic dark night experience from other causes such as depression (*melancholia*). The signs are for spiritual people to notice within themselves. It is important to begin by recognizing what is not the dark night in oneself.

---

68. May, *Dark Night of Soul*, 114.
69. May, *Dark Night of Soul*, 132.

1. Dryness—the first sign is a diminishment of consolation (the soul finds no consolation in God or in any created things).

2. Lack of desire for the old ways of praying.

3. Desire to love God—this third way is certain. Here the soul wishes to remain alone in loving attentiveness to God.[70]

In his own commentary on the first stanza of the dark night poem, John says that three spirits may visit people during the night:

1. The spirit of fornication: Immoral sexual activity; a flailing around in the attempt to procure pleasure

2. The spirit of blasphemy: The impulse to rage against God

3. *Spiritus vertiginis*: The dizzy spirit, which tries to puzzle things out oneself (e.g., "if only I could understand things, I would make them right")[71]

Centuries before Freud, Teresa and John, as perspicacious psychologists, described defense mechanisms, addictions, and depressive disorders. The dark night of the soul is commonly confused with depression. Of course, the dark night can be depressing—liberation involves loss. However, the dark night can't be equated with persistent sadness, pessimism, guilt, hopelessness, lack of energy, insomnia, fatigue, or suicidal ideation, as I said above. In relation to addiction, the first three steps of Alcoholics Anonymous are strikingly reminiscent of the language of the dark night:

1. Admitting we are powerless over alcohol (any addiction)

2. Believing in a Power greater than ourselves

3. Deciding to turn our will over to God (as we understand him)

Spiritual awakenings lead to what May calls the *dark night of recovery*.[72]

If the dark night is experienced in terms of obscurity, daybreak brings clarity and composure. The light at dawn, though, is not like the midday sun—it is, rather, the muted light of early morning. It still partakes of some apophatic mystery. According to May, John speaks of the soul being like a log set afire: warming, steaming, lighting, blazing, finally

---

70. May, *Dark Night of Soul*, 138–42.
71. May, *Dark Night of Soul*, 143–49.
72. May, *Dark Night of Soul*, 161.

being transformed into God's own fire of love.⁷³ May singles out three qualities that characterize contemplation:⁷⁴

1. Freedom
2. Realization
3. Easing/erasing of wilfulness

The intellect, in such a scenario, is transformed into faith, the will into love, and the memory into hope. Ultimately, contemplation is beyond comprehension. Like St. Ignatius and St. Francis, Saints John and Teresa emphasize God's immanence as well as transcendence. For all these mystics, we are always seeking God, as we pray to God, for God, with God, and in God. As Teresa put it in her poem "Buscando a Dios" (Seeking God): "Alma, buscarte has en Mi" (Soul, seek yourself in Me).⁷⁵

In *Shoeless: Carmelite Spirituality in a Disquieted World*, Secular Discalced Carmelite philosopher Donald Wallenfang, together with his wife Megan Wallenfang, in relation to John of the Cross's dark night, observe: "There is no *via negativa* of the dark night without a prior *via positiva* of noonday light."⁷⁶ Apophasis, in other words, happens only against the backdrop and in relation to kataphatic theological correlates. Teresa's five stages of prayer are:

1. Vocal prayer
2. Mental prayer (meditation)
3. Prayer of recollection (first contemplation)
4. Prayer of quiet (second contemplation)
5. Prayer of union (third contemplation)

Aligning this with St. Ignatius, Wallenfang and Wallenfang note: "The *Spiritual Exercises* of Saint Ignatius of Loyola are essential for every person who is serious about knowing how to go about mental prayer."⁷⁷ Before we point to another correspondence, let's remind ourselves of the four different types of water, which is the main metaphor Teresa of Ávila employs to denote the stages of prayer:

73. May, *Dark Night of Soul*, 188.
74. May, *Dark Night of Soul*, 190.
75. May, *Dark Night of Soul*, 199.
76. Wallenfang and Wallenfang, *Shoeless*, 65.
77. Wallenfang and Wallenfang, *Shoeless*, 69.

1. Drawing water from a well
2. The waterwheel
3. Water flowing through a stream
4. Water from the rain[78]

Let's now combine the Juanist two dark nights of the soul with the Teresian seven dwelling places (or mansions) of the interior castle, following Wallenfang and Wallenfang:

1. Active night of sense accords with the first, second, and third dwelling places.
2. Passive night of sense/active night of spirit accords with the fourth dwelling place.
3. Passive night of spirit accords with the fifth and sixth dwelling places.
4. Passive night of the spirit accords with the seventh dwelling places.[79]

So, mapping Teresa's seven stages (in *The Interior Castle*) with John's four (from the *Ascent of Mount Carmel*), we arrive at the following:

1. Vocal and mental prayer correspond to the act of drawing water from a well, to the active night of sense, and to the first, second, and third dwelling places of the interior castle of the soul.
2. The prayer of recollection corresponds to the waterwheel and the transition from the passive night of sense to the active night of spirit, and to the fourth dwelling place of the interior castle of the soul.
3. The prayer of quiet corresponds to the water flowing through a stream, to the beginning of the passive night of spirit, and to the fifth and sixth dwelling places of the interior castle of the soul.
4. The prayer of union corresponds to the water from the rain to the last stages of the passive night of spirit, and to the seventh dwelling place of the interior castle of the soul.

---

78. Wallenfang and Wallenfang, *Shoeless*, 75.
79. Wallenfang and Wallenfang, *Shoeless*, 76.

NIGHT SEA JOURNEY

Teresa and John confronted their shadows; plumbed the depths of their psyches. Carl Jung, the great Swiss psychologist, characterized this inner journey, which Ignatius, Teresa, and John made, to the center of themselves (a Platonic katabasis) as a *night sea journey*, which is a kind of *descensus ad inferos*, a descent into Hades, a journey to the underworld, to the land of ghosts beyond this world and beyond consciousness, as Jung describes it in *The Psychology of the Transference*.[80] The night sea journey is an archetypal motif in mythology that's psychologically associated with depression. It usually involves being swallowed by a sea monster such as a whale or a dragon. It is also represented by crucifixion and dismemberment. At night, the sun goes down, libido is withdrawn—there is a loss of energy, which is a prelude to rebirth. In Jungian terms, St. John of the Cross's experience of the dark night is an encounter with the transpersonal dimensions of the psyche.

We can parallel-map the three well-known mystical stages with three alchemical states thus:

Mystical Stages	Alchemical States
Purgation	*Nigredo* (Blackening)
Illumination	*Albedo* (Illumination)
Union	*Rubedo* (Reddening)

- *Nigredo*: Moonlight
- *Albedo*: Sunrise (dawn)
- *Rubedo*: Midday sun

God loves and wounds/withdraws. The dark night is the death of (our image of) God—the removal of shadow projections. The divine *imago* is cloaked in paradox.[81] The dark night is the *seeming* remoteness of the Absolute. The union (*coniunctio*) that is wrought is the mystical marriage (of ego and self). In terms of alchemical hermeneutics, *nigredo* signifies the dark night. It is meeting the shadow. This gives birth to a more integrated and incarnated self. After the dark night of the ego comes the birth of the more luminous self.

80. Jung, *Practice of Psychotherapy*, para. 455.
81. Odorisio, "Of Gods and Stones."

For Jung, psychology is the science of the soul's interiority—the soul has a logic of its own. The logos of the soul is also evident in the great Carmelites such as Thérèse of Lisieux. The personality is crucified between spirit and instinct. Soul is as much qualified by spirit as it is by body. We never observe an objective event, as it is always filtered by our personality, modified by our subjective experience. Soul is the experiencing subject. To take an example, a pain may or may not be imaginary—it may correspond to a physical object, but it is real all the same as it can be experienced. "We can never get away from the soul."[82] Soul or *psyche* is the proper province of depth psychology.

- Science: Matter
- Philosophy: Mind
- Psychology: Soul

Psyche (soul) is not synonymous with mind, as many philosophers and psychologists erroneously assume. If science deals with perceptions and philosophy with conceptions, soul is that *tertium quid* which is neither mind nor body. Neither *esse in re* nor *esse in mente* but *esse in anima*, to give it its full Jungian flavor and formulation. What follows is this: the meaning of ego or self will derive from the logic of the soul against whose background the other two terms move and live and have their being. Recall that psyche refers to the *experiencing* soul (which, independent of the subject experiencing it, is impossible). Christou asserts: "There is no such thing as an objective psychological experience in the sense in which there is an objective perception of a material object. But there is such a thing as an objective psychological experience provided it also includes the subject, namely the self and the soul."[83] Now, the expression of the meanings of the soul is the symbol—an ontological reality of the soul. (And it is interesting to note the symbolic language of Teresa of Ávila and John of the Cross.)

For Jung, the self is the principle of unity and totality, the spiritualizing center of the personality. Christou (a former student of Wittgenstein, before he trained at the C. G. Jung Institute of Zurich) states, "The personality and its nucleus, the self, are the logical limits of psychology."[84] In this sense, the self is a fiction, an idealized point. If psyche is a process

---

82. Christou, *Logos of the Soul*, 61. The preface was written by James Hillman.
83. Christou, *Logos of the Soul*, 102.
84. Christou, *Logos of the Soul*, 118.

from below upwards, spirit is one from up downwards—the experience of "intrusion" from without—an "interruption" from the Wholly Other. The (Jungian-stated) goal of individuation is the coming into being of one's individualized self.

The reason Jung turned to alchemy was that it was speaking in symbols about the human soul. Jung's own descent into creative illness was an encounter with darkness as *nekyia*. It was similar to Dante's in the *Divine Comedy* where Dante finds himself in a dusky wood (the *nigredo* experience) as well as mirroring T. S. Eliot's *Wasteland*. All three embarked on night-sea journeys to Hades. *Underworld is psyche. Sol niger*—black sun—is an important image of the unconscious. Pseudo-Dionysius had emphasized the divine darkness, the unapproachable light in which divinity dwells.[85]

Following Hillman, Marlan makes the (post-Jungian) point that Jung's "self" is not a substantiated/metaphysical entity. In principle, it is both unknown and unknowable, like God. Jung follows the apophatic alchemical dictum: *Ignotium per ignotius* (The unknown is explained more by the unknown). The self is a no-self. If it was originally modeled on the Hindu notion of Atman/Brahman, it would need to fit too with the Buddhist notion of anatman—a no-self. We need this latter concept as a necessary complementarity principle to keep the self from stagnating into a hypostasized idea. The self has its shadow—its impossible otherness that is essential to it (perhaps approaching the Lacanian *objet petit-a*). James Hillman deconstructs the Jungian transcendental signified. As Marlan makes clear: "When we speak of God or Self, we are naming something whose Being is never fully present and cannot be captured in any signification."[86] When we speak of God or self we always speak under erasure, with an x going through the word—Gxd. This absence of the signified, Derrida calls a trace.

- Jung: Arche-type
- Derrida: Arche-trace

The self shows its otherness when under erasure. It is to symbolize that it is paradoxical, mysterious, "both light and dark, yet neither."[87] We have reached the limits of language as the limits of my world (à la Wittgenstein).

85. Marlan, *Black Sun*.
86. Marlan, *Black Sun*, 184.
87. Marlan, *Black Sun*, 185.

Language does not refer to a nominalist or literalized "thing." Derrida's word for this is *différance*. In psychoanalysis, the subject is decentered, just as in analytical psychology, the ego is relativized and displaced. For Lacan, the subject is an effect of speech. The self is not oneself. It is though, perhaps, oneself as another. The self cannot be totally conscious; it's an unknown mystery that disseminates itself in multiple archetypal images. Marlan quotes Jung as saying: "The concept of the unconscious *posits nothing*; it designates only my *unknowing*."[88] I said that the self casts a shadow; this can be referred to as a divine darkness. In short, the self is like a shooting star which leaves a trail, a trace, in the margins of meaning. The "self" is an image under erasure. As Marlan puts it: "It is a darkness that is light and a light that is darkness,"[89] just like John's *noche oscura*. John experiences spirit as an infinite fire/flame of love. Like the sword that pierced Teresa's heart. *Llama de amor viva*.

ALL AND NOTHING

The spiritual life requires a revisioning in our perceptions, an understanding of polarity and paradox. The lover's quest is everything as well as nothing: *todo y nada*. To want satisfaction in all, desire satisfaction in nothing. The summit of Carmel is space as peace is brought to passion; it is nothing because it holds everything—Presence itself. The gospel is written in poetry, not prose. We are brought to the threshold, not to what is more but to what is less: spiritual subtraction rather than addition. The God of surprises is a God of small things. Phenomenologically, we should let dark night speak, teach, heal. Mystical wisdom comes only through love, union only through night. The young Tobias had to wait *three* nights before he could unite with his bride. This Lover is Three and One. John of the Cross: "As the loved-one in the lover / each in the other's heart resided; / And the love that makes them one / into one of them divided."[90] The process of mystical transformation: from dusk through deep midnight to the light of the rising dawn. *Subir y bajar*: the dialectic of ascent and descent. It may be the case that the soul's center is God, but by participation. "Its substance remains its own," as McGinn puts it.[91] Spiritual marriage

---

88. Marlan, *Black Sun*, 213; emphasis in original.
89. Marlan, *Black Sun*, 214.
90. Cited by McGinn, *Mysticism in the Golden Age*, 247.
91. McGinn, *Mysticism in the Golden Age*, 275.

is communion, deification (theosis), transformation, betrothal, as in the Song of Songs. To put it in Juanist terms, we can say that, eschatologically, the reward of heaven is *serene night* but one on which shines the light of Christ as the Logos of creation.

Ignatian "indifference" is paralleled in John with the latter's emphasis on cleansing and purgation of the passions, which reminds us of the Stoic program, a stripping or divesting (*desnudar*). Dark nights affect both the senses and the spirit, with the passive nights being when God himself works on the soul. On the soul's ascent to the great noonday, alien gods must be dethroned and discarded and the virtues practiced. The road is rocky to the crystalline fount (*cristalina fuente*). With St. Augustine, we get groans, sighs, and tears; with John we get furnace, fire, and flame. The language games differ between Ignatius and John. John is unrelentingly ascetic; he sounds a different note to Augustine, the doctor of grace, and to Ignatius, who deploys none of John's nuptial metaphors. In *Silent Music*, philosopher R. A. Herrera points out that with the coming of the Jesuits on the spiritual scene, supernatural reality became an extension of temporal reality; the religious life was interpreted as no more than an intensification of everyday life (without exceptional episodes). A "devout humanism" characterizes Ignatian spirituality, with Teilhard de Chardin's thought being described/dismissed as grotesque.[92] Herrara cites Gilson's appraisal of Teilhard approvingly—he was "the most Christian of the Gnostics."[93] In light of this harsh (and unfair, I would argue) judgment, we can but state that so much depends on one's own psychology, experience, spiritual and philosophical preferences, temperament, and taste. It also connects to hermeneutics, on how one interprets (and misinterprets) the spiritual masters who but point the way. The night of contemplation is not an end in itself; rather, it prepares us for what is to come: union and joy.

CYNTHIA BOURGEAULT ON THOMAS KEATING

In *Thomas Keating: The Making of a Modern Christian Mystic*, Cynthia Bourgeault, a disciple of Fr. Thomas Keating, distinguishes between the two dark nights thus:

- Dark night of the sense: The deconstruction/dismantling of the false-self system (ego) and our emotional programs for happiness

---

92. Herrera, *Silent Music*, 121.
93. Herrera, *Silent Music*, 122.

- Dark night of the spirit: Affective purification—an upending of the illusion of a separate self-structure

But Bourgeault also hints at a third dark night—*the dark night of self*[94]—the cessation of the separate self-sense, a no-self. She outlines the taxonomy of selfhood, which adds to the Carmelite framework, thus:

- False self: Homemade self, essentially pathological, dismantled in dark night of the sense, beyond which is the illuminative stage
- Ego: Limited autonomous selfhood; disarmed in dark night of spirit, beyond which is the unitive stage
- Separate self: Dualistic perception that divides subject from object; transcended in night of self, beyond which lies unity consciousness
- True self: The Word of God manifesting in our uniqueness; I AM; transcended in night of self, beyond which lies unity consciousness
- Ultimate self: Unmediated participation in the Unmanifest, experienced as pure presence, divine reality reunited as one[95]

The language of one is monism and stasis (for example, the *One without the other* of Advaita); the language of two is polarity and dialectics; the language of three is integration and dynamism. For Keating, union is attained not in the collapse of two into one but in the expansion of two into three, which we can call Trinitarian nonduality or unity consciousness. For example, Jesus's statement: "I and the father are one" (John 10:30). Western theosis—divinization—is best captured and summed up by an epigram attributed to St. Athanasius: "God became man so that man might become God." However, even in transforming union there is still two.

---

94. Bourgeault, *Thomas Keating*, 131.
95. Bourgeault, *Thomas Keating*, 154.

CHAPTER SIX

The Examen of Consciousness in Wittgenstein

WITTGENSTEIN AND CHRISTIANITY

LUDWIG WITTGENSTEIN (1889–1951), THE famous Austrian philosopher and author of the *Tractatus Logico-Philosophicus* and *Philosophical Investigations*, among other seminal works, is regarded by many as one of the greatest thinkers of the twentieth century. He lived without the consolation of belonging to a church, though his religious sense was Christian. Norman Malcolm's opinion is pertinent here: "I am inclined to think that he was more deeply religious than are many people who correctly regard themselves as religious believers."[1] Wittgenstein wasn't a conventionally religious man—he just couldn't help seeing every problem from a religious point of view. For Wittgenstein (as for Kierkegaard), faith was a passion, in a way wisdom was not. Wittgenstein writes: "The Christian religion is only for the one who needs infinite help, that is only for the one who suffers infinite distress."[2] Christianity is less about doctrines and dogmas, for Wittgenstein, and more about direction. He describes religion as "the calm sea bottom at its deepest, remaining calm, however

---

1. Malcolm, *Wittgenstein*, 21.
2. Wittgenstein, *Culture and Value*, 52e.

high the waves rise on the surface."[3] If wisdom is passionless and grey, religion is full of color.[4]

At the outset of the First World War, he was a soldier in the army, and for four years, he wrote his thoughts in six notebooks, of which three survive. His private notebooks, translated by Marjorie Perloff, offer insights into a great mind in dialogue with itself and the world. They were published as late as 2022, having been long withheld by Wittgenstein's estate. The notebooks begin in the summer of 1914 and present the recollections of an infantryman on the eastern front, fresh from his days as a philosophy student in Cambridge. In them, he grapples with his sexuality as much as with philosophical questions and the endless marches and gunfights, as he is assigned to a patrol ship off the coast of Poland. They contain his musings on the meaning of life and death and language. In a way, it's a draft for his *Tractatus*, which was completed in the summer of 1918, and written during 1914–18, a period of great spiritual upheaval for Wittgenstein. Despite his inner turmoil and contemplation of suicide, at the end of his life, he says on his deathbed to his landlady: "Tell them I've had a wonderful life,"[5] words reminiscent of Hopkins's. Wittgenstein would die of colon cancer on April 29, 1951. He came from a very wealthy Jewish family, was baptized a Catholic, and later leaned toward Protestant piety. He lectured philosophy in Cambridge from 1929 until 1947. Three of Wittgenstein's older brothers committed suicide. Wittgenstein, for his part, loved a succession of young men: David Pinsent, Francis Skinner, and Ben Richards. He enjoyed the music of Mozart and Beethoven, employed aphorisms and anecdotes in his works, argued that the limits of my language are the limits of my world, and felt that philosophy was really a form of practice, an attempt to get rid of puzzlement, an endeavor to show the fly the way out of the bottle, as he expressed it himself.[6] All throughout his life, he was searching for the redeeming word (the Johannine Logos), but during these war months, Wittgenstein experienced, as acknowledged by Wittgenstein scholar Marjorie Perloff, "a kind of dark night of the soul."[7] He wanted to change himself; he felt that the sense of the world lay outside of the world, that within the world, everything happens as it happens. "The appeal of Wittgenstein's philosophy has

---

3. Wittgenstein, *Culture and Value*, 61e.
4. Wittgenstein, *Culture and Value*, 71e.
5. Wittgenstein, *Private Notebooks*, 1.
6. Wittgenstein, *Private Notebooks*, 6.
7. Wittgenstein, *Private Notebooks*, 9.

everything to do with what *cannot be said*."[8] This is the mystical—not *what* the world is, but *that* it is, in the first place—*creatio ex nihilo*. If it is true that Hegel always wanted to say that things which look different are really the same, Wittgenstein wished to show that things which look the same are really different—his is a kind of negative theology. In a way, the war saved Wittgenstein's life.

THE NOTEBOOKS: WRITING AS A SPIRITUAL EXERCISE

The dates for the three notebooks are as follows:

- Notebook 1: August 9, 1914—October 30, 1914
- Notebook 2: October 30, 1914—June 22, 1915
- Notebook 3: March 28 (?), 1916—January 1, 1917

The notebooks, which we will explore in this chapter by way of a kind of case history and example of an *examen of consciousness*, detail his depression, his faith-filled moments of consolation, and his periods of desolation. They are packed full of Ignatian and very human themes and can be read as an examen extending over a prolonged period, as Wittgenstein wrestles with his soul and the world. In his journaling, we see him attempting to discern the purpose of his existence.

One typical entry from August 8, 1914, reads "Sometimes a little depressed."[9] He was feeling unwell and had a cough. Two days later, Wittgenstein rages against his shipmates, calling them "a bunch of swine." His spiritual strength as well as sensibility shows through in this quote from the same day: "No choice but to carry out one's work in all *humility* and for God's sake not to lose oneself!!!!"[10] Wittgenstein is intent on striving with all his might to stay alive, but this is hard, as he admits he can't recognize the human being inside the human being.[11] He finds it necessary to maintain distance from everything that happens and "to collect oneself."[12] It seems that Wittgenstein is engaged in some kind of spiritual

---

8. Marjorie Perloff, in Wittgenstein, *Private Notebooks*, 12; emphasis in original.
9. Wittgenstein, *Private Notebooks*, 33.
10. Wittgenstein, *Private Notebooks*, 35; emphasis in original.
11. Wittgenstein, *Private Notebooks*, 37.
12. Wittgenstein, *Private Notebooks*, 39.

exercise here. He resolves to lighten up his outer self, "so as to allow my inner being to be undisturbed." The aim is to practice complete passivity; to accept blows of fate and his destiny, to brave *fortuna* as Boethius did. "One must just be true to oneself!"[13] Occasionally, he sounds a word that becomes a mantra, an affirmation such as "Courage!"[14] as he turns a spotlight on himself and searches himself. When he is in a "hopeless mood" he says over and over the words of Tolstoy, that man is helpless in the flesh but free in the spirit. "God give me strength. Amen. Amen. Amen."[15]

On September 13, 1914, Wittgenstein informs us that he hasn't slept for over thirty hours and feels weak and hopeless again. He writes: "If this is the end for me, may I die a good death, worthy of my best self. May I never lose my self." While peeling potatoes, he prays: "May the spirit enlighten me."[16] The nights pass quietly. Wittgenstein is on watch. He muses: "I am always thinking of how I can keep myself upright."[17] It is hard to serve the spirit on an empty stomach and without sleep. Obeying Ignatius's injunction that during the evening examen, we are to give an account of ourselves and our day, Wittgenstein (while never mentioning St. Ignatius) realizes that "I can't really give an exact account of the immediate cause of my depression,"[18] but he tries, tracing it to a number of factors, not least to his inability to work. From time to time, Wittgenstein works hard but without hope. He is aware he hasn't attained that capacity for self-distancing which permits of a broader perspective and more objective outlook: "I am still lacking an overview."[19] Four days later (on September 29, 1914) he reiterates: "I still don't see clearly and have no overview. I see details without knowing what role they will play in the whole." He needs more courage. "Thy will be done," he prays, and "May the spirit grant me power."[20] When he comes under enemy fire, he prays once more, "May the spirit be with me."[21] It is his duty to fight but also to reserve "my entire being for the spiritual life." He asserts that one must live for the good and the beautiful until life ends of its own accord; until

---

13. Wittgenstein, *Private Notebooks*, 39.
14. Wittgenstein, *Private Notebooks*, 41.
15. Wittgenstein, *Private Notebooks*, 43.
16. Wittgenstein, *Private Notebooks*, 45.
17. Wittgenstein, *Private Notebooks*, 47.
18. Wittgenstein, *Private Notebooks*, 49.
19. Wittgenstein, *Private Notebooks*, 51.
20. Wittgenstein, *Private Notebooks*, 53.
21. Wittgenstein, *Private Notebooks*, 57.

that time, "Every hour of physical well[-]being is a blessing."[22] Ignatius insisted on indifference, and Wittgenstein in an entry of October 11, 1914, accepts that "I must acquire indifference to the hardships of the external life.... God be with me."[23]

Three spiritual exercises stand out here: the practice of gratitude, the attempt to live in the present moment, and the attempt to be indifferent, summed up by Wittgenstein on October 13, 1914: "There are times I cannot live just in the present and for the spirit. One should enjoy the good hours of life gratefully, as a blessing, and otherwise feel indifferent toward life. Today I fought a long time against depression." This fight against is an example of the Ignatian *agere contra* (acting against a natural impulse). Later that same day, he commits this to his journal: "I am all spirit & therefore I am free." He realizes that there are no limitations in the liberty of the spirit. He asks himself: "Will I find the redemptive thought?"[24] He chats, works hard, mans the ship, and longs for David (only first name mentioned, but it is David Pinsent to whom he is referring) amid the cannon fire, wondering whether he will ever see him again. The two spirits are at work within him, vying: "But my spirit speaks within me countering my depression."[25] Around noon on October 13, his depression lifts.[26] His cri de coeur: "Thy will be done."[27] Acceptance. Gratitude. Affirmation. He is now seeing clearly and calmly. The final entry of October 30, 1914, in this, his first notebook, reads: "I will remain firm."[28]

As the winter of 1915 set in, Wittgenstein experienced, according to the editor of the *Private Notebooks*, "what can only be called his Dark Night of the Soul."[29] A poet he had hoped to help died before he reached him in hospital. This was Georg Trakl (1887–1914), who died of a cocaine overdose. Following this tragedy, Wittgenstein became depressed again; on his daily meaningless round, he felt he was losing his very soul/identity. At the time, he was reading Nietzsche's *Antichrist*. He felt that such a life—of an atheist—made no sense. But why not live a life that makes no sense? Doubt remains despite Wittgenstein's insistence that he

22. Wittgenstein, *Private Notebooks*, 59.
23. Wittgenstein, *Private Notebooks*, 61.
24. Wittgenstein, *Private Notebooks*, 63.
25. Wittgenstein, *Private Notebooks*, 67.
26. Wittgenstein, *Private Notebooks*, 71.
27. Wittgenstein, *Private Notebooks*, 73.
28. Wittgenstein, *Private Notebooks*, 75.
29. Marjorie Perloff, in Wittgenstein, *Private Notebooks*, 79.

must always be conscious of the presence of the spirit. When his ship docks, Wittgenstein visits the bathhouses and the cafes. He hints at sexual liaisons and gives himself grief over his daily habit of masturbating. His dark mood and strong sexual desire contribute to his loneliness and loss of hope. He wonders: "Is there a priori an order in the world, and if so, of what does it consist?"[30]

The second notebook opens at the end of October 1914. Wittgenstein continues to provide details in relation to his watch duties. On November 2, 1914, he writes: "It is really fortunate to have one's self & that one can always withdraw into the self."[31] So, despite the daily drama of war and the fact that Wittgenstein was facing mortal danger, he was also practicing self-distancing as he abided serenely in his soul/self, and he continued to write his secret script. This is all the more impressive from somebody who was not overtly religious—at least in any orthodox way—but who seems to have been engaged in some sort of spiritual exercise throughout the war years, at least as documented in his notebooks. There is a constant effort at mental mastery, at (Ignatian) indifference. Witness this entry from November 4, 1914: "I will need much strength to preserve the spirit.—. Be sure not to be dependent on the external world, then you don't need to be afraid of what takes place in it. . . . It is easier to detach oneself from things than from people. But even this is something one must master."[32] Despite being tired, fearful about his future, and "prone to depression," he prays that God may grant him interior strength and that his will be done.[33] "May the spirit not leave me, and may it become more constant in me." He describes his self as a longed-for distant island that has deserted him.[34] He admonishes himself: "Only not to lose oneself!!! Pull yourself together! And don't work just to pass the time but devoutly so as to live! Do no one an injustice!"[35] Effort and ethics are at play in Wittgenstein's soul as he tries to arrive at a clearer picture of both himself and the world. He is thinking a great deal about his life and making an effort to detach from all the happenings—the nonstop comings and goings. Still he prays the same heartfelt prayer to the Almighty: "God

---

30. Wittgenstein, *Private Notebooks*, 82.
31. Wittgenstein, *Private Notebooks*, 87.
32. Wittgenstein, *Private Notebooks*, 87.
33. Wittgenstein, *Private Notebooks*, 89.
34. Wittgenstein, *Private Notebooks*, 91.
35. Wittgenstein, *Private Notebooks*, 93.

give me sanity and strength!!!"[36] In his depression, devoid of all joie de vivre, he begins to work at pulling himself together. He reads Emerson's essays and is much taken by his one on "The Over-Soul" as Wittgenstein endeavors to practice what might be called the *view from above* (a Stoic spiritual exercise aimed at self-detachment). He describes his depression as a stone pressing on his chest.[37] Amid the cannon fire he admits two things—that the redeeming word still has not been articulated and that he is not quite comfortable in his own skin.[38] He peels potatoes, carries coal, sits alone in his cabin, all amid a continuous firestorm and loud cannon thunder. He searches for perspective, peace, and presence of mind. "God be with me!"[39] Above all, Wittgenstein wants a miracle and to develop a "different attitude in order to live."[40] An alteration or adjustment in one's spiritual attitude (mindset) will make all the difference, as well as being true to one's own spirit. "And leave everything to God!"[41] One night when the ship shakes due to cannon fire, Wittgenstein proclaims: "May the spirit protect me!"[42] Everything, he admits, is in God's hands. He reads Nietzsche and despite him recognizes that "Christianity is the only sure path to happiness."[43] The spirit is "the safe haven, protected from the desolate, boundless gray seas of happenings."[44] Despite a flame being extinguished within him, his spirit is active.[45] He lives in the hands of fate. "Only to be in command of oneself!"[46] There is much effort but little letting go for grace. He recognizes the need, and so multiple entries contain these five words: "The spirit be with me."[47]

In February of 1915, Wittgenstein experiences self-reproaches, anger, anxiety, and suicidal ideation.[48] As he wonders whether he will ever work again, he feels "abandoned by all the good spirits.... My soul is worn

36. Wittgenstein, *Private Notebooks*, 93.
37. Wittgenstein, *Private Notebooks*, 99.
38. Wittgenstein, *Private Notebooks*, 101.
39. Wittgenstein, *Private Notebooks*, 105.
40. Wittgenstein, *Private Notebooks*, 107.
41. Wittgenstein, *Private Notebooks*, 109.
42. Wittgenstein, *Private Notebooks*, 111.
43. Wittgenstein, *Private Notebooks*, 113.
44. Wittgenstein, *Private Notebooks*, 117.
45. Wittgenstein, *Private Notebooks*, 123.
46. Wittgenstein, *Private Notebooks*, 127.
47. Wittgenstein, *Private Notebooks*, 133.
48. Wittgenstein, *Private Notebooks*, 133.

out."⁴⁹ Such is his experience of desolation. Wittgenstein struggles against the bad spirit. "I am filled with hatred and cannot let the spirit enter me. God is love.—I am like a burnt-out oven, full of slag and dung."⁵⁰ He now speaks of his depressions (plural), his dark moods, and unchanged situation, as well as somatic symptoms such as pressure on his chest. Writing up his notes on logic helps slightly. *Sehr sinnlich*, "Full of desire."⁵¹ Work becomes a blessing even if he continues to feel broken. Despite being often "*very* depressed," Wittgenstein philosophizes. Indeed, we will meet these insights of his later in the *Tractatus* and *Philosophical Investigations*: "The limits of my language mean the limits of my world."⁵² This second notebook concludes with a confession that he still hasn't found the redeeming word and this: "You are looking into a fog bank and hence persuade yourself that the goal is near. But the fog lifts, and the goal is not yet in sight."⁵³ From confession to catharsis.

Notebook 3 begins on March 28 (maybe) and finishes on January 1, 1917. The notebooks for July 1915 through early March of 1916 were unfortunately lost. In the late autumn, Wittgenstein is transferred to an artillery workshop train where, during the lull in fighting, he reads and writes a great deal and has daily philosophical conversations with a Dr. Max Bieler, who was in charge of a Red Cross hospital train nearby and made friends with Wittgenstein. They compare notes on Dostoyevsky's *Brothers Karamazov*, with Wittgenstein identifying with the *pure* brother Alyosha even if he expresses sympathy for the oldest "sensual" brother Dmitri. Wittgenstein spends a year (1918–19) as a prisoner of war in Casino, Italy. In the meantime, Wittgenstein is sent to the front (present-day Ukraine), where he is assigned to the observation post used for sighting the enemy. Now more than ever does Wittgenstein pray to God. Death gives life meaning, and Wittgenstein is up close and personal to death daily. As we shall see, the summer of 1916, when Wittgenstein was under direct fire, was his turning point. The change that occurs is an inward one. It is the recognition that ethics can't be expressed; ethics can't be said, only shown, and the human, psychological I is not at the center of the universe but only part of it.

49. Wittgenstein, *Private Notebooks*, 137.
50. Wittgenstein, *Private Notebooks*, 139.
51. Wittgenstein, *Private Notebooks*, 141.
52. Wittgenstein, *Private Notebooks*, 147; emphasis in original.
53. Wittgenstein, *Private Notebooks*, 149.

Because he is "close to despair" and suffering the "tortures of hell," Wittgenstein cries out: "God enlighten me!"[54] He counsels that one ought to be of good cheer and satisfied with oneself. He acknowledges that the good life is beautiful, even if he feels he hasn't reached enlightenment yet.[55] As the entry from April 13, 1916, reads: "Still stumbling and falling in the dark. I have not yet awakened to life." Courage. "God make me a better person!"[56] A fortnight later, he is shot at, but "Thy will be done!" He accepts, like Boethius, these blows of fate. He is, however, placing it within a religious register: "Man needs only God."[57] And, as he is being shelled: "I give my soul to the Lord."[58] On July 4, 1916, the question he poses to himself is: What does he know about God and the purpose of his life? He answers with the now-famous litany:

> I know that this world exists.
> That I am placed in it like an eye in its visual field.
> That something about it is problematic, which we call its meaning.
> That this meaning does not lie in it but outside it.
> That life is the world.
> That my will penetrates the world.
> That my will is good or evil.
> That therefore good and evil are somehow connected with the world.
> The meaning of life, i.e., the meaning of the world, we can call God.
> And to that meaning we can connect the image of God as a Father.
> To pray is to think about the meaning of life.
> I cannot bend the happenings in the world to my will; I am completely powerless.
> I can only make myself independent of the world—and so in a certain sense master it—by renouncing any influence on events.[59]

This is an astonishing moment. His religious resignation (can we call it this?) makes him realize that his will is powerless to change things and

---

54. Wittgenstein, *Private Notebooks*, 163.
55. Wittgenstein, *Private Notebooks*, 163.
56. Wittgenstein, *Private Notebooks*, 167.
57. Wittgenstein, *Private Notebooks*, 169.
58. Wittgenstein, *Private Notebooks*, 171.
59. Wittgenstein, *Private Notebooks*, 177.

that meaning is connected with God. A follow-on train of thought is worth quoting in full:

> And in this respect Dostoevsky too is surely right when he says that he who is happy is fulfilling the purpose of being.
> Or one could also say that the person who fulfils the purpose of being, need have no other purpose than to live. That is to say, to be satisfied.
> The solution to the problem of life is to be seen in the disappearance of the problem.
> But can one live so that life ceases to be problematic? So that one is living in eternity and not in time?[60]

In a further important entry of July 8, 1916, Wittgenstein continues in a similar vein, repeating:

> To believe in a God means to understand the question about the meaning of life.
> To believe in a God means to see that the facts of the world are not the end of the matter.
> To believe in a God means to see that life has a meaning....
> I am either happy or unhappy, that's all. One can say: good or evil do not exist.
> He who is happy must have no fear. Not even of death.
> Only he who lives, not in time but in the present, is happy.
> For life in the present there is no death.
> Death is not an event in life. We do not live through it in the world.
> If eternity is understood, not as infinite temporal duration, but as non-temporality, then one can say that he lives eternally who lives in the present.[61]

We must, so: "Live happily!"[62] The present moment is our sacrament. Wittgenstein encourages himself to continue working on becoming good. Meanwhile, being shot at has the effect of him wanting to keep on living. "Ethics and aesthetics are one."[63] Goodness and beauty, so. "Sin" (a surd) is a wrong view of life, Wittgenstein opines. Ethics has nothing to do with punishment. "Ethics is transcendent."[64] In what does it consist,

---

60. Wittgenstein, *Private Notebooks*, 179.
61. Wittgenstein, *Private Notebooks*, 181.
62. Wittgenstein, *Private Notebooks*, 183.
63. Wittgenstein, *Private Notebooks*, 183.
64. Wittgenstein, *Private Notebooks*, 187.

we might well inquire? This: the happy life is good, the unhappy is bad. Wittgenstein knows that the "I" is not an object, even if it makes an appearance in the world by means of the idea that the world is my world. But "everything we see could also be otherwise."[65] The goal: to be happy despite the misery of the world.[66] Difficult? Yes. Impossible? No.

THE IGNATIAN EXAMEN AND BULLET JOURNALING

Usually if one is praying the Ignatian examen, one will do it in the evening and review one's day in terms of one's thoughts, feeling, and actions, discerning where God was present in these experiences. However, one can also do a yearly examen, sifting back over the past twelve months and attending to moments of consolation and grace. Like Wittgenstein, Marcus Aurelius (his famous *Meditations* were originally written as notes to himself), and countless others, Ignatius kept notes. It is something we can do too. One way of systematically doing this is by journaling. And one way of journaling is through the bullet journal method, which enables one to track one's past, order one's present, and plan one's future. It is simply a system that permits one to preview as well as set goals with the aim of more intentional living so that one's beliefs and actions align with meaning and purpose. To take a few examples from the book: one exercise is the mental inventory for decision-making. One writes three columns:

1. In the first column, list all the things you are presently working on.
2. In the second column, list all the things you *should* be working on.
3. In the third column, list all the things you *want* to be working on.[67]

This should provide a clear picture of how you're investing your time and energy. In short, it's a map of your choices. Choices and decisions play a central role in Ignatian spirituality. When you're busy with things, ask:

1. Does it matter?
2. Is it vital?[68]

---

65. Wittgenstein, *Private Notebooks*, 189.
66. Wittgenstein, *Private Notebooks*, 191.
67. Carroll, *Bullet Journal Method*, 38.
68. Carroll, *Bullet Journal Method*, 40.

The journal serves as a mental sanctuary, offering a space to think, reflect, process, and focus. It encourages use of an index, daily log, monthly log, and yearly log to capture events, thoughts, experiences. It also contains a gratitude exercise, which is so congruent with Ignatius. The objective is to cultivate more self-awareness, to pay more attention to one's internal and external life.

In *Reimagining the Ignatian Examen*, Mark E. Thibodeaux (whom I drew on earlier) recommends fifteen minutes per day to spend on the examen. If the traditional examen consists in relishing (asking God to reveal himself at work in my life), requesting (petitionary prayer), reviewing (hour by hour my day), repenting, and resolving to respond better, Thibodeaux includes many more examen-inspired practices, including one called Saving FACE. Many of our problems stem from our:

- *Fears*
- *Attachments*
- Need for *Control*
- Illusions of *Entitlement*[69]

The context of the examen is always in relation to praise, reverence, and service, which is Ignatius's First Principle and Foundation in his Spiritual Exercises. The regular practice of journaling is essential to the contemplative life. To conclude this chapter with a quotation from Viktor Frankl:

> *Everything is recorded in the "logbook" of the world—our entire life and all we have created, our love and suffering.* It is "recorded" in this log and "taken up"; it remains preserved within them. It is not the way a great existentialist philosopher sees it—that the world, so to speak, is a manuscript, which, moreover, is written in a "code language." *No, the world is not a manuscript, which has to be deciphered (and cannot be deciphered)—the world is much rather a record, which we have to dictate!* This record, moreover, has a dramatic character.[70]

Our life is an interrogation; life constantly puts questions to us. "*Constantly we answer life; truly, life is question and answer, seriously.* The logbook of the world cannot be lost. That is our comfort and hope. It is not,

---

69. Thibodeaux, *Reimagining the Ignatian Examen*, 29–31.
70. Frankl, *Rediscovery of the Human*, 98; emphasis in original.

however, only unlosable but also non-correctable."[71] That is a warning but also a reminder. What is of ultimate importance is what we create in the present moment for eternity.

---

71. Frankl, *Rediscovery of the Human*, 98; emphasis in original.

CHAPTER SEVEN

Imagination in the Works of Carl Jung, Ira Progoff, and James Hillman

IGNATIAN IMAGINATIVE PRAYER

ST. IGNATIUS ENCOURAGED PEOPLE to pray using their senses and imagination. One chooses a Gospel scene and begins to see and smell the flowers, touch the surroundings, and taste the food. Considering the Scripture passage—a kind of Ignatian *lectio divina*—involves what's known as the *application of the senses* and *composition of place*. It is a visualizing that is entered into deeply—an imaginative contemplation. For example, in the first week of the exercises, Ignatius will speak of seeing "with the eyes of the imagination" and "in my imagination I will hear"; "I will perceive."[1] In the second week, Ignatius will instruct: "By the sight of my imagination I will see the [divine] persons, by meditating and contemplating in detail all the circumstances around them, and by drawing some profit from the sight."[2] "By my hearing I will listen to what they are saying."[3] "I will smell the fragrance and taste the infinite sweetness and charm of the Divinity."[4] "Using the sense of touch, I will, so to speak, embrace and kiss the places

---

1. *Spiritual Exercises*, in Ignatius, *Personal Writings*, paras. 65–70.
2. *Spiritual Exercises*, in Ignatius, *Personal Writings*, para. 122.
3. *Spiritual Exercises*, in Ignatius, *Personal Writings*, para. 123.
4. *Spiritual Exercises*, in Ignatius, *Personal Writings*, para. 124.

where the persons walk or sit."[5] This continues in the third week[6] and the fourth week.[7]

Similarly with regard to the composition of place: In the first week, Ignatius enjoins us to see in the imagination the composition of place, for example, the temple or mountain where Jesus Christ or Mary happen to be.[8] Or imagine Christ suspended on the cross and converse with him in a colloquy.[9] How is it that the Creator came to be a human being and to die? In the second week, this is given to contemplate (imaginatively see): the synagogues, villages, and castles through which Christ passed as he preached. I will hearken to the call of the King. I will (also) imagine the noises and rooms of Our Lady, in the city of Nazareth, in the province of Galilee.[10] I will see the road from Nazareth to Bethlehem. "Consider its length and breadth, whether it is level or winds through valleys and hills."[11] Again, in this second week, I will imagine myself standing before God and the saints to desire and know what will be more pleasing to the divine persons.[12] In the third week, I will see the road from Bethany to Jerusalem: Is it broad or narrow? How is the room arranged for the supper?[13] Finally, in the fourth week, I will see the arrangement of the holy sepulchre, also the house where Our Lady was,[14] as well as to see myself standing before God, the angels, and saints who are interceding for me.[15] These exercises would come to life, of course, on any pilgrimage, for example, to the Holy Land,[16] but they are primarily carried out by the feat and faculty of imagination.

This kind of imaginative, close scriptural praying has a parallel in Carl Jung's technique of *active imagination*. Indeed, we can interpret the Ignatian contemplations as *exercises in Christian active imagination*

---

5. *Spiritual Exercises*, in Ignatius, *Personal Writings*, para. 125.
6. *Spiritual Exercises*, in Ignatius, *Personal Writings*, para. 208.
7. *Spiritual Exercises*, in Ignatius, *Personal Writings*, paras. 226–27.
8. *Spiritual Exercises*, in Ignatius, *Personal Writings*, para. 47.
9. *Spiritual Exercises*, in Ignatius, *Personal Writings*, para. 53.
10. *Spiritual Exercises*, in Ignatius, *Personal Writings*, para. 103.
11. *Spiritual Exercises*, in Ignatius, *Personal Writings*, para. 112.
12. *Spiritual Exercises*, in Ignatius, *Personal Writings*, para. 151.
13. *Spiritual Exercises*, in Ignatius, *Personal Writings*, para. 192.
14. *Spiritual Exercises*, in Ignatius, *Personal Writings*, para. 220.
15. *Spiritual Exercises*, in Ignatius, *Personal Writings*, para. 232.
16. See Martin, *Jesus*; Grogan, *Alone and on Foot*.

without doing hermeneutic violence to St. Ignatius.[17] Before we turn to this psychological method as it figures in Jung's work, let's first briefly enumerate the story of the imagination as it has developed in the history of philosophy.

THE IMAGINATION IN PHILOSOPHICAL HISTORY

It would take the Romantic poets such as Wordsworth, Keats, Shelley, and, above all, Coleridge to emphasize the visionary and properly reproductive, rather than just productive, uses of the imagination. They understood the imagination as the exact opposite of what is unvented or unreal; imagination underpins mere perception. For the Neoplatonists, soul or psyche was the underlying principle of reality. The world soul, which is both transcendent and immanent, animates the world. Another strand from which imagination came was depth psychology. Jung, in contrast to Freud's conception of a personal unconscious, postulated the existence of a collective unconscious (our phylogenetic psyche), which was common to all and consisting of archetypes, which, like their historical precedents—Kant's a priori categories and Plato's Forms—are abstract entities constituting the substrate of reality. While unknown in themselves, they manifest themselves in images.[18] As Harpur notes: "Jung's hierarchical scheme of the psyche looks much like the Neoplatonic cosmos, except that it is located inside us."[19] Analytical and archetypal psychologists make imagination the cornerstone of their thought. The imaginal is the realm of the in-between (*metaxy*). James Hillman (the father of archetypal psychology) identifies Heraclitus as the founder of depth psychology, as he was the first to speak of psyche's depth.[20] In the beginning is the image. Post-Jungians may be reluctant to interpret images, but they do suggest we amplify them through association.

The question as to what is innate versus what is learned still rages today, with some coming down on the side of nature (such as contemporary American psychologist Steven Pinker) and others (the behaviorists) coming down on the side of nurture. Modernity began with Descartes,

---

17. For a further discussion of Jung and Ignatius, see Costello, *Ignatian Mysticism*.
18. Harpur, *Philosophers' Secret Fire*, 35–44.
19. Harpur, *Philosophers' Secret Fire*, 41.
20. Harpur, *Philosophers' Secret Fire*, 42.

who believed in innate ideas. John Locke, by contrast, redefined the mind by reviving the Aristotelian idea about the mind being a tabula rasa (blank slate), like a sheet of paper, which experience writes up. David Hume opined that the imagination simply reproduces the sensory experiences impressed on the mind. For Immanuel Kant, human cognition is channeled through the mind's categories.[21] Kant, thus, links the tradition that comes from Plato through Bonaventure and anticipates Jung. But for our purposes, it is important just to get the connection between archetype (innate predispositions) and image. Harpur explains: "Jung's collective unconscious whose archetypes, unknowable in themselves, are paradoxically knowable through particular manifestations of themselves—that is, through archetypal images."[22]

For much of its philosophical history, psychic image has been marginalized, sandwiched between reason and matter, mind and body. But as young children, we begin to imagine before learning to speak. As Aristotle noted in his *Metaphysics*: "The soul never thinks without an image."[23] Plato had conceived of images as reproductions of reproductions whereas Aristotle had shifted the inquiry from the metaphysical to the psychological. For Aristotle in his *De Anima* images are mental intermediaries between sensation and reason. However, neither Plato nor Aristotle conceived of images as autonomous products of the creative process. Images remained largely a reproductive activity: imaging, so, as imitation rather than creation. Both the Judeo-Christian and Greek traditions continued this line. It was not until the Renaissance and the work of Paracelsus, Ficino, and Bruno that a new version of imaging was proposed—one that was transformative. Imagining was now central to creativity. Kant liberated the image while Romanticism in the works of Blake, Shelley, Byron, Coleridge, and Keats celebrated the image. All this paved the way for the work of Jung who rehabilitated psychic reality. As he wrote in a letter: "I am indeed convinced that creative imagination is the only primordial phenomenon accessible to us, the real Ground of the psyche, the only immediate reality."[24]

---

21. Harpur, *Philosophers' Secret Fire*, 217–22.
22. Harpur, *Philosophers' Secret Fire*, 220.
23. Aristotle, *Metaphysics*, para. 431a.
24. Jung, *1906–1950*, 60.

JUNG ON ACTIVE IMAGINATION

Carl Jung (1875–1961) shifted the object of depth psychology from sexuality (Freud's main concern) to psychic image. "The psyche consists essentially of images."[25] The psyche creates reality every day in the form of fantasy. If *esse in intellectu* lacks tangible reality and *esse in re* lacks mind, Jung's approach offers a third way of *esse in anima*.[26]

Jung discovered this technique of active imagination between the years 1913 and 1916, following his break with Freud. This was a period of inner turmoil and disturbance for the great Swiss founder of analytical psychology. Jung was searching for something that would heal his personality from within. He would engage and dialogue with the images and fantasies from his unconscious. It was through rediscovering the importance of symbolic play that Jung was able to reconnect with his creative spirit. He termed this therapeutic method *active imagination*, which is based on the natural healing function of the imagination. One chooses an image from a dream or vision or fantasy and concentrates on it; more often than not, these protoplasmic images from the organ depths of the psyche emerge spontaneously. It could be a visual image (as it was predominantly in the case of St. Ignatius) or an inner voice or even a psychosomatic symptom. One concentrates upon it; one becomes absorbed by it. Attention is turned inward. Jung observes: "*Looking*, psychologically, brings about the activation of the object; it is as if something were emanating from one's spiritual eye that evokes or activates the object of one's vision."[27] Active imagination takes place mainly in the mind. It has two stages:

1. Letting the unconscious up: It is a natural process, a form of meditation that involves the suspension of the rational or discursive mind. *Wu wei* is the Taoist term for letting things happen, doing by not doing. Here we gain greater access to the contents of the unconscious.

2. Coming to terms with the unconscious: Here the ego enters actively into the experience; a spontaneous string of insights may emerge which later will need to be evaluated and integrated. A kind of inner dialogue ensues.

---

25. Jung, *Structure of the Psyche*, para. 618.

26. See Kugler's fascinating work *Raids on the Unthinkable* for a further discussion on this central topic.

27. Jung, *Jung on Active Imagination*, 7.

We, thus, empty the mad mind of the ego to let the unconscious fantasy image arise from the unconscious depths. There may be occasions when this procedure is contraindicated, for example, with a psychotic patient who is already enveloped in phantasmagoria. The meaning resides in the image; image *is* psyche. It's an inner psychodrama. Jung's and Ignatius's approaches are equivalent, albeit emerging from different cultural contexts. Active imagination is the way to individuation. It's the imaginative alternative (also extension) of Freud's free association. When patients would report their dreams or fantasies to Jung, he would simply ask them: What comes to mind? What occurs to you in connection with that? Their replies were associations that would become amplified or enlarged through conversation. It would be important to stick as closely as possible to the images themselves. One simply allows the images and inner voices to speak, sometimes by writing them down. There's usually always an image in an emotion. Jung's own inner images and visions, as well as paintings and drawings, would be transferred to the Red Book. Jung listed every item of his psychic inventory, and he did so meticulously over the course of his long life.

Active imagination is more often than not done away from the analyst and the clinic. Dream interpretation, by contrast, is practiced clinically in the presence of the analyst. Both represent two distinct methods, although in later years, Jung suggested that his dream interpretation method was based on active imagination.[28] Both are ways to self-knowledge based on symbolic contents born from a mythopoetic matrix. One way to contain all these images is within a circle or mandala. "Formation, Transformation, Eternal Mind's . . . recreation,"[29] which is the self—the wholeness of the personality. The mandala is the path to the center, to individuation, which is the goal. The self is the archetype of meaning. In his *Memories, Dreams, Reflections* of 1961, Jung muses:

> The years when I was pursuing my inner images were the most important in my life—in them everything essential was decided. It all began then; the later details are only supplements and clarifications of the material that burst forth from the unconscious, and at first swamped me. It was the *prima materia* for a lifetime's work.[30]

---

28. Jung, *Jung on Active Imagination*, 17.
29. Jung, *Jung on Active Imagination*, 38.
30. Jung, *Jung on Active Imagination*, 41.

The aim is to establish contact and connection with one's unconscious, such that consciousness and unconsciousness are in a relationship of complementarity and collaboration. Active imagination is, thus, an important auxiliary method. What Jung calls the (psychological) *transcendent function* arises from the union of conscious and unconscious contents. According to Jung, the unconscious behaves in a compensatory manner toward the conscious. The strict separation between the two systems—conscious and unconscious—is thus discarded. The analyst's function is to mediate the transcendent function for the patient—in other words, to help him to bring the conscious and unconscious together and so arrive at a new attitude. Dream images are the pure product of the unconscious. Since the dream originates in sleep, it has all the characteristics of the *abaissement du niveau mental* (Janet's frequently used term)—of low-energy tension. In both dreams and active imagination (which is like waking dreaming), the fantasy pictures appear hypnagogically. What happens with any inner work through which one confronts the unconscious is that consciousness is continually widened. Jung describes it succinctly: "This transformation is the aim of the analysis of the unconscious."[31] To give a concrete clinical example, if someone is depressed, it would be important for this person to give his depression a hearing, "to try to get his mood to speak to him."[32] Through active imagination, one actively participates in and through the fantasy images that emerge. We don't literalize or concretize our fantasies, though. We let things happen in the psyche.

Jung prefers the term "imagination" to "fantasy." *Opus nostrum* (our work) ought to be done *per veram imaginationem et non phantastica* (by true imagination and not a fantastical one). If fantasy is fleeting and insubstantial, imagination is purposeful creation. Images have a life of their own, and symbols develop according to their own logic.[33] Our unconscious, in the process of active imagination, will produce a series of images that will complete our story (rather than possessing a myopic account of personality that leaves half the reality—the unconscious—out of the mix). This process will not be linear but, rather, will be carried out in a spiral, like a walk around (*circumambulatio*) the *temenos* or sacred center (the self) symbolized by a mandala. It's a centering process. In active imagination, one literally steps into the picture. In a letter to a Mr. O dated May 2, 1947, Jung writes:

31. Jung, *Jung on Active Imagination*, 61.
32. Jung, *Jung on Active Imagination*, 64.
33. Jung, *Jung on Active Imagination*, 145.

> I'm somewhat astonished that you haven't learned yet to apply what I call "active imagination" . . . that is really meant to go to the roots. . . . The point is that you start with any image. . . . Contemplate it and carefully observe how the picture begins to unfold or to change. Don't try to make it into something, just do nothing but observe what its spontaneous changes are. Any mental picture you contemplate in this way will sooner or later change through a spontaneous association that causes a slight alteration of the picture. You must carefully avoid impatient jumping from one subject to another. Hold fast to the one image. . . . Step into the picture yourself, and if it is a speaking figure at all then say what you have to say to that figure and listen to what he or she has to say. Thus you can not only analyse your unconscious, but you also give your unconscious a chance to analyse yourself, and therewith you gradually create the unity of conscious and unconscious without which there is no individuation at all.[34]

PROGOFF ON TWILIGHT IMAGING

It was a pupil of Jung's called Ira Progoff (1921–98), founder of the intensive journal method, who adapted Jung's active imagination. His equivalent was twilight imaging/psyche evoking, which he sets out in his book *The Symbolic and the Real*, which he dedicated to Jung.

For Progoff, the meaning of one's life is dependent on knowledge of the nature of the deep psyche. He deploys the metaphor of the seed to denote the latent possibilities and potentialities of our nature, of what the species can become. He observes: "The fullness of the oak tree is latent in the acorn."[35] In terms of dreams and active imagination, symbols appear spontaneously from the organ depths of the personality; they do not refer to specific objects. The symbol embodies the open future, the seed depths of the individual in his or her unfoldment. Just as Socrates's *daimon* (his inner oracle) called him and drew him on to understand the meaning of his personal existence, so he stung his fellow Athenians into an awareness of their ignorance. As such, Socrates was the first psyche evoker, contends Progoff.[36] Where Socrates goaded, Progoff would evoke. Psyche evoking

---

34. Jung, *Jung on Active Imagination*, 164.
35. Progoff, *Symbolic and Real*, 21.
36. Progoff, *Symbolic and Real*, 41–66.

is simply a rousing of latent potentials in the depths of the person; it is the equivalent of Jung's active imagination, just reframed and rearticulated.

Depth psychology no longer has therapy as its primary goal but rather the development of the personality as a whole. Therapy will be the inevitable by-product of this process, of course. Progoff notes: "Only a unifying experience that establishes anew a sense of wholeness as a principle working within the person can have a lastingly healing effect."[37] For Progoff, psyche is the principle of direction and the place of depth. Integrative wholeness is the operative principle in man. Progoff sees the unconscious as creatively constructive and purposive rather than regressive and repressive. Where Jung used the term (especially in the writings of his later years) "objective psyche," Progoff would use the term "organic psyche" to emphasize the close connection between the psyche and natural evolution.[38] Psyche is the directing principle in the individual; it sets the pattern of growth. Outwardly, it discloses itself in a person's biography—in his works and in his social relationships; inwardly, it comprises dreams, images, intuitions, desires. Progoff avers: "The essence of the psyche is that it is the directive principle by means of which meaning unfolds in the individual's essence."[39] Thus, purpose emerges in the life of a person. The psyche is a mirror of the patterns of meaning that make up a life. The stuff of the psyche is images, and images are symbolic—they portray meaning. This symbolic imagery requires no translation. *Tradurre e tradire*: to translate is to betray—it is to do hermeneutic violence, to commit textual terrorism. The meaning of the image/dream is in its movement. To understand symbolic images does not require a theory of analytical interpretation but a sensitivity to their flow. Progoff recommends the method of twilight imaging:

> In the method of twilight imaging, the individual relaxes, closes his eyes, and permits himself to observe and describe the flow of imagery that moves upon the screen of his mind's eye. This flow, which is a product of the image-making faculty of the psyche, is kaleidoscopic.[40]

This principle of direction and place of depth in man is a visualizing symbol (psychic reality). Progoff gives the example of a patient called Carl,

---

37. Progoff, *Symbolic and Real*, 64.
38. Progoff, *Symbolic and Real*, 72.
39. Progoff, *Symbolic and Real*, 80.
40. Progoff, *Symbolic and Real*, 92.

whom he instructs to lie back, relax, and close his eyes. A screen will appear, Progoff says, and images will appear on the screen of his mind's eye. There will be sounds, perhaps words, feelings, intimations. As they come up, report them, he instructs him. This process is an open reverie conducted at the twilight or intermediate level between waking and sleep. The content of the material connects to the nonconscious depths but flows freely in the midst of consciousness.[41] When Carl did this, an antelope appeared, then an arc, a feeling of reaching out, a statue appeared and rose, then a rocket. The imaging session (a kind of semi-trance) lasted half an hour, and Carl felt refreshed afterwards. Progoff asks some gentle question, probes his psyche.[42] Carl answers and associates freely, gains creative insights into his being, and enters into a larger dimension of reality.

The psyche produces its own symbols out of its own need and wisdom. "The alternative to the analytical way in psychotherapy is to work to stimulate the depth of the psyche until it brings forth symbolic contents that make possible a vital new experience of meaning in the individual's life."[43] According to Progoff, when a meaning of life is experienced deeply and symbolically in terms of a person's inherent imagery, symptoms disappear for lack of attention.[44] Symptoms are simply out of place in symbolic reality. Attention gets shifted from the specific problems to the depth level of the psyche. By permitting the elemental symbols to unfold, a new quality of awareness is achieved; the original problem is thus placed in a new perspective. The guidelines are to keep a record of such imagery in a psychological workbook but resist interpreting it when we begin to enter the symbolic realm of human experience. Psyche evoking and twilight imaging are Progoff's program for growth by which the human person touches transcendence and discovers the ever-enlarging meaning of his/her existence. Progoff describes it as "an act of participation in the wholeness of life, and by means of it the individual enters a larger dimension of reality."[45] By Progoff's particular methodology, "the psychological way of reaching toward reality fulfils the ideal of Socrates."[46] By so doing, fresh and continuing experiences of spirit will break through the psyche, and one "will have forged out of his personal experience a new awareness

41. Progoff, *Symbolic and Real*, 113.
42. Progoff, *Symbolic and Real*, 114–52.
43. Progoff, *Symbolic and Real*, 143.
44. Progoff, *Symbolic and Real*, 144.
45. Progoff, *Symbolic and Real*, 172–73.
46. Progoff, *Symbolic and Real*, 204.

of what spiritual reality is, not as an object of dogma but as the place of meeting in the depth of man where meaning unfolds."[47]

JAMES HILLMAN ON IMAGINATION

No discussion on imagination would be complete without mention of James Hillman (1926–2011), the American post-Jungian founder of archetypal psychology. Hillman articulates a poetic basis of mind, maintaining that the archetypal world is also the *mundus imaginalis*. Soul (psyche) is revealed as being the first principle, placing it as a *tertium* between the perspectives of the body (matter) and of the mind (spirit). This tripartite anthropology of body, mind, and spirit separates archetypal psychology from dualistic divisions (such as those of Aristotle and Descartes). Psyche has its own logos. Hillman states: "The *datum* with which archetypal begins is the image."[48] The soul is constituted of images; psyche is an imagining activity. The source of images is the self-generative activity of the soul. We are our images. Image is irreducible. We are imagined. Archetypal psychology is a way of seeing. Its golden rule: stick to the image, because the image is the primary psychological datum. As such, it refuses Jung's distinction between noumenal archetype per se and phenomenal archetypal image: "its concern is with the phenomenon: the archetypal image,"[49] which is universal and transhistorical as well as being intentional and necessary. Images are *daimones* and angels (message bearers). The verbal work with images is the recovery of soul in speech. Archetypal psychology is mythical realism.[50]

Psyche is the anima mundi, the (Neoplatonic) soul of the world, but soul understood less as a substance and more as a perspective, as a viewpoint toward things rather than a thing itself: the soul, thus, as a symbol that makes meaning possible. Psyche permeates all fields. The heart of psychology's mission is to reawaken consciousness to a sense of soul, to soul making. Hillman recognizes the fact that "fantasy is the archetypal activity of the psyche,"[51] which is not subject to a phenomenological

47. Progoff, *Symbolic and Real*, 226.
48. Hillman, *Archetypal Psychology*, 14.
49. Hillman, *Archetypal Psychology*, 20.
50. Hillman, *Archetypal Psychology*, 24; see also Avis, *God and Creative Imagination*, ch. 14, "Mythic Realism."
51. Hillman, *Archetypal Psychology*, 33.

epoche (à la Edmund Husserl), as fantasy is always going on. Hillman keeps the distinction between soul (symbolized by vales) and spirit (imaginally represented by peaks), recognizing that "the spirit perspective must place itself above (as the soul places itself as inferior) and speak in transcendent, ultimate, and pure terms."[52] This demarcation guards against psychological analysis becoming confused with Eastern or Western meditative disciples, which conceptualize psychic events in spiritual terms. Following poets such as William Blake and John Keats, Hillman calls the world (and the work) "soul-making." Hillman observes: "The curative or salvational vision of archetypal psychology focuses upon the soul in the world which is also the soul of the world."[53] The act of soul making (psycho-poesis) is imagining, "since images are the psyche, its stuff, and its perspective."[54] If the dream makes soul each night, images are the means of translating life events into soul. Archetypal psychology sees the ego as a fantasy of the psyche that it seeks to dissolve, like certain Eastern philosophies; indeed, it's comparable, in this regard, to a Zen exercise.[55]

However, Hillman contends that archetypal psychology's perspectivalism goes beyond Nietzsche as it regards perspectives as forms of vision and lived styles. Soul is the first metaphor. We are multiple personalities; to be imagined polytheistically (rather than pantheistically), like the old Greek gods, who can't be literalized but psychologized, personified. In short, Jung's analytical psychology is reenvisioned within an archetypal hermeneutic, one which respects and exalts the polycentricity of the psyche. Archetypal psychology is "an image-focused therapy."[56] The examination of presentational images is a further refinement of Jungian active imagination, which becomes the method of choice in therapy. "There is a direct perception of and engagement with an imaginary figure."[57] Such images are taken seriously but not literally—like the Bible. By taking soul seriously, archetypal psychology is metaxological through and through. Images have been reduced to feelings in traditional psychology—this reductive personalism is rejected by Hillman and his

52. Hillman, *Archetypal Psychology*, 34.
53. Hillman, *Archetypal Psychology*, 35.
54. Hillman, *Archetypal Psychology*, 36.
55. Hillman, *Archetypal Psychology*, 41.
56. Hillman, *Archetypal Psychology*, 55.
57. Hillman, *Archetypal Psychology*, 56.

followers. "Emotions reinforce ego psychology."[58] Emotions aren't merely personal—they belong to imaginal reality. Personality is conceived of as a peopled drama in which the subject, I, takes part but is not always the main character or even present on stage. The ego is simply a partial capacity that has been elevated in a monotheistic tradition of psychology, one that has placed unity over multiplicity. Archetypal psychology "presents the polytheistic structure of a post-modern consciousness,"[59] whose inspiration is fundamentally Platonic, but without the metaphysics—a phenomenological Neoplatonism, as it were.

Hillman, as *puer aeternus* and trickster figure, interchanges mythology and psychology. In *The Dream and the Underworld*, he states: "Mythology is a psychology of antiquity. Psychology is a mythology of modernity."[60] He proposes an archetypal hermeneutics. For him, this endless activity of soul making is psychologizing, and he uses the term unapologetically. The reason: because consciousness depends upon fantasy images. All we know about anything—our bodies, the mind, the world, the spirit—comes to us through images. For the Greeks, the soul was an image (*eidola*). Our dreams (both night and day) speak in images—indeed, *are* images. Dreaming is imaging. The archetypal method doesn't interpret dreams (along the lines of an a priori ideology, be it Jungian or Freudian), as the dream is its own interpretation; rather, it returns us back to the underworld of psychic images by amplifying their mythic parallels. The soul in *psycho*-therapy is the patient. "There is only the image."[61] The dream is an initiation, not a compensation (Jung) or distortion (Freud). Images get killed through interpretation. The psyche makes images—that is its work. Hillman's emphasis is on shaping psychic stuff. As such, it is "a psychology of craft rather than a psychology of growth."[62] He pays special attention to depth—to what is below (suppression, subconscious, shadow). To repeat: image is psyche, and it can't revert except to its own imaging. Archetypal praxis is an exercise in imagination, not interpretation. There is something liberating about this. Psyche does its own work.

In her book *Alchemical Active Imagination*, Marie-Louise von Franz imagines a theologian saying to a depth psychologist, "You turn everything into psychology," but she maintains that one cannot say "only

58. Hillman, *Archetypal Psychology*, 58.
59. Hillman, *Archetypal Psychology*, 65.
60. Hillman, *Dream and Underworld*, 23.
61. Hillman, *Dream and Underworld*, 82.
62. Hillman, *Dream and Underworld*, 138.

psychological" because that presupposes that psyche is "nothing but."[63] Psyche is objective, for the Jungians, that is to say, not reducible, not an epiphenomenon. And soul is not ego. In analysis, we don't reflect on our personality. Franz says that that would be completely sterile—"to me that would be like the dog who tries to catch his own tail."[64] True knowledge of oneself is knowledge of the objective psyche, of what Jung terms "the self" (a concept criticized by Hillman and replaced by the term "soul"). Franz draws on the Platonic idea of a metaphysical realm of ideas. She observes that "everything on earth has its archetypal model in the *unus mundus*,"[65] which is a variation of the collective unconscious (objective psyche).

In *Archetypal Ontology: New Directions in Analytical Psychology*, two contemporary thinkers continue the discussion. Philosopher-psychoanalyst Jon Mills and psychiatrist Erik Goodwyn exchange views on the nature of archetypes. Mills maintains that archetypes are unconscious schemas, and that the notion of a collective unconscious is dubious if not superfluous,[66] while Goodwyn questions the assertion that we need to eliminate or redefine the idea of "biologically inherited archetypes-as-such."[67] Mills favors *esse in anima*: being/to be in soul. Soul is an aperture to consciousness. Psyche is existence; the world is psyche; psyche is world, as he puts it.[68] Goodwyn, for his part, states: "Psyche exists, and I (currently) exist within it."[69]

CRITICISMS OF HILLMAN'S ARCHETYPAL PSYCHOLOGY

Now, there are critiques of this postmodern Jungian position (and some commentators and clinicians hold that it is not even Jungian). For example, in *The Pursuit of the Soul: Psychoanalysis, Soul-Making, and the Christian Tradition*, Peter Tyler devotes chapter 6 to a critique of Hillman,

---

63. Franz, *Alchemical Active Imagination*, 68.
64. Franz, *Alchemical Active Imagination*, 70.
65. Franz, *Alchemical Active Imagination*, 148.
66. Mills and Goodwyn, *Archetypal Ontology*, ix.
67. Mills and Goodwyn, *Archetypal Ontology*, 29.
68. Mills and Goodwyn, *Archetypal Ontology*, 72–73.
69. Mills and Goodwyn, *Archetypal Ontology*, 80.

labeling him the "heretic trickster."[70] Tyler's main objection: that psychology is a religious act for Hillman and that religion becomes "religion without the transcendent."[71] It is true that Hillman seems to collapse what is transcendent (outside) into what is immanent (inside), but, for Hillman, there is no *outside*! Or better put, the outside can be seen only from inside, from within psyche itself. The same criticism has been leveled against Jung's position on religion—that he subsumes the transcendent into the psychological, despite Jung's numerous objections to the contrary. Yes, Hillman defies easy categorization—it is "a bit like trying to pin down an eel!"[72] Tyler inquires as to whether Hillman believes in the gods of which he speaks. Hillman sees gods as metaphors. His polytheistic psychology is not meant literally. Like Jung, he simply won't comment on the existence or nonexistence of God outside psyche. Certainly, we have images of God, and that is all Jung and Hillman can work with; this will not be enough for some. There is an unconscious God, a spiritual unconscious, an unconscious religious sense, in Viktor Frankl's view.[73] But what about extramental reality? Needless to say, this is a pressing issue for theologians and religious philosophers, even if archetypal psychologists maintain silence on the subject. For Tyler, Hillman's system is "unsatisfactory" on this account.[74] By subsuming spirit into soul (as Tyler sees it), Hillman's polyvalent perspective becomes "an illusion."[75] The charge: "the sublimation of the transcendent into the immanent."[76] However, in *Archetypal Psychology*, Hillman puts forward soul as first principle, soul as *tertium*, as *esse in anima* (Jung), as a figure of the Platonic *metaxy*. He writes, acknowledging our threefold structure: "Body, soul, spirit: this tripartite anthropology further separates archetypal psychology from the usual Western dualistic division, whose history goes back to Descartes."[77] As soul (psyche) is the privileged province of psychology, this is what Hillman prioritizes. But he doesn't dismiss the notion of spirit. As the above quotation suggests, he is aware of spirit's place—he just thinks this is the proper dimension of religion. I am reminded of Teresa of Ávila's

70. Tyler, *Pursuit of the Soul*, 121.
71. Tyler, *Pursuit of the Soul*, 127.
72. Tyler, *Pursuit of the Soul*, 128.
73. Frankl, *Man's Search for Ultimate Meaning*.
74. Tyler, *Pursuit of the Soul*, 129.
75. Tyler, *Pursuit of the Soul*, 130.
76. Tyler, *Pursuit of the Soul*, 132.
77. Hillman, *Archetypal Psychology*, 13.

admission in her autobiography: "I cannot understand what mind is, or how it differs from soul or spirit. They all seem one to me."[78] Tyler recognizes what is good in Hillman and acknowledges his enterprise has a philosophical precursor in Plato: "a return to the Platonic in postmodern clothes."[79] Summing up his position and concluding, Tyler accuses Jung not of destroying Christianity but of transforming it. Furthermore, just as Jung *transformed* Christianity, Hillman *transcended* Christianity.[80] He recommends the figure of a saint-philosopher to us—Edith Stein—as a Carmelite psychologist who recognizes that "only in the radical notion of the Trinity can the unity and diversity of the soul be held together."[81] We might also mention the work of philosopher Daniel Helminiak, whose work *The Human Core of Spirituality: Mind as Psyche and Spirit* offers an alternative Lonerganian perspective on the topics we have been considering, on psyche, soul, spirit, the unconscious, etc. Let's see, however, what a well-known defender of Hillman might say by way of response to these criticisms.

ROBERT AVENS'S ARCHETYPAL PSYCHOLOGY

Roberts Avens (1923–2006) was a Latvian poet and professor of religious studies. As a psychological philosopher, he penned the first comprehensive account of archetypal psychology's place within a major tradition of modern thought—that of mythical thinking—in his work *Imagination Is Reality*. This essay can, at least theoretically, provide a defense of Hillman's perspective in light of Tyler's critique. Whether it's persuasive as an apologia, only the reader can judge for him- or herself. Hillman and Avens abjure the heights of spirituality in favor of the caverns of imagination, as "there is a risk of a monistic adulation of the spirit principle."[82] Avens argues that there is no spiritualization without imagination because it is the imagination that *images* the spirit, even if the spirit pretends to be independent from the imagination.[83] The soul is in the middle (*metaxy*), between the sensible and intelligible worlds, and endows all else with

78. Teresa of Ávila, *Life*, 122.
79. Tyler, *Pursuit of the Soul*, 139.
80. Tyler, *Pursuit of the Soul*, 140.
81. Tyler, *Pursuit of the Soul*, 146.
82. Avens, *Imagination Is Reality*, 9.
83. Avens, *Imagination Is Reality*, 10.

being and meaning. Oriental spirituality proceeds by way of a denial and disparagement of the imaginal soul. The dark and psychological side of human existence is ignored or spiritualized. The issue is between the northern Protestantism of Europe and America with its exaltation of ascension and unity and spirit and wholeness on the one hand, versus, on the other hand, the southern and Catholic Mediterranean tradition with its emphasis on "a pathologizing polytheistic imagery of the soul."[84] The predominant intellectual Cartesian framework has given us a fuzzy conglomerate of mind, psyche, and spirit. We have lost the middle position, which is the place of soul—a world of imagination that is neither physical and material nor spiritual and abstract. Psychology is neither a physical science nor a spiritual metaphysics. Imagination is the common ground of both. Archetypal psychology embraces the essential polycentricity of life. The essence of the psyche is myth, and psychology is mythology, that is to say, the study of stories of the soul.[85] Psyche is a symbol; it is the subject of our experience and the object of psychology simultaneously. If the Second Council of Nicaea depotentiated images in AD 787, the Council of Constantinople reduced the soul to the rational spirit in AD 868, Avens contends.[86] By contrast, Jung and Hillman resuscitated images. Psyche is not brain or mind or spirit but soul: "*esse in anima* as a third reality between the *esse in intellectu* (the mind, the idea) and *esse in re* (the matter, the thing). In the psyche, idea and thing come together and are held in balance. The psychic reality (*tertium quid*) is the creative realm of emotions, fantasies, visions and dreams. Its language is that of images, metaphors, and symbols."[87] Images are the only reality we apprehend directly. Nothing can be known unless it first appears as a psychic image. Fantasy images are the fundamental facts of human experience. It is from the stuff of these images that we create reality/our world. Man is an image maker. We are such stuff as dreams are made on.[88] Image and meaning are identical. Archetypes are patterns, motifs, partial personalities appearing in myth, art, literature, and religions. Jung gave them names: shadow, ego (hero), *persona*, *anima*, *animus*, the great mother, the wise old man, the self. Jung remained (epistemologically) a Kantian (tied to the noumenal-phenomenal distinction) while undoing Kant and

---

84. Avens, *Imagination Is Reality*, 11.
85. Avens, *Imagination Is Reality*, 15.
86. Avens, *Imagination Is Reality*, 41.
87. Avens, *Imagination Is Reality*, 42.
88. Shakespeare, *Tempest*, act 4, scene 1, lines 1887–88.

making this distinction unnecessary by saying that the archetypes are unknowable in themselves. We know archetypes only indirectly, metaphorically, mythically, as images or metaphors. There is no privileged position within the image. The archetype is immanent in its image. Avens wishes to apply Occam's razor—which states that things should not be multiplied without necessity—to Kant's noumenon "by eliminating pseudo-explanatory sounding spiritual constructs,"[89] which are fantasies of the imaginal psyche. Avens proclaims: "Psyche is precisely nothing in itself because it is absolutely implicated in everything."[90] The soul is the experiencing subject—a viewpoint or perspective; it is the middle of three hypostases, between *nous* and *physis*. Wholeness is not in the self (a fiction) "but in a multidirectional psychic structure that takes nothing statically or literalistically."[91] The I is not single but many; it is *samsaric*. The I is imaginal. So, everything is revisioned. As Avens puts it: "Western psychology has been looking at soul in the ego's mirror instead of seeing the ego in the mirror of the soul."[92]

The unconscious, which was originally a hypothesis, has been reified into a hypostasis. In archetypal psychology, *the unconscious* is the process of deepening interiorizing. What psyche is not, is a tabula rasa (blank slate). Things are simply so—*suchness*—from the perspective of soul. A question arises: Is it not about integrating the unconscious into consciousness? No, not according to the archetypal psychologists. Like Zen, the aim (if it has one) is to break up the dualistic structure of consciousness and unconsciousness. Hillman is doing for Jung what Lacan did for Freud. Finally, can we still speak of anything spiritual anymore, something like meditation? Yes. But meditation as soul making. Soul is imagination. Only soul, which is the imaginal realm, is not reducible to anything else and so constitutes our ontological reality. The soul is not in us; we are in soul. Spirit is like a steeple, pointing us to transcendence, while soul is the valley beneath.

Both Jung and Hillman are uncompromisingly psychological; they see everything through that lens (one of psychological immanentism, according to their detractors, who interpret their psychologizing as a form of psychologism and reductionism).

89. Avens, *Imagination Is Reality*, 59.
90. Avens, *Imagination Is Reality*, 68.
91. Avens, *Imagination Is Reality*, 90.
92. Avens, *Imagination Is Reality*, 93.

Hillman is the dancing Derrida of depth psychology, its main deconstructor. Gone is the Jungian self and wholeness and unity. Even in the biblical/patristic and philosophical tripartite anthropology of body (organism), psyche, and spirit—*the apex mentis*, the lines between Spirit and spirit begin to blur, and between soul and spirit. (Such an analogical approach to theological anthropology has been magisterially articulated by John Betz in *Christ, the Logos of Creation: An Essay in Analogical Metaphysics*). We have a tridimensional ontology in figures as diverse as St. Paul, Plato, Frankl, Lonergan, Edith Stein, and James Hillman. Any ternary metaphysics/Trinitarian theology will want to maintain the distinction between transcendence and immanence and so overcome both monism and dualism. This emphasis on the *analogia entis* is fulfilled, for Betz, in a Christological metaphysics, "which is the key to an analogical anthropology of the human being ordered to the incarnate Logos, in whom all things are reconciled in their distinction: God-man, man-woman, body-soul, essence-existence, image-likeness. . . . My own view is that we need to recover the biblical/Patristic tripartite anthropology of body, soul, and spirit—spirit being the 'heart' or '*nous*' or '*apex mentis*.'"[93] Hillman would agree. Indeed, he leaves the notion of spirit to the theologians while concentrating, together with the poets and mystics, on the soul. Archetypal psychologists will continue to insist that the ego/self is a *psychological* fantasy; that the goal of analysis, as in life, is to develop a sense of *soul*; and that the psychic image is far more profound than any comprehension of it.

A CATHOLIC SOUL PSYCHOLOGY?

In *A Catholic Soul Psychology*, Randolph Severson, a family therapist and early student of and assistant to James Hillman, bewails the fact that diagnosis has replaced (phenomenological) description in psychotherapy, as the model of covenant with patient is replaced by contracts with clients. He proposes an archetypal Catholic psychology with "amplification" being the primary method. He doesn't regard archetypal psychology as an ideology of polytheism (à la David Miller and the Syracuse school) nor soul (à la Thomas Moore), nor as a post-Jungian approach (à la Andrew Samuels and many of Hillman's followers), but as a craft, as a way

---

93. Email from John Betz to the author, ca. Jan.—Mar. 2022.

IMAGINATION 171

of doing psychology.[94] Severson argues that archetypal psychology is a Western psychology, at once Catholic and classical, the goal of which is "individuation as eccentricity"[95] rather than existential authenticity, an archetypal psychology "that could be *sui generis* shorn away from its Jungian baggage."[96] The symbolic life and soul making would be at the heart of this (ethical) enterprise. There are similarities between analytical psychology and Catholicism, Severson contends: a sacred rite (analysis), devotional practices (active imagination and dreamwork), saints (the people of the psyche), a pope (Jung himself), but "although the Jungian enchantments were strong, the allure was finally unsatisfying. It was Merlin's glimmering, shimmering magic, not the sensual-spiritual comforts and historical continuity of the Sacramental Mass."[97] As to Hillman, the founder of archetypal psychology, Severson says in a coda, which is an appreciation of James Hillman that concludes his book: "Some say he built on Jung. I wonder. Jungianism, as I experienced it, which was, admittedly, at the margins, was a Church."[98] That said, what Hillman did, as Severson recognizes and relates, was to recover the soul as psychological; in other words, Hillman restored the soul to the world, to the world understood as the vale of soul making. Hillman himself pointed out that there was not one but many archetypal psychologies. This alone justifies Severson's position. In conclusion, we can list some charges one might make against Hillman:

- He repudiates the (factual) existence of the inherited archetype.
- His phenomenology combined with Neoplatonic conceptions is a hodgepodge and clashes, methodologically, with Jung's *analytical* psychology.
- His phenomenology would argue that we have access only to archetypal images that are conscious, but Jung will argue for the archetype *as such*, which cannot be made conscious.
- Metaphor replaces metaphysics.
- Other schools of psychology are routinely dismissed and discarded.

---

94. Severson, *Catholic Soul Psychology*, 8.
95. Severson, *Catholic Soul Psychology*, 13.
96. Severson, *Catholic Soul Psychology*, 70.
97. Severson, *Catholic Soul Psychology*, 184–85.
98. Severson, *Catholic Soul Psychology*, 184.

- His psychological polytheism replaces Jung's notion of the integration of the unconscious.
- His aesthetic paradigm overestimates psychic images (at the expense of symbols?).
- His poetic basis of mind would have us all live in a phantasmagoria of fantasies.
- His ontology is nothing more than a subjective idealism.
- He plays, enjoys, and observes psychical images but doesn't interpret their meaning.

Ultimately, Jung and Hillman—a wayward Jungian—point in different directions. As Corbin scholar Tom Cheetham puts it: "Hillman's Greek gods lack the sense of profound transcendence that is integral to the Abrahamic tradition, and his loose-limbed polytheism is a far cry from [Henry] Corbin's *kathenotheism*."[99]

DORAN'S LONERGANIAN REJOINDER TO JUNGIAN PSYCHOLOGY

In *Subject and Psyche*, which draws on Lonergan and Jung (more so on the former to correct some errors in the latter), Jesuit theologian Robert Doran makes this point:

> While I have long been convinced that spiritual direction ought to profit from the best insights of depth psychology, my experience at the C. G. Jung Institute in Zurich has convinced me also that Jungian analysis not informed by and related to the insights of the spiritual traditions of the various world religions is proceeding blindly and headlong for the romantic agony.[100]

Doran takes issue with Hillman for insisting that soul making and spiritual direction are two quite separate processes.[101] The aim, for Doran, is to become individuating existential, self-transcending subjects, with the help of Ignatius, Jung, and Lonergan. The principles of Jung "may become an avenue to profound and genuine religious experience," as Doran puts

---

99. Cheetham, *All the World an Icon*, 199.
100. Doran, *Subject and Psyche*, 119n3.
101. Doran, *Subject and Psyche*, 118n3.

it.[102] However, it has to be pointed out in relation to Jung that the "absence of a clear notion of cognitional self-transcendence prevents Jung from vigorously accenting the dynamism to self-transcendence immanent in the psyche itself."[103] Method is an interiorization of both logos and mythos. This is the meeting place between theology and depth psychology. The key to method is the presence of the subject to himself. The psyche can't be given the upper hand in this process. (Why not?) Doran notes: "The failure of Jung adequately to distinguish psychic energy and intentionality is, I fear, the basis of a potential psychic totalitarianism on the part of his followers."[104] According to Doran, what we have in Jung is a conception of the self as integrator (self as psychic totality) but not of the self as operator as one has in Lonergan's cognitional theory. Doran remarks: "The Jungian notion of individuation, then, is quite susceptible of reinterpretation within the context of the self-appropriation of the existential subject. Individuation is the psychic complement of the self-appropriation of intentionality aided by Lonergan."[105] Doran finds Jung's views on God and evil to be woefully inadequate. The solution to the problem of evil is not by integrating it into the psyche as Jung suggests but by transcending it in the Crucified.[106] Moreover, some Jungian terms are woolly. Doran would like to replace "the unconscious" with "the undifferentiated," and "the collective unconscious" with "the archetypal function."[107] While Doran is correct to alert us to the conceptual philosophical dangers of these terms, namely, in substantializing and reifying them, it seems unrealistic at best to seek, at this point of their intellectual history, to replace them.

Where does all this leave us with Jung and Lonergan? Let the final word on this topic go to Doran: "Jung tends to swallow all the functions into the psyche and frequently speaks as though a human being were *only* a psychic being. Lonergan's *Insight* is an aid to the differentiation of what Jung is reaching for."[108] In other words, the whole matter would be better understood within a context more sensitive to intentionality and its differentiation from the psyche. What is lacking in Jung's work is a critical

102. Doran, *Subject and Psyche*, 23.
103. Doran, *Subject and Psyche*, 19.
104. Doran, *Subject and Psyche*, 65n17.
105. Doran, *Subject and Psyche*, 162.
106. Doran, *Subject and Psyche*, 166.
107. Doran, *Subject and Psyche*, 173.
108. Doran, *Subject and Psyche*, 216.

method such as the one advanced/provided by Lonergan, according to Doran. In short, what is needed in analytical psychology is the adoption of Lonergan's transcendental method with the addition of (Doran's) notion of psychic conversion. This last point has also been made by the late Jungian analyst Paul Ruefli, in a doctoral psychology thesis.[109] A professor of depth psychology sums it up best: "There is much to criticize in Jung and much to save."[110]

RETURNING TO IGNATIUS

To return to Ignatius in light of the above—Ignatius encountered a God within human experience, an immanent God. Ignatius received frequent mystical experiences throughout his life, though, according to Irish Jesuit Brian O'Leary, there is "no evidence that Ignatius underwent a Dark Night of the Soul, such as that described by St John of the Cross."[111]

If we imagine Ignatius consulting with a Jungian analyst about his visions and form of imaginative praying, they might suggest he try active imagination and dialogue with his fantasies, as a mental strategy to communicate with his unconscious. The key to active imagination is to restrain the waking mind from exerting influence on the internal images as they unfold. A Jungian analyst might suggest to Ignatius just to observe the scene, watch for changes in whatever is transpiring, respond to, and report them. He would urge Ignatius to enter into the process as if the drama being enacted before his mind's eye were real. The images and fantasies of the unconscious mind naturally rise to become conscious. By visualizing, one lets them act themselves out. The technique allows for communication to take place between the conscious and unconscious aspects of the psyche as well as between the personal and collective unconscious. Perhaps this is what Ignatius was in fact doing hundreds of years before the arrival on the scene of Freud and Jung.

The problem is, from a Jungian perspective, that the Ignatian practice of actively imagining a scene from the Gospel is more an act of reproductive than productive imagining (even though it can lead to the latter), that it is a technique involving not spontaneous emergences from the creative and spiritual unconscious but of directed, New Testament–centered

---

109. Ruefli, "Via Intention to Personal Authenticity."
110. Wood, *Archetypal Artist*, 76.
111. O'Leary, *Ignatius Loyola*, 70n37.

a priori images. (Of course, I take it that an "image" may not just be visual—it can be any impressive or expressive sensation.)

Finally, one should note that archetypal psychology distinguishes between the *imaginary* and the *imaginal*, with this latter term signifying the metaphysically objectively real.[112] Perhaps too there is some conceptual confusion around definitions that needs to be cleared up. One does get the impression that Hillman's work has not been a source of serious or sustained study by some of Jung's detractors.

Any original explanatory principle—such as self or spirit or signifier—explains everything except itself. This realization doesn't lead to relativism or nihilism necessarily but to psychological realism, because it is based on the recognition that all systems of interpretation gain their authority precisely by a grounding in a transcendental signifier that is no longer so absolute or ultimate. Why? Because the ultimate ground of depth psychology is not a known God term but the unknowable, which is the unconscious itself.

---

112. Bourgeault, *Eye of the Heart*.

CHAPTER EIGHT

The Enneagram and Christianity

Throughout this book, we have been looking at key Ignatian themes through the lenses of various philosophers, depth psychologists, theologians, and poets. It is fitting we include the Enneagram, which offers nine lenses through which we perceive the world with our personalities. Jesuits and former Jesuits such as Jim O'Brien, Robert Ochs, Jerome Wagner, Don Riso, and Tad Dunne, to name but a few, were among the first students of the Enneagram and responsible for its growth, dissemination, popularity, and application, especially in the arena of spiritual direction. In the Cova Sant Ignasi in Manresa, a course is offered entitled "Spiritual Exercises with Enneagram Intuitions."[1]

The purpose of the Spiritual Exercises is to gain an authentic experience of the Love that is the source of everything. In Manresa, Ignatius experienced a spiritual renewal and gained an intellectual clarity that guided his own life from that point (1522) on until his death in Rome in 1556. It opened his eyes to his essence. And this is exactly what the Enneagram does too. It advances one in the process that Saint Ignatius proposes. Consolation and desolation, as movements of the spirits, indicate authentic lines of integration or disintegration, of which the Enneagram speaks. (Indeed, we would lose nothing in translation or meaning if we replaced "essence" with "authentic selfhood.")

---

1. For a current listing of courses, see https://www.covamanresa.cat/ca/propostes-i-formacio-espiritual.

Members of other religious orders have engaged with Enneagram teachings too, most notably, Suzanne Zuercher, a Benedictine, and Richard Rohr, a Franciscan. As I have written on the Enneagram in four other books,[2] in this chapter, I would like to concentrate on showing the congruence/compatibility between the Enneagram and Christianity, as well as outlining some interesting Ignatian parallels.

RICHARD ROHR ON THE CHRISTIAN ROOTS OF THE ENNEAGRAM

In *The Enneagram: A Christian Perspective*, Richard Rohr, OFM, and Andreas Ebert suggest that the Enneagram has Christian roots dating at least to the Desert Fathers, with pre-Christian sources. Rather than stemming from Sufism, as has been claimed by many, it is, these authors contend, genuinely Christian. In the preface, Andreas Ebert, a Lutheran minister, notes: "Since the first edition we have become convinced that the Enneagram does not derive from mediaeval Islamic (Sufi) sources, but can be traced back, at least in part, to the Christian desert monk Evagrius Ponticus (d. 399) and the Franciscan Blessed Ramón Lull (1236–1315)."[3] Ebert recognizes that a "number of Jesuits and the Catholic 'Communities of Christian Living' had used it [the Enneagram] for retreats and the training of spiritual counsellors."[4] Self-knowledge, such as the Enneagram provides, is the presupposition of the inner journey. The roots of the Enneagram "go back at least as far as the early monasticism of the Desert Fathers, perhaps even back to pre-Christian times (Pythagoras). Later, it was presumably passed on orally through the Islamic wisdom tradition of Sufism. Thus, although it seems to be genuinely Christian, it draws from pre-Christian sources and has had an influence on non-Christian mystical traditions."[5] In relation to the discernment of spirits (1 John 4:1), Rohr writes: "The Enneagram, like the Spirit of truth itself, will always set you free, but first it will make you miserable!"[6] Such is the cost of self-knowledge.

---

2. See Costello, *Nine Faces of Fear*; *Dynamics of Discernment*; *Between Speech and Silence*; and *Alchemy of Addiction*.
3. Rohr and Ebert, *Enneagram*, ix.
4. Rohr and Ebert, *Enneagram*, x.
5. Rohr and Ebert, *Enneagram*, xi–xii.
6. Rohr and Ebert, *Enneagram*, xiii.

The Enneagram was presented in the West by George Ivanovich Gurdjieff in 1916 as a comprehensive symbol of the harmonic structure and inner dynamism of the cosmos. Only later did it become a typology of character. One of Gurdjieff's disciples, J. G. Bennett, maintained that Gurdjieff had learned the Enneagram from Sufis in Asia. Oscar Ichazo developed the Enneagram of fixations in the 1970s and likewise referred to hidden Sufi sources. In 1995, Andreas Ebert stumbled on a text by the Desert Father Evagrius that he felt must have had something to do with the Enneagram. He wondered whether the Enneagram had Christian origins. Rohr and Ebert ask:

> So were the origins of the Enneagram Christian—and not Sufi—after all? The Jesuit Robert Ochs, one of the Enneagram disciples of Claudio Naranjo, was convinced that the Enneagram was profoundly rooted in Christian mysticism. . . . Ochs recognised the tradition of the Desert Fathers, a group of fourth-century monks who had developed the view of the seven deadly passions that charge the types with their energy. In 1992 the German Benedictine Anselm Grün had also noted some astonishing parallels between the Enneagram and the teaching of the passions developed by Evagrius.[7]

Evagrius, an anchorite, lived in a hermitage in the Nitrian desert and was influenced intellectually by Origen. His teachings, including those of other Desert Fathers, exerted an enormous influence on Eastern Orthodox monks. "The work of Evagrius closely coincides at two points with the Enneagram: in his *Teaching on the Passions* and in the description of a figure that is based on Pythagorean numerological speculation, which displays the essential features of the Enneagram symbol. Evagrius developed a list of eight—or even nine, in one passage . . . vices"[8] or distracting thoughts ("demons"). The following is a list of the eight vices (sins) corresponding to the Enneagram number:

Vice	Enneagram Point
Anger	One
Pride	Two
Vanity	Three
Sadness or Envy	Four
Avarice	Five

---

7. Rohr and Ebert, *Enneagram*, 8.
8. Rohr and Ebert, *Enneagram*, 10.

Gluttony	Seven
Lust	Eight
Laziness/Acedia	Nine

Fear, which is classified in Type Six, is missing. Pope Gregory I later reduced this list to the one prevalent today consisting of the seven classical deadly sins, dropping vanity and sadness and leaving anger, pride, envy, greed, gluttony, lust, and sloth. Although Evagrius mentions nine vices in one passage, he doesn't provide a systematic account of the fixations, which Ichazo developed in the 1970s.

Rohr and Ebert make much of the number 153. At the end of John's Gospel, we are told that after his resurrection on Easter, Jesus ordered his disciples to cast their fishing net into the Sea of Genesareth. They did so and caught 153 large fish (1 plus 5 plus 3 add up to 9). Numerological symbolism was rampant in antiquity and the early church. Evagrius refers this number to Pythagorean theory. Origen was influenced by Pythagoras, for whom numbers were the building blocks of reality, who, in turn influenced Evagrius. Evagrius wrote a little book entitled *153 Chapters on Prayer*! These 153 chapters are also part of the *Philokalia*—a collection of instructions on prayer from the ancient church that is the foundation of the mysticism in the Eastern Church. *Logismoi* are assaultive thoughts—toxic or troublesome thoughts that lead us away from Christ. Evagrius informs us that this number is symbolic and "contains the form of both a triangle and a hexagon,"[9] just like the Enneagram symbol. The triangle, he tells us, represents the Trinity, and the hexagon represents the ordered cosmos. The number 100 is, by itself, a square; the number 53 is made up of the sum of 25 and 28. The number 28 is a triangular number, and the number 25 is a circular number (5 times 5). "And so in this number you have a square figure to express the fourfold number of the virtues, but also the spherical which, because of its form, represents the circular movements of time and is an apt symbol for deep knowledge of this world."[10] The triangle, represented by the number 28, symbolizes the knowledge of the Trinity (and of the theological virtues—faith, hope, and charity). Pythagoras had distinguished triangular, square, octagonal, and circular numbers:

---

9. Evagrius Ponticus, *Chapters on Prayer*, 54.
10. Evagrius Ponticus, *Chapters on Prayer*, 54–55.

- Triangular numbers—The sum of consecutive numbers beginning with 1. Thus: 3 equals 1 plus 2; 6 equals 1 plus 2 plus 3, etc.

- Square numbers—The sum of numbers beginning with 1, from which one number is left out. Thus: 4 equals 1 plus 3 (2 left out).

- Hexagonal numbers—The sum of numbers, beginning with 1, from which three numbers have been left out. Thus: 6 equals 1 plus 5 (2, 3, and 4 left out).

- Circular numbers—A number that is the product of a number that, upon being squared, is repeated in the last place. Thus: 25 equals 5 times 5; 36 equals 6 times 6.[11]

This means that the number 153 is triangular and hexagonal, thus standing for the Trinity and the created world (six days of creation). Evagrius sketched a symbolic psychology of characters based on eight (and in one case, nine) evil thoughts or passions, which is depicted in the modern Enneagram of personality, as well as outlining a cosmology symbolically represented by a combination of circle, square, and hexagon, which one sees in the Enneagram symbol. We can't say that the Desert Fathers constructed the Enneagram (at least in toto), but what we can say is "that the two most important elements of modern Enneagram lore (a cosmic symbol that contains triangle, circle, and hexagon), plus a teaching about character based on the 'deadly sins' can be traced back to Evagrius, that great Christian expert on the world and the human soul."[12] But even simpler than this are the numbers themselves, which, when added, come to 153: 1 plus 5 plus 3 equals 9, which is the number of Enneagram types! Evagrius came from (modern-day) Turkey, which is right beside Armenia, where Gurdjieff resided, which is an interesting coincidence/synchronicity. Later, St. Augustine talked about the seven gifts of the Holy Spirit and the Ten Commandments, which, when added together, result in 17, which is a triangular number—the sum, in fact, of numbers 1 plus 2 plus 3, etc., up to 17 equals 153!

Another great figure whose work amazingly anticipates the Enneagram was Ramón Lull (1232–1315/6), who was a member of the Third Order of Franciscans. He was interested in a new language of spirituality, one that would contribute to the conversation between Christians, Jews, and Muslims. What does he do? The starting point for the common

11. Rohr and Ebert, *Enneagram*, 12.
12. Rohr and Ebert, *Enneagram*, 14.

quest for truth would be nine (!) names of God that he distributes clockwise around the circumference of his circular figure A standing in this schema for God's essence, while the nine qualities of God bear the letters *b* to *k*. They are linked to the center and one another. There is a second figure T, which represents relative principles that characterize the nearness and difference between Creator and creatures but coincide in God. Figure T is a circle filled with three triangles (3 times 3 equals 9). "The closeness of both these figures to the Enneagram figure is unmistakeable. Like the figures of Evagrius, Lull's schemata could also be called 'proto-Enneagrams.'"[13]

It seems likely that Gurdjieff was influenced by the Desert Fathers (who were highly prized in Orthodox spirituality) and by Sufism. Gurdjieff had originally trained to be a Russian Orthodox priest. He had traveled to Egypt, India, and Tibet. In a monastery of the Sufi Sarmoun brotherhood, he is supposed to have come to know the tradition on which the Enneagram is based. He called himself, throughout his life, a "Pythagorean Greek" and an "esoteric Christian."[14] He compared the Enneagram to the legendary philosopher's stone. But as a teaching of psychological types, the Enneagram played no role in Gurdjieff's thought. That form goes back to Ichazo, who claims he learned it from Sufi masters in Afghanistan. In the 1960s, Ichazo taught in Bolivia and Chile before emigrating to the USA in 1971 where the psychiatrist Claudio Naranjo adopted Ichazo's model in the Esalen Institute. Thereafter, a "series of American Jesuits, above all Father Robert Ochs, ran into the model while working with Naranjo. After long years of testing and theological scrutiny many Jesuits decided to adopt the Enneagram as a tool for spiritual counselling and as a model for retreat work."[15]

In Rohr and Ebert's opinion, St. Ignatius developed a method for spiritual direction that is both intellectually and psychologically sensitive, based on the discernment of spirits, which is carried out in three steps.[16] The aim was:

1. To sense the various stirrings in the soul

---

13. Rohr and Ebert, *Enneagram*, 16–17.
14. Rohr and Ebert, *Enneagram*, 18.
15. Rohr and Ebert, *Enneagram*, 20.
16. Rohr and Ebert, *Enneagram*, 22.

2. To recognize and understand their origin and end, and to make a judgment on whether they lead constructively to the meaning-goal of my life or destructively away from it

3. To take a position on such movements within me by accepting or rejecting them

Rohr and Ebert conclude with this observation: "The Enneagram is a related tool, and in some ways a still more precise tool, for reaching this goal. That is one of the reasons a series of retreat houses have begun to introduce the Enneagram alongside the traditional Ignatian Exercises."[17] The encounter with the Enneagram, Rohr says, has been one of the great overwhelming experiences of his life.[18] He is in no doubt whatever as to its spiritual efficacy: "The Enneagram can promote spiritual enrichment."[19]

ESSENCE AND THE ENNEAGRAM

In *The 9 Dimensions of the Soul*, David Hey relates the Enneagram personality types to essence, thus integrating the psychological aspects of the Enneagram with its spiritual dimension. Like Rohr, Hey recognizes that there is "no doubt that it [the Enneagram] had a place in the wisdom of ancient Egypt, in Christian and Jewish mysticism."[20] We need to be clear as to how the Enneagram conceives of essence before detailing its relationship with Christianity, specifically with the Ignatian tradition. Essence relates to qualities of Being, which is our true nature. "Essence defines the different aspects of our true nature. These are essential qualities such as Joy, Strength, and Will."[21] Each of the nine points on the Enneagram circle represents not only a personality type but an essential reality. Essence connects us with being. With each stage of childhood development, there is an experience of essence. For example, Type Eight (the Controller or the Boss) strongly experiences the red essence of strength in the separation phase of six to twelve months of age. Type Two (the helper or giver) has strong experiences of the gold essence of merging love during the symbiotic phase of childhood, which is from zero to six

---

17. Rohr and Ebert, *Enneagram*, 22.
18. Rohr and Ebert, *Enneagram*, 23.
19. Rohr and Ebert, *Enneagram*, 24.
20. Hey, *9 Dimensions of Soul*, 6.
21. Hey, *9 Dimensions of Soul*, 7.

months of age. At the moment of birth, we are in full contact with Being. Over time, our ego-personality loses this essential connection; the ego will try to compensate for this loss by promoting a fixation. Below, I summarize the names associated with each type on the Enneagram:

Type	Name
One	Perfectionist/Reformer
Two	Giver/Helper
Three	Achiever/Performer
Four	Romantic/Creative
Five	Thinker/Observer
Six	Skeptic/Loyalist
Seven	Planner/Enthusiast
Eight	Challenger/Controller
Nine	Peace Lover/Mediator

Here is Hey's essence of the Enneagram list:[22]

Nine	Universal Love	Daylight Essence
One	Perfect Love	Pink Essence
Two	Merging Love	Gold Essence
Three	Autonomy	Pearl Essence
Four	True Self	Rainbow Essence
Five	Inner Guidance	Diamond Essence
Six	Will	White Essence
Seven	Joy	Yellow Essence
Eight	Strength	Red Essence

Different colors are associated with essence. Essence is holy humanity. We are born into essence before we develop personality traits and lose touch with who we are in truth. What the Enneagram tradition calls the Holy Ideas (which are akin to Platonic Forms) are positioned as the antidote to each type's fixation. The Holy Idea is, to quote Christopher Heuertz, "the mental clarity of the True Self when the mind is at rest, while the Virtue of each type is the emotional objectivity of the True Self

---

22. Hey, *9 Dimensions of Soul*, 8.

that comes forward in a heart at peace."[23] Taken together, our Holy Idea and virtue express who we are created to be. Here is the list of Holy Ideas connected to type:

- One: Holy Perfection
- Two: Holy Will
- Three: Holy Harmony
- Four: Holy Origin
- Five: Holy Transparency
- Six: Holy Strength
- Seven: Holy Wisdom
- Eight: Holy Truth
- Nine: Holy Love[24]

In relation to our (Enneagram) essence, Heuertz observes: "Moving beyond a caricature of personality traits to understand the essence behind type unearths the true offering of the Enneagram: access to incredible transformation."[25] To do this, we need to approach the Enneagram from a contemplative perspective, from a spirituality characterized by stillness and silence, for whole-person growth. The modern Enneagram was brought the United States by South American psychiatrist Claudio Naranjo and then, in Heuertz's words, "unleashed by a spiritual community (the Jesuits)."[26] Conversion is the aim of the Enneagram, wherein we become freed from the prison of our passions and fixations. A truly contemplative spirituality will succeed in calming the body, stilling the emotions, and quietening the mind.

Sandra Maitri, a member of the first group to whom Naranjo presented the Enneagram system, likewise explores in her books the spiritual context of the Enneagram. She suggests that two versions of the Enneagram are promulgated, one that relates to *egoic* experience (that of personality) and the second to *essential* experience (that which is beyond

---

23. Heuertz, *Sacred Enneagram*, 36.
24. Heuertz, *Sacred Enneagram*, 37.
25. Heuertz, *Sacred Enneagram*, 60.
26. Heuertz, *Sacred Enneagram*, 165.

the conditioned self.[27] She also insists on pursuing spiritual work in tandem with the Enneagram.

Let me summarize her exposition of the Holy Ideas in relation to the nine types.[28] With Point Nine (Holy Love), we see that the ultimate nature of all that exists is love and that we are created out of such love; we are an expression of this love. Moving clockwise around the Enneagram, we come to Holy Perfection at Point One, which suggests to us that the fundamental nature of everything is inherently good and perfect just as it is. When experiencing reality through the vantage point of Point Two, Holy Will, we see that the universe's unfoldment has its own momentum and direction and that which occurs within each of us is a result of the divine plan/project. From the perspective of Point Three, we see that everything that happens is part and parcel of the changing pattern of the universe and that none of us acts separately from the source/whole. When experiencing reality from the angle of Point Four (Holy Origin), we see that true nature is the source of all manifestation, and that everything is inseparable from it. From Point Five's idea of Holy Omniscience, we see that each of us is a holon, a part of the fabric of reality, and that the boundaries which distinguish us are not ultimate. With Point Six—Holy Faith—we see with certainty that our inner nature is essence not ego, and this sustains us, giving us faith and fortitude. At Point Seven (Holy Plan), we see that there is an inner logic and progression to the unfoldment of the human soul, whose natural tendency is to teleological individuation. With Holy Truth at Point Eight informing our perception, we see that Being is the ultimate nature of all that exists, so that all distinctions, even between ego and essence, are ultimately illusory. With loss of contact with essence, which takes place over the first three to four years of life, Type Nine loses, to take just one example from above, the perception of Holy Love, which results in the belief (fixed cognitive fixation) that who he is, is not lovable, significant, valuable, worthwhile.

CHILDHOOD LOSS

- Types One as children might have felt criticized, been punished, experienced being not good enough. The rules of the house might

---

27. Maitri, *Spiritual Dimension of Enneagram*, 7.
28. Maitri, *Spiritual Dimension of Enneagram*, 11–12.

have been applied inconsistently. Increasingly, Type One children felt they couldn't make mistakes.

- Types Two as children felt loved only if they helped others; their personal needs felt selfish. So, as a result, they closed off their personal needs and feelings, turning to others. Love became giving to get as a way of compensating for the love they didn't feel they received or was reciprocated.

- Type Three children felt rewarded when they accomplished/achieved. Their feelings were disowned and discounted. Only performance mattered. Admiration replaced love, and in the process, it harmed their ability to love themselves.

- Type Four children felt abandoned by one or more of their primary caregivers, feeling alone and cut off, for reasons they couldn't understand. They were neither seen nor mirrored. As a result, they turned inward with their imagination helping them to cope with their isolation.

- Type Five children received no meaningful interaction, emotion, or affection from caregivers, or they had an intrusive and controlling parent and felt defenseless in the face of such intrusion. Over time, they built a wall around themselves and retreated to their safe mental realm.

- Type Six children were raised in an unpredictable situation with no safe place to go. They lost faith that they would be protected, so they turned to inner doubting, disbelieving reality and rejecting their own gut instincts and inner guidance.

- Type Seven children were deprived of nurture, or it was removed from them. They handled this loss/lack by distraction to minimize the pain. They focused on all their options and relied on themselves to fulfill their desires.

- Type Eight children grew up in an emotionally and/or physically unsafe environment and had to mature precociously. They didn't feel safe to show any vulnerability or perceived weakness, as it was frequently used against them, so they focused on building strength.

- Type Nine children were neglected or overlooked. They were ignored for having needs or for expressing themselves (especially anger) and decided to keep a low profile, focusing on the needs of others instead.[29]

Question to consider: How did you experience wounding as a child? Does that pain continue to today? How did you learn to cope when you were young?

APPLYING THE ENNEAGRAM TO JESUS

Holy Cross priest Robert J. Nogosek directly relates the Enneagram to Christianity in that he applies it to Jesus in his *Nine Portraits of Jesus: Discovering Jesus Through the Enneagram*. The Enneagram, like the Ignatian exercises, is a call to conversion. (A similar work is by Irish Jesuit priest Peter Hannan, entitled *Nine Faces of God*.) Nogosek persuasively relates Christ to all points on the Enneagram, citing stories from Scripture, as he progresses, thus:

- One: His discipline
- Two: His solicitude
- Three: His ambition
- Four: His sensitivity
- Five: His wisdom
- Six: His loyalty
- Seven: His joviality
- Eight: His assertiveness
- Nine: His serenity[30]

The words of Christ that he associates with each Enneatype are the following:

- One: "Be perfect . . ." (Matt 5:48)
- Two: "Be . . . servant of all" (Mark 9:35)
- Three: "Go . . . to all nations" (Matt 28:19)
- Four: "I am deeply grieved" (Mark 14:34)

---

29. Heuertz, *Sacred Enneagram*, 54–55.
30. Nogosek, *Nine Portraits of Jesus*, 31–109.

- Five: "Be like a wise man" (Matt 7:24)
- Six: "Believe also in me" (John 14:1)
- Seven: "Come and have breakfast" (John 21:12)
- Eight: "Woe to you ... hypocrites" (Matt 23:13)
- Nine: "My peace I give to you" (John 14:27)[31]

THE IGNATIAN ENNEAGRAM

Clare Loughrige coins the term "iEnneagram" to show the connections she tries to make between the Enneagram and Ignatian spirituality in her eighty-page booklet *Motions of the Soul: The Enneagram and Ignatian Spirituality*. Motions of the soul are the discernment of spirits. While recovering from his war wound, St. Ignatius discovered engagement of what the Enneagram calls the three centers of intelligence: head, heart, and gut. Inner motions are experiences of desire, imagination, emotion, intellect, and instinctive reactions—both attraction and repulsion, which Ignatius categorized as good and bad spirits, consolation and desolation. Loughrige was taught the Enneagram, she tells us, from Jesuits.[32] Ignatius paid attention in his imaginative prayer to his thoughts (head), desires (gut), and feelings (heart). He practiced discernment. As Loughrige puts it: "Wise intellect, healthy emotions, and gut instincts describe the presence of each of the persons of the Trinity and God's work in integrated human beings."[33] Where Nogosek applied the Enneagram to Jesus's life, Loughrige proposes Ignatius as a model of Enneagram wisdom, albeit not altogether satisfactorily in this author's opinion. The Trinitarian motions of the soul are, she contends:

- Father: Head
- Jesus: Heart
- Holy Spirit: Gut[34]

The head or thinking triad in the Enneagram consist of Types Five, Six, and Seven. The heart or feeling triad consists of Types Two, Three, and

---

31. Nogosek, *Nine Portraits of Jesus*, 117.
32. Loughrige, *Motions of the Soul*, 9.
33. Loughrige, *Motions of the Soul*, 12.
34. Loughrige, *Motions of the Soul*, 13.

Four. The gut or instinctive triad consists of Types Eight, Nine, and One. Loughrige applies the three centers to the three theological virtues, relating the gut to hope, the heart to love, and the head to faith, asking: Am I moving toward faith, hope, and love in my life?[35] Each type, existing from presence/essence, will embody uniqueness. Thus, in Loughrige's words:

- One: Goodness creates joy.
- Two: Love contemplates, then decides.
- Three: Effective loyalty harmonizes.
- Four: Originality joyfully reforms.
- Five: Wisdom lovingly directs.
- Six: Faithfulness produces peace.
- Seven: Joy is deeply stable.
- Eight: Justice is contemplative love.
- Nine: Peace effects team.[36]

Ignatian imaginative prayer is engaging the head, the heart, and the gut. We allow ourselves to observe the sights, sounds, smells, tastes, and experiences of the Gospel event. We let our affective responses emerge. Loughrige poses three questions:

1. What is happening in your gut when you're reading some Scripture? Do you have any instinctual reactions?
2. At the level of the heart, is there an emotional response?
3. Does the story speak to a situation in your life and what are you thinking about that—head?[37]

The aim of the Enneagram: to enable one to be present to the divine Presence itself. The perfection of the One keeps them from (experiencing) Presence; the possessiveness and people-pleasing of the Two keep them from Presence; the performance and pragmatism of the Three keep them from Presence; the personalizing and pouting of the Four keep them from Presence; the pontificating and private nature of the Five keep them from Presence; the paranoia and pledges of the Six keep them from Presence;

---

35. Loughrige, *Motions of the Soul*, 13.
36. Loughrige, *Motions of the Soul*, 23–48.
37. Loughrige, *Motions of the Soul*, 67.

the playing and preoccupation of the Seven keep them from Presence; the power and persecutions of the Eight keep them from Presence; and the powering down and procrastinating nature of the Nine keep them from Presence.[38] It is not for nothing that the changes which use of the Enneagram results in are called inner *work*.

Jean-Marc Laporte, SJ, wrote an article in 2017 entitled "A Christian Transposition of the Enneagram: With Paul of Tarsus and Ignatius Loyola," in which he reexpresses Enneagram categories within Pauline anthropology. He realizes that there are some conservative Catholic critics of the Enneagram (for example, Mitch Pacwa, SJ, who studied under Fr. Robert Ochs, SJ, but who had a change of heart later on in relation to the Enneagram), not to mention some fundamentalist Protestant pastors who object to it on spurious grounds. Laporte argues in favor of the Enneagram, maintaining that it has a both "positive" and "liberating" impact on the lives of many.[39] Pauline anthropology is based on a tridimensional ontology and revealed in the following passage: "May the God of peace himself sanctify you entirely; and may your soul and spirit and body be kept sound and blameless at the coming of our Lord Jesus Christ" (1 Thess 5:23). There are the three categories mentioned: body (soma), soul (psyche), and spirit (pneuma). The spirit of man, Paul also calls the heart, which is the locus of fundamental conversion. In the Enneagram, this mysterious center is called essence (which is distinct from personality) or self (as distinct from ego). Soul or psyche is closer to spirit, while the body is closer to the outside world.[40] In Enneagram terms, the two functions of the psyche—knowing/thinking and feeling—are termed head and heart. It is through the body that stimuli from the outside awakens the psyche and the spirit. In terms of our biology and bodies, the Enneagram describes three instincts:

1. Self-preservative
2. Social
3. Sexual

Taken together, they refer to "gut," thus yielding the triad of head, heart, and gut. Just as the distinction between psyche and soma is blurred within *personality*, the distinction between God and the human self is blurred in

---

38. Loughrige, *Motions of the Soul*, 69.
39. Laporte, "Christian Transposition of Enneagram," 2.
40. Laporte, "Christian Transposition of Enneagram," 4.

essence. However, theological anthropology is clear: between God and the self there is distinction but not separation, "union but not absorption."[41] Where Christianity speaks of original sin, the Enneagram will speak of the false ego, with its nine patterns, one of which predominates in each human being. When the mind is constricted, we get (mental) fixations, just as when the affective disposition is warped, we get compulsions. The nine fixations are:

- One: To be good/perfect
- Two: To be helpful/self-sacrificing
- Three: To be successful/efficient
- Four: To be original/refined
- Five: To be observant/wise
- Six: To be on guard/loyal
- Seven: To be joyful/enthusiastic
- Eight: To be in control/assertive
- Nine: To be peaceful/unobtrusive[42]

The nine compulsions/disordered passions/capital sins are the vices we enumerated above. According to Laporte, it is the indwelling Spirit who cuts through my biases, fixations, compulsions, making me aware of the distorted patterns of my personality. With the work of the Enneagram and Ignatian spirituality, one gains the ability to center oneself, and a habit of "genuine self-presence takes root in me."[43] When I abide in the still point of the soul, I experience (Ignatian) consolation. Change and growth are the result of acting against (*agere contra*) the fixations and compulsion of my type. This means going against the grain of my unredeemed nature; it will involve unlearning fixations and mechanical habits. Moving against the (Enneagram) arrows is moving against the grain. The Ignatian term *agere contra* signifies precisely this countermovement/behavior in the soul, so I can reach the virtues:

- One: Serenity
- Two: Humility

---

41. Laporte, "Christian Transposition of Enneagram," 6.
42. Laporte, "Christian Transposition of Enneagram," 15.
43. Laporte, "Christian Transposition of Enneagram," 21.

- Three: Veracity
- Four: Equanimity
- Five: Generosity
- Six: Courage
- Seven: Sobriety
- Eight: Innocence
- Nine: Alertness

A further approach: to observe the five fundamental precepts that apply to all humans, irrespective of their Enneatype. Laporte cites Lonergan:

- Be attentive.
- Be intelligent.
- Be reasonable.
- Be responsible.
- Be loving.[44]

If we take the first and last "be" attitudes—be attentive and be loving—these are similar to Ignatius's two standards meditation: the forces of sin (symbolized by Luther—the enemy of our human nature) and the play of grace (Christ). Where do I see this dynamic playing in my life?

Finally, each type belongs to a triad: Eight, Nine, One: instinctive (root system); Two, Three, Four: emotional (limbic system); and Five, Six, Seven: cognitive (neocortex). These three correspond with gut, heart, and head, respectively. The focus in the first group is *survival* in the world as it is here and *now*, the focus in the second group is *recognition* by others on the basis of *past* performance, and the focus in the third group is finding a *secure path* into the *future*. The underlying affects that need to be addressed, pertaining to the types/triads, are:

- Aggression
- Shame
- Anxiety[45]

---

44. Laporte, "Christian Transposition of Enneagram," 26–28; see also Dunne, *Enneatypes*.

45. Laporte, "Christian Transposition of Enneagram," 35.

Within the instinctive reactors, Eight is aggressive, Nine is withdrawing, and One is dependent. Within the emotive types, Three is aggressive, Two is dependent, and Four is withdrawing. In the thinking types, Seven is aggressive, Six is dependent, and Five is withdrawing.[46]

Finally, Dominican Maria Beesing, Holy Cross Father Robert Nogosek, and Jesuit priest Patrick O'Leary place the Enneagram within the arena of spiritual psychology in their co-written book *The Enneagram: A Journey of Self Discovery*. Ones are perfectionists (sticklers) who avoid anger, Twos are people pleasers who avoid recognizing they have needs, Threes are success-driven achievers who avoid failure, Fours are romantic individualists who avoid ordinariness, Fives are thinkers who try to avoid emptiness, Sixes are skeptics who avoid being disloyal, Sevens are enthusiastic future planners who avoid pain, Eights are bosses who avoid appearing weak, Nines are peace-loving mediators who avoid conflict.[47] Usually, in terms of typology, each type is described in terms of their compulsions. For example, if we were to align a symbolic animal to each type, we would have the following:

- The compulsive One is like a *terrier* with his bark and bite.
- The compulsive Two is like a *cat* who rubs up against a person until they are satisfied, then strolls away.
- The compulsive Three is like a *peacock* showing off and displaying their success.
- The compulsive Four is like a *basset hound* with droopy eyes expressing sadness as a way to connect with people.
- The compulsive Five is like a *fox* silently watching and slinking around.
- The compulsive Six is like a *rabbit*, always scared and twitching.
- The compulsive Seven is like a *monkey*, inquisitive and always on the go.
- The compulsive Eight is like a *rhinoceros*, thick skinned and nearsighted.

---

46. Laporte, "Christian Transposition of Enneagram," 37.
47. Beesing et al., *Enneagram*, 10.

- The compulsive Nine is like an *elephant*, all ears and ponderously slow.[48]

What the above authors do is to study the personality of Jesus as an antidote to this prevailing focus on the compulsions of the types. A compulsion is a kind of mistake in how to live out one's good qualities or essence. By pushing the good quality to extremes, compulsions are formed. "The compulsion is a *sin against wholeness*."[49] Christ lived all nine ways of human personality without their compulsions and so can be truly taken as a model in our journey to freedom. These nine good qualities in Jesus associated with the Enneatype can be adumbrated thus:

- One: Jesus is an idealist and reformer but compassionate.
- Two: Jesus serves and helps others without clinging and attachment.
- Three: Jesus works for success and the coming of the kingdom but accepts failure.
- Four: Jesus is deeply sensitive and emotionally attuned but avoids self-pity and melancholy.
- Five: Jesus loves wisdom but doesn't remain aloof.
- Six: Jesus is loyal without being self-righteous.
- Seven: Jesus is optimistic but can stay in the present moment.
- Eight: Jesus confronts injustice while also being vulnerable.
- Nine: Jesus is patient but never indolent.[50]

The Enneagram shows the way to conversion for the compulsive self. We can distinguish three types of conversion, as explicated by the Enneagram:

1. Head center: *Intellectual conversion through the Holy Ideas.* (For example, the holy idea of growth releases Ones from their trap of perfection.)
2. Heart center: *Affective conversion: passions healed by the virtues.* (For example, Twos move from the passion of pride to the virtue of humility.)

---

48. Beesing et al., *Enneagram*, 120–23.
49. Beesing et al., *Enneagram*, 50.
50. Beesing et al., *Enneagram*, 49–98.

3. Gut center: *Instinctual conversion: discernment of spirits.* (Here, following the lead of Ignatius Loyola, we test the movements of consolation and desolation to choose what to do and what not to do.)

This is the way Beesing, Nogosek, and O'Leary describe what we might call an Ignatian Enneagram process:

- The *consolation* of Ones is the experience of peace, which is a characteristic of their head center because moving toward the Seven *against* the arrow they must move into the head center. The *desolation* of Ones is in the heart center because moving *with* the arrow they move toward the Four. The experience is that of distaste and restlessness.

- The *consolation* of Twos is in the heart center because positive growth is moving *against* the arrow toward Four. Their consolation is being thankful (grateful). The *desolation* of Twos is in the gut center. When they move *with* the arrow, they move toward the Eight. They experience desolation as a profound darkness.

- The *consolation* of Threes is in the head center because they grow less bound by their moving *toward* the Six. They are consoled by being at peace. The *desolation* of Threes is in the gut center because they move *with* the arrow of compulsion toward the Nine. Their desolation is to feel in turmoil.

- The *consolation* of Fours is in the gut center because they move *against* the arrow by moving toward the One. Their consolation is an experience of being on fire. The *desolation* of Fours is in the heart center because moving *with* the arrow is moving toward the Two. Fours experience desolation as distasteful.

- The *consolation* of Fives is in the gut center because they move toward the Eight by moving *against* the arrow. Their experience is of being on fire. The *desolation* of Fives is in the head center because their negative movement is *with* the arrow toward the Seven. The experience is that of selfishness.

- The *consolation* of Sixes is in the gut center because they grow positively by moving *against* the arrow toward Nine. Their consolation is to see things in the context of God. They become on fire with zeal. The *desolation* of Sixes is in the heart center because they move toward the Three by moving *with* the arrow. The experience is that of frenetic restlessness.

- The *consolation* of Sevens is in the head center because they move toward the Five by moving *against* the arrow. Here they are strengthened. The *desolation* of the Sevens is in the gut center because they move toward the One by moving *with* the arrow. The desolation experience is that of darkness.

- The *consolation* of Eights is in the heart center because they move *against* the arrow by moving toward the Two. Their consolation is being thankful. The *desolation* of Eights is in the head center because they move *with* the arrow by moving toward the Five. The experience is that of selfishness.

- The *consolation* of Nines is in the heart center because their positive growth is in moving *toward* the Three. The experience is that of being thankful. They experience God loving them just as they are. The *desolation* of Nines is in the head center because they move *with* the arrow by moving toward the Six. The experience is that of despair.[51]

The symbolic animals we can now associate with the *redeemed* types are the following:

- Redeemed Ones are characterized by the *ant* (industrious, well-organized, and purposeful).

- Redeemed Twos are characterized by the *Irish setter* (warm, loyal, and emotionally effusive).

- Redeemed Threes are characterized by the *bald eagle* (larger than life, unmistakable, and at ease with themselves).

- Redeemed Fours are characterized by the *black stallion* (free spirits, self-possessed, and special).

- Redeemed Fives are characterized by the *owl* (alertly restful, silent, and adaptable).

- Redeemed Sixes are characterized by the *deer* (tuned in, sensitive, and drawing strength from the group).

- Redeemed Sevens are characterized by the *butterfly* (radiating beauty, passion, and hope).

---

51. Beesing et al., *Enneagram*, 205–10.

- Redeemed Eights are characterized by the *tiger* (carefully camouflaged, selective, and strong).
- Redeemed Nines are characterized by the *porpoise* (intelligent, eager to learn, and peacefully cooperative).[52]

We began this book with an external pilgrimage; here we have been considering an inward journey, depicted by the Enneagram, which is such a powerful path leading to liberation. The way ahead for us all will consist of light and shadow, ignorance and inspiration, joy-filled days and dark nights of the soul, consolation and desolation, fixations and moments of fullness, compulsions and conversion experiences.

---

52. Beesing et al., *Enneagram*, 210–18.

CHAPTER NINE

Care of Creation, the Great Chain of Being, and Catholic Social Teaching in E. F. Schumacher, *Laudato Si'*, and Simone Weil

THE IGNATIAN *CONTEMPLATIO*

IGNATIUS BEGAN HIS *SPIRITUAL Exercises* with the notion of creation when he said in the Principle and Foundation that human beings are *created* to praise, reverence, and serve God. Other things on the face of the earth are created for humans "to help them in the pursuit of the end for which they are created."[1] This opens the first week of the exercises. Ignatius concludes his work with the contemplation to attain love in the fourth week, which has the retreatant realize that he/she has received his creation from God himself,[2] which is the first point of the meditation, while in the second point, he/she should consider how God dwells in creatures:

- In the elements, giving them existence
- In the plants, giving them life
- In the animals, giving them sensation
- In human beings, giving them intelligence

---

1. *Spiritual Exercises*, in Ignatius, *Personal Writings*, para. 23.
2. *Spiritual Exercises*, in Ignatius, *Personal Writings*, para. 234.

Ignatius alerts us to how God abides in me too, giving me existence, life, sensation, and intelligence, making me his temple, "since I am created as a likeness and image of the Divine majesty."[3] In the third point, Ignatius draws our attention to God laboring and working for me "in all the creatures on the face of the earth."[4] Ignatius is offering a cosmic perspective here. Let's amplify this by taking a brief look at (1) E. F. Schumacher's systems theory; (2) Pope Francis's encyclical on creation, *Laudato Si'*; and (3) Catholic social teaching.

SCHUMACHER'S GREAT CHAIN OF BEING

E. F. Schumacher (1911–77) was a British economist and protégé of John Maynard Keynes who was born in Germany and greatly influenced by Mahatma Gandhi, even if Catholicism exerted its appeal on him from the late 1950s. He is known for two publications in particular: *Small Is Beautiful* (1973) and *A Guide for the Perplexed* (1977), which was a critique of materialist scientism. He was a leading figure in the ecological movement. There are similarities between his own views and the teaching of papal encyclicals on socioeconomic concerns (for example, Leo XII's *Rerum Novarum*, John XXIII's *Mater et Magistra*, and Pope Francis's *Laudato Si'*) as well as the distributism promoted by Catholic thinkers such as G. K. Chesterton and Hilaire Belloc. Philosophically, Schumacher absorbed Thomism and was deeply read in St. Teresa of Ávila and Thomas Merton. He converted to Catholicism in 1971. His legacy consists of a Schumacher circle, center, society, and college dedicated to his philosophy. Schumacher's *Guide for the Perplexed* is a reference to Maimonides's *Guide for the Perplexed*. In it, he argues that the current philosophical maps that dominate Western thought are overtly narrow. He interprets the world as a hierarchical structure with at least four levels of being, which is a restatement of the great chain of being, derived from Plato and Plotinus in the main, which begins with God and descends though the angels, humans, animals, and plants to minerals. It is congruent with Ignatius's mystical vision in his *contemplatio*. God, angels, humans, animals, and minerals are all links in a chain. These are the four kingdoms/levels of being; there are differences of kind between each level of being, which he conceptualizes thus:

---

3. *Spiritual Exercises*, in Ignatius, *Personal Writings*, para. 235.
4. *Spiritual Exercises*, in Ignatius, *Personal Writings*, para. 236.

1. Mineral = m
2. Plant = m + x
3. Animal = m + x + y
4. Human = m + x + y + z[5]

X, y, and z represent ontological discontinuities: matter, life, consciousness, self-awareness. Moreover, there is a change in the movement between each level, with humans having free will:

1. Cause: Mineral kingdom
2. Stimulus: Plant kingdom
3. Motive: Animal kingdom
4. Will: Humanity

According to Schumacher (and preempting the work of Ken Wilber), there are four quadrants of human existence/experience, four worlds:

1. I—inner: What is going on in my inner world
2. The world (you)—inner: What is going on in the inner world of other beings
3. I—outer: What I look like in the eyes of other beings
4. The world (you)—outer: What I observe in the world around me[6]

What St. Ignatius and St. Francis, St. Bonaventure and Teilhard de Chardin, Schumacher and Pope Francis want to draw our attention to is this: that all life is shot through and saturated with divinity and comes from the Creator through a free act of love. God's goodness is diffusive (*bonus est diffusivum sui*). All layers and levels of being participate in the divine reality. This all-encompassing perspective, derived from Ignatius but also from St. Francis of Assisi, is dealt with more systematically by Pope Francis in his encyclical of 2015, entitled "*Laudato Si'*: Care for Our Common Home."

---

5. Schumacher, *Guide for the Perplexed*, 28.
6. Schumacher, *Guide for the Perplexed*, 74.

LAUDATO SI'

The pope begins his encyclical by quoting St. Francis of Assisi's beautiful canticle to all of God's creatures, to Mother/Sister Earth, who produces fruits and flowers for us. However, humans have harmed the natural environment; this is evident in the soil and sea and air. Consumption, pollution, the rapid rate of human evolution, waste, climate change, and our throwaway culture have inflicted much damage, so much so that we can speak of an ecological disaster.[7] By contrast, St. Francis is proposed as a model par excellence of "integral ecology."[8] Nature is the first book in which God speaks to us, granting us glimpses of his glory. However, presently the planet is in peril. What is needed to combat this tragedy is "universal solidarity"[9]—global consensus rather than denial, indifference, or nonchalant resignation. The pope's expressed hope is that this encyclical is "added to the body of the Church's social teaching."[10] Throughout it, the pope links the plight of the poor with the plight of the planet. The culprits are depletion of natural resources, loss of biodiversity, exploitation,[11] extinction of mammals and birds, decline in the overall quality of life, breakdown in society, and global inequality.[12]

Chapter 2 is explicitly called "The Gospel of Creation." Francis asserts that the Catholic Church "is open to dialogue with philosophical thought" in seeking "paths of liberation."[13] The book of Genesis is cited as God's plan for creation, even if the language is symbolic. Human life is grounded in three relationships: with God, neighbor, and the earth itself. Genesis will speak of dominion over the earth (Gen 1:28), which we are to till and keep (Gen 2:15). We humans are stewards, sojourners, strangers on the land. The Psalms, for their part, ring out paeans of praise to the God of creation and consolation. The world does not derive from chaos or chance but from a decision.[14] Francis invokes his namesake in mentioning Brother Sun, Sister Moon, Brother Wind, Sister Water, Brother

---

7. Francis, *Laudato Si'*, paras. 20–26.
8. Francis, *Laudato Si'*, para. 10.
9. Francis, *Laudato Si'*, para. 14.
10. Francis, *Laudato Si'*, para. 15.
11. Francis, *Laudato Si'*, para. 27.
12. Francis, *Laudato Si'*, paras. 48–49.
13. Francis, *Laudato Si'*, para. 64.
14. Francis, *Laudato Si'*, para. 77.

Fire.[15] We creatures exist in communion with the rest of nature. There is the common destination of goods—peace and prosperity for all God's children. The natural environment is a collective good, a common home, the patrimony of all humanity. We should, thus, be attentive to the beauty of the world, as we seek to live in harmony with creation.[16]

Politically, cultural relativism has negatively affected/impacted social ecology. Here, Pope Francis invokes the notion of "communitarian salvation," which is the principle of the common good (social ethics)—the sum of social life by which individuals access their own fulfillment/flourishing.[17] Subsidiarity is mentioned too.[18] The pope insists that politics must not be subject to the economy.[19] Life is not fundamentally about the maximization of profits; such compulsive consumerism leads to collective selfishness.[20] There is a covenant between humanity and the environment; what's needed is environmental education, an "ecological conversion."[21] St. Francis shows us the way to sublime fraternity with all creation; indeed, this Italian Franciscan friar radiantly embodied it.[22] It was an attitude of the heart.

Pope Francis commends us to practice St. Thérèse of Lisieux's "little way of love."[23] She emphasizes small things such as showing a smile to a stranger to contribute to a civilization of love.[24] Community actions such as designing a public square or restoring an old building can become "intense spiritual experiences."[25] Indeed, it is possible to construe everything as a sacramental sign. The pope, as a faithful son of St. Ignatius, poetically proclaims:

> The universe unfolds in God, who fills it completely. Hence, there is a mystical meaning to be found in a leaf, in a mountain trail, in a dewdrop, in a poor person's face. The ideal is not only

---

15. Francis, *Laudato Si'*, para. 87.
16. Francis, *Laudato Si'*, para. 97.
17. Francis, *Laudato Si'*, para. 149.
18. Francis, *Laudato Si'*, paras. 156–58.
19. Francis, *Laudato Si'*, para. 189.
20. Francis, *Laudato Si'*, para. 203.
21. Francis, *Laudato Si'*, para. 217.
22. Francis, *Laudato Si'*, para. 221.
23. Francis, *Laudato Si'*, para. 230.
24. Francis, *Laudato Si'*, para. 231.
25. Francis, *Laudato Si'*, para. 232.

to pass from the exterior to the interior to discover the action of God in the soul, but also to discover God in all things.[26]

In fact, all things are God.[27] That said, it is the sacraments that are the privileged pathway and the means by which God mediates supernatural life. We find our true meaning in the incarnate Word. "It is in the Eucharist that all that has been created finds its greatest exaltation"—unsurpassable grace, cosmic love, inexhaustible life.[28] Just as the Eucharist pervades, penetrates all creation, the Trinity is the ultimate source of everything.[29] The divine persons are subsistent relations intimately involved in the world, understood and interpreted as a web of relationships. "Everything is interconnected."[30] The task is to develop a spirituality of that global solidarity which flows or issues from the heart of the Trinity. Francis makes the point that Mary is to be regarded as the queen of all creation. He concludes his "lengthy reflection"[31] saying that we journey toward the "Sabbath of eternity, the new Jerusalem, towards our common home in Heaven," and cites the book of Revelation: "I make all things new" (Rev 21:5).[32] The encyclical ends on that promise and a prayer: praise be to God.

CATHOLIC SOCIAL TEACHING

Catholic social teaching (CST) is a vast corpus of work. Here, I merely want to mention some salient aspects. CST has always emphasized the dual poles of individual dignity and the common good. The twin principles of subsidiarity (from the Latin *subsidium*, meaning "help") and solidarity guide Christian action in creating a just social order. Where the former (the principle of subsidiarity) is mindful of personal dignity, the latter (the principle of solidarity) is mindful of the common good. There is this unceasing interplay at work. The church critiques neoliberal capitalism as much as state socialism. Many see in CST an alternative third

---

26. Francis, *Laudato Si'*, para. 233.
27. Francis, *Laudato Si'*, para. 234.
28. Francis, *Laudato Si'*, para. 236.
29. Francis, *Laudato Si'*, para. 238.
30. Francis, *Laudato Si'*, para. 240.
31. Francis, *Laudato Si'*, para. 246.
32. Francis, *Laudato Si'*, para. 243.

way.[33] CST never loses sight of the primacy of the person—the individual is both the source and end of society, which is man writ large. Putting it another way, the person is the purpose of every social organization (as man is made in God's image). The family is the fundamental cell and the foundation of both church and society. We are by nature social beings. We are free under the law of God; we know the good through our conscience. Human society is a community that goes beyond simple self-interest. The object is to create justice in society. Justice is right relationships, the ordering of the soul to the good, to give it a Platonic flavor. Human rights may have to be backed up by law courts. Man has rights—the right to live, to work and worship, to form free associations, to take an active part in civic life, etc. He is entitled to legal protection of his rights. The state derives its authority from God. The common good of the state is achieved when all citizens possess their human rights. The state's nature is purposive—developing individual and public well-being. Totalitarianism and moral relativism debase man. There is a right to revolt against an unjust aggressor (just war theory). Work has spiritual significance. The legitimate title to ownership of the means of production lies in the service of labor. The right to ownership of private goods is a natural right. Property is viewed as an extension and expression of personality. A morally responsible capitalism (a social as distinct from market economy) can meet the needs of the poor. The market is not an autonomous moral force but a social mechanism and as such is subject to control of the state for the common good.

A CATHOLIC THIRD WAY

There is so much more to say, but perhaps a Catholic third way that mediates between the Scylla of laissez-faire monetarism and the Charybdis of Marxist-Leninism can best be described as some form of, or interplay between, center-left social democracy and center-right Christian democracy, as the political ideology closest to CST. James Alison the Girardian theologian argued that "Social Democracy is the closest political philosophy for Catholic Christianity at the moment. I think it was the (good) tension between Christian Democracy and Social Democracy in the post-war years that made them a time of such huge growth. . . . And yes, I think neo-liberalism ultimately sucks the soul out of every

---

33. See Jesuit Centre, *Catholic Social Teaching*; Charles, *Catholic Social Teaching*.

sort of centrism that 'dallies' with it. And that leaves people focused on (a) money and no meaning, or (b) being against other people as the only available source of meaning."[34]

Worried conservatives balk at the prevailing/dominant culture of gender ideology wars, the rainbow alphabet, the clash of cultures, moral relativism, wokeism, mass/uncontrolled and illegal immigration, so-called jihadism, cancel culture, laws limiting free speech, abortion, and what some see as the Islamization of Western (Christian) society. American conservatives and/or nationalists react through MAGA Trumpism and Project 2025; UK conservatives and/or nationalists support Brexit, and the Reform Party is set up to further a right-wing populist message/agenda; French conservatives and/or nationalists vote for Marine Le Pen and Jordan Bardella's National Rally party, to cite a few examples. Of course, one can be culturally conservative[35] while, within the order of economics, being social or liberal[36] or Christian democratic. James Alison observed: "Personally, I think that getting worked up into Christo-national fundamentalism (a) is against Christianity, and (b) does Islam the mistaken favour of thinking that the only way to beat it is to become like it. Attempting to be Christian in the midst of all this, is much more interesting."[37] Others will favor a form of post-liberalism aligned with CST.

Unfortunately, there are others who invoke the noble name of St. Benedict to argue for enforced exile and the construction of a resilient counterculture out of disenchantment and distaste for modernity. I refer to Rod Dreher (who is Orthodox, not Catholic) and what Dreher calls "the Benedict option" (which has nothing to do with Benedictine spirituality) in his depressing book of the same title. His suggestions sound suspiciously like proposals for a sect. Charles Taylor's penetrating analysis of secularity and Christianity is a much more lucid and convincing one than Dreher's desperate effort.[38]

Clearly, in light of the cultural crises that are besieging contemporary society, a mixed constitution will be preferable. The common good

---

34. Email from James Alison to the author, July 12, 2024. See Annet, *Cathonomics*; and "Theology of Social Democracy," where he likewise argues that social democracy is the political application of CST. See also Hart, "Three Cheers for Socialism."

35. See Scruton, *How to Be Conservative*.

36. Walsh, *Growth of Liberal Soul*.

37. Email from James Alison to the author, July 12, 2024.

38. See Taylor, *Secular Age*; and *Cosmic Connections*.

needs to be enshrined (and perhaps radically reimagined) lest individual ideological interests (which are often sectarian), reconfigured to suit and benefit the elites, proliferate and predominate. Economics is important but so also are social, environmental, and spiritual factors. Flourishing (what the ancient Greek philosophers called *eudaimonia* with its close links to *arete* or virtuous living) is a requisite for well-being. Small is still good, be this seen in terms of a classical education or of a working democracy. Big government and big business are not good for the soul. We shouldn't aim to immanentize the *eschaton*. In other words, apropos of St. Augustine, we should not think it possible to fully realize the city of God on earth—this was the delusional dream of many totalitarian regimes. One philosopher who follows Plato and Augustine in a radical way in an attempt to rethink the central liberal place of human rights as well as the needs of the soul is French philosopher Simone Weil (1909–43), and so it is to her thought that we now turn.

FROM RIGHTS TO OBLIGATIONS: SIMONE WEIL

In a talk I gave entitled "From Rights to Obligations: Simone Weil's Alternative Philosophical Perspective," at the Symposium of Human Rights and Reconciliation, which was held in Parliament Buildings at the Stormont Assembly in Northern Ireland in 2005 and attended by many politicians, especially Unionist ones, I shifted the emphasis from rights to our (eternal) obligations to the Other, deploying the discourse not of politics but of ethics. I include it here by way of an addendum to the above discussion. Just as Pope Francis refers to the figure of St. Francis in *Laudato Si'*, so too does Simone Weil, whom I invoke in what follows, call upon the Italian friar by way of adducing and amplifying her own mystical political perspective.

They were once called natural rights—rights that are ours by virtue of our nature or being. Now we call them *human* rights. The question is: What rights do we have? And what exactly is a right? Is a right a mere freedom to do what we want? How many rights may be justified? Do rights even exist? There is in today's culture a proliferation and plethora of so-called rights. Few to say from where these alleged rights stem/derive.

The language of rights is the language of *demand* addressed to an Other, which can often come from people who have a gripe. They say or imply: "I have a right to education; I have the right to have a say over my own body; I have the right to assemble a bomb; I have the right under the guise of freedom of expression to incite others to hatred. I have a right to do what I want, when I want, and in the way I want." The more these demands are met, the more they grow. This is the nature of demand. I want to locate *some* of the language of rights (not all) within the (ego) speech of demand. Before proceeding it may be helpful to situate the discussion historically and philosophically.

Human rights are not just a political issue; they are first and foremost a philosophical problem. The whole notion of rights can be deconstructed or, at least, hermeneutically revisited. We would have to wait for the Enlightenment in the seventeenth and eighteenth centuries before the notion of rights came to the fore. John Locke, the English empiricist, lists a series of so-called rights: life, health, liberty, and property; safety and reputation for Thomas Hobbes. For Locke, the authority of rights derives from God and reason. Immanuel Kant, the German rationalist, spoke of the absolute and unconditional value of moral obligation. In the Kantian perspective, rights are ways of expressing and protecting our dignity and autonomy as free, rational, moral agents. Moral rights are foundational. A person's rights are built on the duties of others.[39] Kant influenced Simone Weil, the twentieth-century mystic French Platonist philosopher, whose work I will draw on, in a way that the other Enlightenment thinkers did not. Kant was the first philosopher to connect a duty with a right. *A duty is the correlative of a right*. For Kant, duty—what Weil will call an obligation—is the necessity of acting out of reverence for the (moral) law. We would have to wait for twentieth-century philosophy, in particular Jean-Paul Sartre and his brand of existentialism, together with Frankl's logotherapy, for the notion of responsibility to be stressed. With rights come responsibilities lest liberty become license.

What we have in the twentieth century is the formalization of rights enshrined in various declarations such as the United Nations Universal Declaration of Human Rights and the Council of European Convention for the Protection of Human Rights and Fundamental Freedoms. These two explain the inherent dignity and equality of all human persons with respect to their inalienable rights. Rights that are emphasized include: the right to life, liberty, security, equality before the law, freedom from arbitrary arrest, detention, and exile. We are not to be subjected to slavery,

---

39. See, for example, Gorman, *Rights and Reason*, for an informative philosophical analysis and historical survey of the notion of rights.

torture, or cruel treatment. We have a right to freedom of movement, asylum from persecution; we have a right to peaceful assembly and to freedom of expression and opinion. We have the right to work, to vote, to equal pay for equal work, to rest and leisure and education, etc.

What happens, though, when there's a clash, a conflict of rights? Who wins? Usually it is decided by the government in a referendum or simply by passing a statute, so that the alleged right becomes enshrined in law. So, does the law make a right, right? In Ireland, we had to vote on abortion. There was much heated debate and bitter disagreement between the rights of the mother and the rights of the unborn child. The language of rights is often contentious and conflictual. That much is obvious. Now, if there is no agreement on the above, then what rights, I want to ask, are universal or objective or binding or self-evident or axiomatic? For the moment let's park this question.

Philosophically, it's instructive to explore the reflections of Simone Weil because she offers a serious and sustained critique of rights. Weil was a religious philosopher and political activist. She lived only thirty-four years, and all her writings were published posthumously; she was a mystic as well as a Marxist. Jewish by upbringing, she found a spiritual home with Catholicism (though remained an outsider, not joining the church) and enjoyed several mystical experiences that deeply affected her thought. There are two sources from which I wish to draw out her philosophy on rights. There is her remarkable essay "On Human Personality" and her book *The Need for Roots*. Weil worked in a factory and on a farm, in the field and on the shop floor, taught philosophy in a lycée and fought against Franco's fascists in the Spanish Civil War. The first sentence of her *The Need for Roots* (originally published in France in 1949) reads thus: "The notion of obligation comes before that of right, which is subordinate and relative to the former."[40] However, to set this in context, we need to look first at her essay on the human personality. Weil begins her essay "On Human Personality" by saying that the "notion of rights, which was launched into the world in 1789, has proved unable, because of its intrinsic inadequacy, to fulfil the role assigned to it."[41] What does she mean by this? Why does she say it? For Weil, there is nothing sacred except the good, and the expectation of good is not what is involved, according to her, when we "agitate" for our rights.[42]

40. Weil, *Need for Roots*, 3.
41. Cited by McLellan, *Simone Weil*, 273.
42. Cited by McLellan, *Simone Weil*, 274.

What is sacred in man is not the person per se but the impersonal; truth and beauty dwell on the level of the impersonal. Our personality, by contrast, is the ego. The mystic's whole effort involves moving away from the ego, so that there is nothing left in his soul to say "I." This is attained through *attention*, through attending to the source of good, which is God. She calls this *de-creation*. Creation is the work of gravity; de-creation is the work of grace. For Weil, the language of rights is the language of (plea) bargaining. She observes, "This bargaining spirit was already implicit in the notion of rights which the men of 1789 so unwisely made the keynote of their deliberate challenge to the world. By so doing, they ensured its inefficacy in advance."[43] One can see Weil's logic here: if rights are dependent on the person and if Weil wants to get away from the sphere of the personal toward the sphere of the impersonal (universal), this likewise involves a transition away from rights and toward obligations. The sphere of rights belongs to commerce. The sphere of obligations pertains to the spiritual sphere. Weil writes, "The notion of rights is linked with the notion of sharing out, of exchange, of measured quantity. It has a commercial flavor, essentially evocative of legal claims and arguments. Rights are always asserted in a tone of contention; and when this tone is adopted, it must rely upon force in the background, or else it will be laughed at."[44] For Weil, rights are simply alien to the sphere of the supernatural. She is opposing this tradition of natural rights stemming from the eighteenth century. "The Greeks," by contrast, "had no conception of rights. They had no words to express it. They were content with the name of justice."[45] She gives as an example Antigone, the daughter of the doomed house of Oedipus, about whom Sophocles writes in his Theban trilogy. She breaks the law to bury her brother and goes against the law of the state embodied by Lord Creon. According to Weil, this unwritten law that Antigone obeyed had nothing at all to do with rights. It was love, the same absurd and extreme love that led Christ to the cross.[46] Weil explains: "It was justice, companion of the gods in the other world, who dictated this surfeit of love, and not any right at all. Rights have no direct connexion with love."[47] Weil is assigning a supreme place to love, to virtue, to attention, to de-creation. The notion of rights is as alien to the Greek mind as it is

43. Cited by McLellan, *Simone Weil*, 279.
44. Cited by McLellan, *Simone Weil*, 279.
45. Cited by McLellan, *Simone Weil*, 279.
46. McLellan, *Simone Weil*, 280.
47. Cited by McLellan, *Simone Weil*, 280.

to Christianity, she contends, when the latter hasn't been contaminated by the Roman, Hebraic, or Aristotelian heritage. Weil proclaims: "One cannot imagine St. Francis of Assisi talking about rights."[48]

However, according to Weil, if you say to someone that what they are doing to you is not just, you may awaken the spirit of attention and love. This is not the same as saying: "I have the right to . . ." This evokes a war and the spirit of *contention* rather than *attention*. As Weil observes: "To place the notion of rights at the centre of social conflicts is to inhibit any possible impulse of charity on both sides."[49] She continues: "Thanks to this word, what should have been a cry of protest from the depth of the heart has been turned into a shrill nagging of claims and counter-claims."[50] Weil here calls the language of rights talk a "shrill nagging"; I have called it the language of *demand*, while Alasdair MacIntyre talks of the "self-assertive shrillness of protest" surrounding rights talk.[51] For Weil, the language of rights talk is even "meaner than bargaining."[52] It is the language of envy. In this sense, it is actually harmful. Notions such as rights do not dwell in heaven. This is so because one can make good or evil use of an alleged right. Contrariwise, it is always good to fulfill an obligation. Weil prefers the language of justice, obligation, attention, and love to the language of rights. As she exclaims, "Justice, truth, and beauty are sisters and comrades. With three such beautiful words we have no need to look for any others."[53]

Justice, for Weil, consists in seeing that no harm is done to man. When a man cries out, "Why am I being hurt?" harm is being done to him. There is another cry, a less noble one, and it is this one: "Why has he got more than I have?" This references rights. This second cry must be hushed with the help of a code of justice, tribunals, and the police. Minds capable of solving it "can be formed in a law school."[54] But to the cry "Why are you hurting me?" the spirit of truth, justice, and love is indispensable. These words are also dangerous. They are dangerous because they are not humanly conceivable. And this is why they are indispensable.

---

48. Cited by McLellan, *Simone Weil*, 280.
49. Cited by McLellan, *Simone Weil*, 280.
50. Cited by McLellan, *Simone Weil*, 280.
51. MacIntyre, *After Virtue*, 71.
52. Cited by McLellan, *Simone Weil*, 281.
53. Cited by McLellan, *Simone Weil*, 281.
54. Cited by McLellan, *Simone Weil*, 286.

Weil has put in question the mainstream of Western political and moral thought from the founding of the United States to the Charter of the United Nations. She is not against the whole notion of rights, and nor am I. Of course not. But the language of rights can be misused, so she prefers the notion of obligations. I am merely gesturing here in the direction of Plato via Weil. Obligations, as we have said, come before that of rights, which are subordinate to the former. Weil writes:

> An obligation which goes unrecognised by anybody loses none of the full force of its existence. A right which goes unrecognised by anybody is not worth very much. . . . Rights are always found to be related to certain conditions. Obligations alone remain independent of conditions. They belong to a realm situated above all conditions, because it is situated above this world.[55]

Obligations are binding only on human beings, and there exists an obligation toward a human being by the sheer fact and sole reason that he/she is a human being. Obligations are eternal; they are coextensive with the divine destiny of human beings. "Duty towards the human being as such—that alone is eternal."[56] The recognition of this obligation is expressed in a confused and imperfect form by human rights. In the light of this, Weil draws up her list of eternal duties toward each human being. She makes the transition from *rights (ego)* to *obligations (self)*. If we were all living up to our obligations, there would be no need for rights.

We can put it this way: *rights operate within a horizontal social exchange based on symmetry whereas justice operates within a vertical asymmetry based on a cosmic scale.* Justice brings the kingdom closer to earth. To become godly or Christlike means (and this is only one way of speaking) to empty oneself (kenosis), to become as a slave with no sense of rights at all. This is achievable through effort and grace.

If I could put on a ring and become invisible, why wouldn't I go out to rob or rape because I felt like it? This is the famous myth of Gyges's ring in Plato's *Republic*. Weil's answer is that it is not because of the other person's alleged rights, nor is it because of the law. It is because to do so would involve violating something sacred in the other person. No, we are not born into a quid pro quo relation or with rights. What we receive comes as a *gift*, as a grace. Love is the basis of justice and of everything else for that matter. Obligation, not rights, is the requisite of justice. Rights are

---

55. Weil, *Need for Roots*, 3–4.
56. Weil, *Need for Roots*, 5.

conditional; obligations are eternal. Weil rejects, so, a contractual view of social order. And obligation's object, in the Levinasian sense, is the (face of the) Other. In "The Rights of Man and Good Will," Emmanuel Levinas observes, "The categorical imperative would be the ultimate principle of the rights of man."[57] For Levinas, the rights of the Other constitute a juncture in which God comes to mind.

"I have a right to . . ." This speech frequently stems from the fat, illusion-making, deceitful ego. In rights talk, it may merely be the imperial ego asserting itself in the language of *me, me, me*. But what of the Other, the Other we must never abandon, that Other who is always the selfsame me or, as Paul Ricoeur put it, oneself as another and the other as oneself?[58] Behind rights talk may lurk a hidden narcissism, an unconscious aggressivity in all this pseudo-philanthropy, to put it in Lacanian terms.

Neither rights nor obligations can be prescribed. Rights bypass desire. They are the language of law and politics but not of ethics. They are the language of (Nietzschean) will to power. Either I demand my rights be met, in which case I am a master, or I feel obliged or duty bound to give you yours, in which case I am a servant (the Hegelian master-slave dialectic). But it is a servant one should be.

There is one philosopher who has gone even further than Weil in dismissing and dismantling rights altogether, and the view that rights are *fictions* is expressed in his 1981 book *After Virtue*. According to Alasdair MacIntyre, whose lecture on this very subject I attended as a student in University College Dublin, rights imply the existence of a socially established set of rules, but such a set of rules comes into existence only in particular historical periods under certain social circumstances. They are not universal features of the human condition. Rights presuppose some ground to entitlement, and they are expressed in the language of *protest* and *unmasking*, contends MacIntyre. The opposite of a right is a *gift*.

Thomas Jefferson famously exclaimed, "We hold these truths to be self-evident: that all men are created equal; that they are endowed by their Creator with certain inalienable rights; that among these are life, liberty, and the pursuit of happiness." These words are enshrined in the American Declaration of Independence. In the eighteenth century, such rights were defined negatively, as rights *not* to be interfered with. But in

---

57. "The Rights of Man and Good Will," in Levinas, *Entre Nous*, 157.
58. See Ricoeur, *Oneself as Another*.

our own century, rights are spoken of in positive terms and added to. MacIntyre maintains that every attempt to show how these alleged rights are self-evident and every attempt to give good reasons for believing there are such rights has failed. Why? Because there are no self-evident truths. MacIntyre notes:

> In the United Nations declaration on human rights of 1949 what has since become the normal UN practice of not giving good reasons for *any* assertions whatsoever is followed with great rigor. And the latest defender of such rights, Ronald Dworkin (*Taking Rights Seriously*, 1976) concedes that the existence of such rights cannot be demonstrated, but remarks on this point simply that it does not follow from the fact that a statement cannot be demonstrated that it is not true (p. 81). Which is true but could equally be used to defend claims about unicorns and witches.[59]

Rights, MacIntyre argues, purport to provide us with an objective and impersonal criterion, but they do not. He concludes his argument by asserting that there are no such things as human rights, and belief in them is one with a belief in witches and unicorns.

Yes, but is he *right*? It is not time to give the last rites to rights. Rights should not be rejected out of hand but be placed in proper perspective. As Patrick Riordan, SJ, an Irish political philosopher, argues in his *A Politics of the Common Good*, "The rhetoric of rights . . . seems to rely on an assertion of a moral claim which seeks recognition in the law," and these are sometimes dubious.[60] In rights debates, the focus is usually on moral rights and legal entitlements with little attention paid to the philosophical basis on which these rights are asserted or how these alleged rights can even be known. Many people merely assume they are self-evident even when they are incompatible and irreconcilable with other alleged rights. The language of rights cannot be used in these debates since the point is to establish what rights are to be recognized in the first place. The language of rights is legal in origin; it is not ethical. Its force comes from courts of law, as I said. The individualism permeating this liberal model of rights talk forecloses on questions of the common good, so central to CST, and the assertions behind them become reduced to a mere slogan.

Obligations, by contrast to rights, disturb and overpower me; they seize me. Obligations bind me to the Other (*ligare, ob-ligare, re-ligare*),

59. MacIntyre, *After Virtue*, 69–70.
60. Riordan, *Politics of Common Good*, 106.

to this Other to whom I am beholden through ties of disinterested love, though, of course, (Ignatian) discernment is called for. Obligation disturbs my sleep. This is why insomnia is ethical. Perhaps obligation is the "whisper of the will of God in our ear" and of his holy desire.[61]

Obligation consorts with "the widow, the orphan, the stranger," as Exodus would have it (Exod 22:21). Ethics is about our obligations to the Other. The Other claims our attention and commands us, but it is no Kantian categorical imperative. The claim of the Good is finite and fragile, like a child's face, in whom we may detect Trinitarian traces of the absent God. Yes, traces of God and still, small voices of conscience more than the echoes of evil that resound all round us, in these days of the world's night. So, what I am recommending is *an ethics of obligation instead of a rhetoric of rights*. Meanwhile, the discussion will continue. As John Caputo, the American philosopher and deconstructionist disciple of Derrida, put it: "Obligations rebound after philosophical debate, after every academic conference, just shortly after the invited plenary speaker has collected his check and is headed for the airport."[62]

THE RETURN TO PLATO

We have, in this book, been considering the themes of pilgrimage, psyche (with its dialectic of consolation and desolation), pneuma, and polis. It was Plato who linked soul (the individual) with city-state (society). So, it seems fitting to conclude with a postscript to Plato, whose thought informed Simone Weil's. Any call to action results from an exercise in contemplation. The Good of which Plato speaks is a magnetic center of ultimate attraction. The right order of man and society is, for Plato, an embodiment of the idea of the Good (*Agathon*). The ideal polis is built by Socrates in the soul. The (Heraclitean) depth of soul cannot be measured. Plato employs the symbol, as I said earlier, of depth and descent (*kateben*). Philosophy is the light of wisdom that falls on the struggle to achieve a just polis and well-ordered psyche. Eric Voegelin summarizes the Platonic position succinctly thus: "The substance of society is psyche."[63] Voegelin reorients the modern psyche to its transcendent ground. The disorder of society is a disease in the psyche of its citizens/

---

61. Caputo, *Against Ethics*, 19.
62. Caputo, *Against Ethics*, 25.
63. Voegelin, *Plato and Aristotle*, 123.

members. Society is the person written in larger letters. A polis is in order when it is run and ruled by men with well-ordered souls. Plato's good polis is the philosopher written large, while a corrupt society is the greatest of sophists.[64] A disordered society comes about through derailment, when *doxa* (opinion) replaces *aletheia* (truth). *Daemon* is the divine substance of the soul (be it Socrates attending to his daemon or St. Ignatius attending to the movement of the spirits within him). This attunement has two components: the experience of *depth* and of a *direction* from the depth upward. If we get our souls in order—this is a Platonic way of speaking—we can create justice in society, thereby realizing Plato's dream. Voegelin observes, "The depth of experience is not unrelieved night; a light shines in the darkness."[65] There is a growing luminosity of the depth; the Logos is victorious over darkness as well as death. There are levels of penetration, of increasing clarity. There is a correlation between the order of man's soul and the order of society.

Plato sees the person in three dimensions. In the soul, we can distinguish these forces: the appetitive, the spirited, and the rational (the highest organizing principle of the soul). The virtues bring about order in the soul: these ordering powers/forces are wisdom (*sophia*), courage, temperance, and justice. Justice is the keystone of the system. Politics is founded on ethics, one might say. Moreover, the right ordering of both psyche and polis in Plato's model points toward transcendent reality as the source of such order. This is why these three—ethics, politics, mysticism—cohere/interrelate. It is the story of the self/soul, society, and cosmos (the mystical body of Christ). Plato's term for what lies beyond being is the *epekeina*, about which nothing can be said. As Voegelin notes, "The transcendence of the Agathon makes immanent propositions concerning its content impossible."[66] Plato's parable of the cave illustrates this truth allegorically. The *periagoge* (turning) taking place in the parable, whereby the prisoners ascend from the shadows into the sunlight, is nothing other than conversion. The soul turns away from becoming toward being and ultimately dwells in the region/dimension of the most eudaimonic being. Voegelin expands:

> Eudaimonia is not a beatific vision in the Christian sense, but literally a heightened state of Daimonia, which the Daimon in

---

64. Voegelin, *Plato and Aristotle*, 124.
65. Voegelin, *Plato and Aristotle*, 138.
66. Voegelin, *Plato and Aristotle*, 166.

the psyche of man will reach when he engages in cultivation (*paideia*) through association with the eudaimonic Agathon. The philosopher who has reached the state of Eudaimonia will be inclined to linger at the height of contemplation. He will be reluctant to return to the darkness of the Cave and to dispute shadows with the prisoners.[67]

The philosopher (viz., the one who make this pilgrimage) will have seen nothing less than the truth of the beautiful, the just, and the good. The philosophizing person will have to engage in an anamnestic exploration of his/her own consciousness in order to discover the flow of presence, the divine draw. This is what Plato, Ignatius, Lonergan, and Voegelin all insist upon. The descent into the depth of the psyche will be complemented by the meditative ascent toward its beyond. The structures of consciousness are moving forces in the process of reality becoming luminous. Voegelin muses, "Plato and Aristotle recognised these forces in the experiences of a human questioning (*aporein*) and seeking (*zetein*) in response to a mysterious drawing (*helkein*) and moving (*kinein*) from the divine side."[68] In the quest for the ground of existence and the truth of reality, the soul is drawn in loving response to the divine Beyond and the vision of beatific Mystery that resides at its core.

---

67. Voegelin, *Plato and Aristotle*, 170.
68. Voegelin, *Published Essays*, 326.

Conclusion

I WOULD LIKE TO do three things in this conclusion. First, I want to analyze some criticisms of both Jung and St. Ignatius that have been made by a Jungian analyst of some renown—Dr. Anthony Storr—as well as citing some criticisms of the Jesuit Order that have been put forward by a Jesuit priest. Second, I would like to confront the statistics pertaining to child sex abuse in the church and in the Jesuits more specifically. Third, I will suggest a positive path going forward into a radically uncertain future.

ANTHONY STORR'S CRITICISMS OF JUNG AND IGNATIUS

Feet of Clay, by British Jungian psychiatrist and analyst Anthony Storr, is about gurus—a Sanskrit word meaning "heavy," but which has come to mean spiritual leader. In it, Storr discusses ten people, including Jung and St. Ignatius. It will be instructive to see what he has to say about these two towering figures. In relation to Jung, Storr argues that Jungian psychology offers a "secular form of salvation."[1] Perhaps. Perhaps not. Jung actually encouraged lapsed believers to return to the faith, and I am not familiar with any passage in his *Collected Works* where he uses the term "salvation" to refer to his own school of analytical psychology.

Jung endured a long period of psychological disturbance after his break from Freud. He emerged from what Storr calls his "mental illness" toward the end of the First World War with overt claims to be a prophet, even though Storr quotes Jung in a paragraph later, saying, "I am a researcher and not a prophet," in a letter Jung wrote in 1935 to a lady

1. Storr, *Feet of Clay*, 85.

seeking his views on Rudolf Steiner.[2] It could be called—perhaps disingenuously—a mental illness, but equally it might be labeled a period of creative illness. Storr makes much of the fact that Jung was alone for the first nine years of his life and that his mother suffered a breakdown (this is simply stated, rather than biographically backed up). Later in childhood, Jung experienced, according to Storr, visual hallucinations and distortions that "closely resemble those described by schizophrenics."[3] So, does it *resemble* schizophrenia, or *was* it schizophrenia, and if Jung was later "cured" of it, to what end is Storr making the point? Storr suggests that Jung passed through a psychotic episode and that when he met Jung on April 14, 1951, Jung said about his *Answer to Job*, which he was writing at the time, that it is "pure poison" but "I owe it to my people," and Storr felt no psychiatrist would ever say "to my people."[4] Storr deduces from this that Jung wanted to present himself to people as a religious prophet. Generalizations, inferences, and contradictions abound. He ends by saying that Jung's loss of faith (curious, as Jung said himself, he *knew* God existed, in a famous television interview) "led to his discovery of God in the unconscious."[5] I am not sure what this means. Jung repeatedly says when he is talking about God, he is talking about the god image in man. For Storr (himself a Jungian), Jung's views are "only mildly eccentric,"[6] even if on the next page Storr states that Jung's typology "has been adopted by experimental psychologists"[7] and that Jung is an empiricist. Turning now to Storr's profile of St. Ignatius.

Storr sees Ignatius of Loyola as also going through a mental illness, which transformed him from a *hidalgo* into a spiritual teacher. During his enforced convalescence after the cannonball, Ignatius suffered "severe depression," according to Storr, which continued from July to October 1522. Storr writes, "There can be little doubt that Iñigo was temperamentally manic-depressive."[8] No evidence is produced from any source, psychiatric or psychological, to assert that it was manic depression. These months of depression could be said to constitute a dark night of the soul, he contends, although we have seen that others have ruled this out. Storr

2. Storr, *Feet of Clay*, 85.
3. Storr, *Feet of Clay*, 89.
4. Storr, *Feet of Clay*, 96.
5. Storr, *Feet of Clay*, 103.
6. Storr, *Feet of Clay*, 104.
7. Storr, *Feet of Clay*, 105.
8. Storr, *Feet of Clay*, 132.

says that Jung discusses the archetypal significance of Ignatius's vision in his essay "On the Nature of the Psyche," but there is no doubt that such visions "occur in manic-depressive illness."[9] Storr can't seem to make a differential diagnosis between psychological and spiritual phenomena—one must be able to distinguish hallucinations and mystical visions.

Storr spots the link between Ignatian imaginative prayer and Jungian active imagination but has an issue with Ignatius's emphasis on obedience.[10] He does admit Ignatius was sensitive to the spiritual needs of others; brought comfort to those who were distressed, especially those in hospitals and prisons; and was empathic and hugely talented as an organizer and administrator, as well as being an effective leader, skilled diplomat, and powerful personality.[11] Before we see what a Spanish Jesuit has to say by way of his critical comments pertaining to the order, we must deal with the revelations of sexual misconduct by members of the clergy, lest we ignore what in Jungian psychology is known as the "shadow."

JESUIT STATISTICS AND CLERICAL SEX ABUSE

A somber note must now be sounded if I am to avoid accusations of naïve optimism or worse, ostrichism, when it comes to discussing the church, first, due to the fact that the immediate future looks ostensibly bleak for the continuance of many religious orders, at least in their present form; and second, due to the culture and context of clerical sex abuse cases and their cover-ups. This shadow side can't be shied away from.

The Society of Jesus was founded in 1540 by St. Ignatius of Loyola. Since then, it has grown from the original 7 to 25,000 members in 2015, who worked out of 1,825 houses in 112 countries. As of 2022, according to the statistics of the Society of Jesus itself, there were 14,437 Jesuit priests, brothers, scholastics, and novices worldwide, thus making them the largest male religious order in the Catholic Church. In 2013, there were more than 17,200 Jesuits, which means that in just over ten years, the society has decreased by more than 3,000 members.[12] In the intervening five hundred years since its inception, many Jesuits have become renowned for their sanctity, having within their ranks 52 canonized and

9. Storr, *Feet of Clay*, 133.
10. Storr, *Feet of Clay*, 134.
11. Storr, *Feet of Clay*, 135–39.
12. Compiled from figures found at www.jesuits.global.

157 beatified, totalling 209 saints as of 2022, and some have been removed through laicization for clerical sex abuse.[13]

In Ireland, in 2005, there were fewer than two hundred Irish Jesuits; now just under twenty years later, there are approximately ninety Irish Jesuits, according to Irish Jesuit Tom Casey, SJ, and the majority of these are elderly, most well past retirement age.[14] In the Irish Province, one young man has passed through the two-year novitiate, as of July 2024. The society (together with most other orders) is in deep decline, with the vocations' crisis showing no sign of abating, at least in Western Europe, a significant source of which has to be connected to the scourge and scandal of clerical sex abuse.

To take a few international Jesuit examples: Prominent Slovenian mosaic artist and Jesuit Marko Rupnik was expelled from the society in 2023 for committing serious sexual and spiritual abuse against at least twenty women.[15] The late Spanish Jesuit Fr. Luis ("Lucho") Roma Pedrosa abused more than one hundred minors in Bolivia. Many of these indigenous young girls were between the ages of eight and eleven. He photographed and videoed them as well as documenting his crimes in writing.[16] In another case, Fr. Alfonso Pedrajas ("Padre Pica"), who also kept a diary detailing his assaults, admitted perpetrating pedophilic acts in several Latin America countries, abusing up to eighty-five boys and adolescents, which was subsequently covered up by Catholic authorities.[17]

Here in Ireland, if we take as an example just the Jesuit Order, thirty-four complaints of sexual abuse were received against nineteen Jesuits at three Jesuit-run schools—Belvedere College in Dublin, Crescent College in Limerick, and Clongowes Wood College in Kildare. Worldwide, more than forty Jesuits have been accused, and 7.4 million euros have been paid out in settlement cases in 2020 for incidents going back to the 1940s.[18] There were ninety-three child abuse complaints against the late Irish Jesuit Fr. Joseph Marmion alone.[19] Sexual abuse complaints were made against the two directors (now deceased) of St. Declan's Special School for children in Dublin, Ireland: Fr. Paul Andrews, a Jesuit

---

13. Jesuits in Ireland, *Naming Regarding Sexual Abuse.*
14. Text message from Tom Casey to the author, June 25, 2024.
15. Brockhaus, "Father Marko Rupnik."
16. Núñez, "Charagua Manuscripts."
17. Wikipedia, "Alfonso Pedrajas."
18. McGarry, "More Than 40 Priests."
19. McGarry, "More Than 40 Priests," para. 5.

psychologist and spiritual director (with whom I consulted for weekly sessions for a couple of years and whom I held in the highest regard; I was made aware of the allegations made against him just before they became public knowledge in February 2024, news I received with shock and sadness) and Fr. Dermot Casey. The present provincial of the Irish Jesuits, Fr. Shane Daly, acknowledged that these crimes were a source of deep shame and asked for forgiveness.[20] Finally, on February 12, 2025, the Jesuit Order in Ireland published a list of fifteen names of deceased Jesuits regarding child sexual abuse complaints.[21] The stories of clerical sexual abuse with all their sordid details are, alas, all too common, unfortunately, in the Catholic Church and relate to all orders as well as to secular clergy worldwide.

As of March 2025, a commissioned sculpture by artist John Coll has been placed in the portico of St. Francis Xavier Church in Dublin, as a symbolic gesture agreed upon between past pupils who have suffered abuse and the Irish Jesuits. Five smaller pieces are due to be displayed in each of the five Jesuit secondary schools in the country. The sculpture sits on a plinth that is inscribed with the following words: "In tribute to all the victims of abuse by those who should have protected and nurtured you." It is a heart wheel with a quotation from *Murder in the Cathedral* by T. S. Eliot running on the track: "Forgive us, pray for us, that we may pray for you out of our shame."

CRITICISMS OF THE JESUIT ORDER

On May 24, 2024, Jesuit priest the Reverend Doctor Julio Fernández, rector of the Catholic University of Uruguay, wrote a widely circulated critical essay about the problems besetting the Jesuit Order. The essay by the (then) seventy-year-old is titled "Ad Ucum Nostrorum III" (For Our Use III) and is addressed to his Jesuit confrères. It was published by the Spanish journalist Francisco José Fernández de la Cigoña on his blog on Infovaticana. It was third in a series that began in 2022 when Fernández admitted that he felt dissatisfied with the situation in the society while making it clear that his dissatisfaction was not related to a vocational crisis and that he was intending to remain in the society. He published

---

20. Jesuits in Ireland, "Naming Andrews and Casey," closing paras.
21. Jesuits in Ireland, *Naming Regarding Sexual Abuse*.

the second essay a year later in April 2023, proposing a revision of the order. Fr. Fernández referenced the following:

- Marko Rupnik, whom I have already referenced above.
- The scandal of sex abuse committed by (some) Jesuits in Bolivia and the (alleged) cover-up, especially the case of Alfonso Pedrajas, which I have also mentioned above.
- The drop in the number of admissions to the society, with high numbers leaving the order too. In a few years the society will have disappeared from several European countries and will be insignificant in others, he contends. Fernández maintains that this is not due to a secularized society or to changing times but to the fact that the Jesuits don't know how to respond to today's challenges with courage or creativity.
- The vision of the Jesuits resembles that of a secular think tank with ties to a left-wing political party.
- The absence of a transcendent outlook, giving the impression that Jesuits belong to a woke nongovernmental organization (NGO).
- His conclusion: the society is in deep decline.[22]

Despite all this, Fr. Fernández wants to recover the order's wonderful charism with passion, boldness, and generosity. He urges the society to stop being so politically correct. He hopes and prays that the Jesuits can still rise once more to be of great service to the church and the world.

THE IGNATIAN OPTION

What the future holds for the Jesuits and, indeed, for other religious orders no one can know or predict with any precision. Some have experienced an influx of lay associates or tertiaries, for example, Third Order Dominicans, Secular Carmelites, and Benedictine oblates. This is a possible route and choice for some who wish to attach to a particular charism or way of life, but unfortunately it is not possible within the Ignatian tradition—it should be! St. Ignatius originally gave the Spiritual Exercises as a layman. It is probable (and increasingly the case) that the laity, informed by Ignatian spirituality and the contemporary findings of

---

22. For timeline of essays and links, see Silva, "Prominent Jesuit."

psychology and trained in the Enneagram, will give the exercises to a new generation of spiritual seekers and committed Christians.

In *Christendom Lost and Found: Meditations for a Post Post-Christian Era*, Jesuit father Robert McTeigue sets out a series of meditations on how a Christ-centered culture can be renewed and retrieved, inspired by St. Augustine's *City of God*. Christendom can be reclaimed and restored. He maintains that we have witnessed the dissolution of three dimensions of public life:

1. Civil society
2. The institutional dimension of the church
3. Academia[23]

Despite these derailments, we have to live as a people of hope. Dreher's dreary and dismal so-called "Benedict option" (referred to earlier) is a form of splendid isolation. Any thought of such self-sufficiency that would keep us all safe from the fray is, in McTeigue's words, "a dangerous fantasy."[24] So, what shall we do? McTeigue suggests that we return to Ignatius of Loyola's First Principle and Foundation in the *Spiritual Exercises*, which states that man is created to praise, reverence, and serve God and so save his soul. It is also to recognize that all the other things on the face of the earth are created for man to help him attain that end. We are all created with a purpose. The First Principle and Foundation "is a divinely ordained teleological mandate."[25] If the diagnosis of our cultural disorder is secular humanism, the prescription is in reclaiming Christian humanism. McTeigue quotes Hilaire Belloc approvingly: the choice is Christ or chaos.[26] Four strategies/responses to our malaise have been put forward/proposed:[27]

1. *Circle the wagon*: This short-term strategy involves hunkering down, sticking together, and waiting for the storm to pass. (But the problem is that this is a short-term strategy.)
2. *Build an ark like Noah*: This is similar to the first option but with the expectation that the storm could last a long time. This is akin to the

---

23. McTeigue, *Christendom Lost and Found*, 55.
24. McTeigue, *Christendom Lost and Found*, 70.
25. McTeigue, *Christendom Lost and Found*, 97.
26. McTeigue, *Christendom Lost and Found*, 107.
27. McTeigue, *Christendom Lost and Found*, 110–13.

Benedict option. (But there might not be time to build an ark, and anyway with this option one will not survive outside the ark.)

3. *Flee to the catacombs*: This involves staying away from prying eyes long enough to do what is so distinctively Christian that it would get us killed above ground. (But this is fraught with peril due to the possibility of betrayal or discovery.)

4. *Riding forth or reconquista*: This option prioritizes defiance over endurance. It involves pushing back and deploying the virtues of hope, anger, and courage. McTeigue quotes Augustine: "Hope has two beautiful daughters; their names are Anger and Courage. Anger at the way things are and Courage to see that they do not remain as they are."[28]

We must study, pray, discern, and exercise the virtue of prudence, both individually and collectively, as McTeigue recommends. "Remember that you must not do nothing; you must do something; and you cannot do everything."[29] This will amount to something like an Ignatian option, with all that that entails: prayer, discernment (especially in relation to the dialectic of consolation and desolation), a commitment to a faith that does justice, the exercises, spiritual direction, practice of the Ignatian examen, etc. Needless to say, such an Ignatian option can be deployed from outside of the Jesuit Order itself.

McTeigue, for his part, offers eight principles to help us act:

1. Be Christ centered.
2. Be not anxious about the world's wickedness.
3. Move from self-seeking to self-donation.
4. No passivity, procrastination, or excuses allowed—ever.
5. Everything truly important should be important to you.
6. Grace builds on nature—strive to give your best self.
7. Do the hard things first.
8. Improvement begins by doing what needs to be done.[30]

---

28. McTeigue, *Christendom Lost and Found*, 113.
29. McTeigue, *Christendom Lost and Found*, 116.
30. McTeigue, *Christendom Lost and Found*, 117.

Christendom is a matter of life and death—souls are at stake. Such a *post post*-Christian era will not only be good for the human person but will be for the greater glory of God. We are at Gethsemane. It is winter. We've to prepare for Easter. Come what may down the tracks, we are called to have confidence that the Spirit is (still) at work in the world, especially in the church. Of course, it needn't necessarily be an Ignatian option; it could well be a Carmelite option based on Teresian or Juanist contemplation or a Benedictine option based on hospitality and liturgical prayer.

Following on from this, I would like to add and encourage take-up of some of the following effective methods/techniques/procedures in one's personal and professional life outside of any religious order's charism:

- Analysis
- Therapy (logotherapy and/or psychosynthesis, with their emphasis on the spiritual core of the human person)
- Enneagram coaching
- Spiritual direction (ideally from someone trained in either psychoanalysis and/or the Enneagram)
- The Ignatian examen
- The Spiritual Exercises
- Lonergan's transcendental method
- *Lectio divina*

THE FUTURE OF THE CHURCH?

What does the future hold for the church and the religious orders? Well, there is an old story within the Society of Jesus that alleges that St. Ignatius said that should the society ever be disbanded, he would need fifteen minutes of prayer to recover and reconcile himself with that. I suspect that many of us would need considerably more time to accept and adjust.

In *Dilexit Nos*, referencing St. Ignatius, Pope Francis observes that the theology underlying the Spiritual Exercises is based on *afectus* (affection), which pertains to the order of the heart.[31] The structure of the exercises assumes the desire to rearrange one's life in the service of the mystery of the human heart. The interior movements of which St. Ignatius

---

31. Francis, *Dilexit Nos*, para. 24.

speaks are the inbreaking of God's desire amid the orderly progression of the meditations. Something unexpected and starts to speak in our heart. So, regardless of what happens to the church and in the church, divine communication will never cease, as we will not be left orphans by the divine Majesty/Mystery.

One thing is certain: just as fear is the enemy of love, so is hopelessness the work of the bad spirit. We trust an unknown future to a known God because, to cite Hebrews: "Faith is the substance of things hoped for, the evidence of things not seen" (Heb 11:1). Indeed, throughout the journey of life, as we weave the threads together that make up its tapestry, we are beckoned by Being Itself. In the process, we are transformed to find not only God in all things but all things in God.

Bibliography

Annet, Anthony. *Cathonomics: How Catholic Tradition Can Create a More Just Economy.* Washington, DC: Georgetown University Press, 2022.
———. "The Theology of Social Democracy: Catholic Social Teaching Guides Us Beyond Neoliberalism." *Commonweal*, Apr. 5, 2024. https://www.commonwealmagazine.org/theology-social-democracy.
Aristotle. *Metaphysics.* Translated by Richard Hope. Ann Arbor Paperbacks. Ann Arbor: University of Michigan Press, 1952.
Arraj, James. *Christian Mysticism in the Light of Jungian Psychology: St. John of the Cross and Dr. C. G. Jung.* Chiloquin, OR: Inner Growth, 1986.
Avens, Roberts. *Imagination Is Reality: Western Nirvana in Jung, Hillman, Barfield and Cassirer.* Woodstock, CT: Spring, 2020.
Avis, Paul. *God and the Creative Imagination: Metaphor, Symbol and Myth in Religion and Theology.* London: Routledge, 1999.
Ballacer, Robert. *Jesuit Pilgrimage.* iPad ed., v. 1.1.3. Robert Ballacer, 2025. https://jesuitpilgrimage.app.
Balthasar, Hans Urs von. *Two Sisters in the Spirit: Thérèse of Lisieux and Elizabeth of the Trinity.* San Francisco: Ignatius, 1998.
Beesing, Maria, et al. *The Enneagram: A Journey of Self Discovery.* Denville, NJ: Dimension, 1984.
Bell, Richard, ed. *Simone Weil's Philosophy of Culture: Readings Toward a Divine Humanity.* Cambridge: Cambridge University Press, 1993.
Betz, John R. *Christ, the Logos of Creation: An Essay in Analogical Metaphysics.* Renewal Within Tradition. Steubenville, OH: Emmaus, 2023.
Boethius. *The Consolation of Philosophy.* Translated by Victor Watts. Penguin Classics. London: Penguin, 1969.
Bourgeault, Cynthia. *Eye of the Heart: A Spiritual Journey into the Imaginal Realm.* Boulder: Shambhala, 2020.
———. *The Holy Trinity and the Law of Three.* Boulder: Shambhala, 2013.
———. *Thomas Keating: The Making of a Modern Christian Mystic.* Boulder: Shambhala, 2024.
Brockhaus, Hannah. "Father Marko Rupnik, Accused of Abuse and Returned to Ministry: A Timeline." *National Catholic Register*, Mar. 13, 2025. https://www.

ncregister.com/cna/father-marko-rupnik-accused-of-abuse-and-returned-to-ministry-a-timeline.

Buber, Martin. *Eclipse of God: Studies in the Relation Between Religion and Philosophy*. New York: Humanity, 1988.

Caputo, John D. *Against Ethics: Contributions to a Poetics of Obligation with Constant Reference to Deconstruction*. Studies in Continental Thought. Bloomington: Indiana University Press, 1993.

Carroll, Ryder. *The Bullet Journal Method: Track Your Past, Order Your Present, Plan Your Future*. London: 4th Estate, 2018.

Casey, Fr. "Was St. Ignatius a Franciscan in Disguise? Reclaiming Catholicism." YouTube, Oct. 4, 2021. https://www.youtube.com/watch?v=GPjTBfhN3GI&list=PLRnXSS4SzUG7DD2qwZKYnpZO6KiH3Tp02&index=2.

Center for Ignatian Spirituality. "19th Annotation of the Spiritual Exercises." Center for Ignatian Spirituality, n.d. https://www.bc.edu/bc-web/offices/missionministry/sites/center-for-ignatian-spirituality/prayer/19th-annotation.html.

Charles, Rodger. *An Introduction to Catholic Social Teaching*. San Francisco: Ignatius, 1999.

Cheetham, Tom. *All the World an Icon: Henry Corbin and the Angelic Function of Beings*. Berkeley, CA: North Atlantic, 2012.

Christou, Evangelos. *The Logos of the Soul*. Edited by James Hillman. Putnam, CT: Springer, 1976.

Clark-Stern, Elizabeth. *Timeless Night: Viktor Frankl Meets Edith Stein*. Canada: Piccolo, 2014.

Clayton, Eric A. *Cannonball Moments: Telling Your Story, Deepening Your Faith*. Chicago: Loyola, 2022.

———. *My Life with the Jedi: The Spirituality of Star Wars*. Chicago: Loyola, 2023.

Comerford, Brendan. *The Pilgrim's Story: The Life and Spirituality of St. Ignatius Loyola*. Chicago: Loyola, 2021.

Connor, James L., and Fellows of the Woodstock Theological Center. *The Dynamism of Desire: Bernard J. F. Lonergan, S.J., on "The Spiritual Exercises" of Saint Ignatius of Loyola*. Saint Louis, MO: Institute of Jesuit Sources, 2006.

Costello, Stephen J. *The Alchemy of Addiction: Carl Jung, the Enneagram, and Contemplative Wisdom Traditions*. London: Routledge, 2024.

———. *Between Speech and Silence: From Communicating to Meditating*. Postmodern Ethics 12. Eugene, OR: Pickwick, 2022.

———. "Beyond Flourishing: 'Fullness' and 'Conversion' in Taylor and Lonergan." In *The Taylor Effect: Responding to a Secular Age*, edited by Ian Leask, 39–52. Cambridge, UK: Cambridge Scholars, 2010.

———. *Beyond Hope: Philosophical Reflections*. Newcastle upon Tyne, UK: Cambridge Scholars, 2020.

———. *Dynamics of Discernment: A Guide to Good Decision-Making*. Postmodern Ethics 13. Eugene, OR: Pickwick, 2022.

———. "The Ethical Dimension of Boethius' *The Consolation of Philosophy*: A Logotherapeutic Reading." In *An Ethics of/for the Future?*, edited by Mary Shanahan, 30–42. Newcastle upon Tyne, UK: Cambridge Scholars, 2014.

———. *The Ethics of Happiness: An Existential Analysis*. Oregon, OH: Wyndham Hall, 2010.

———. "From Rights to Obligations: Simone Weil's Alternative Philosophical Perspective." Lecture at Symposium of Human Rights and Reconciliation, Stormont Assembly, Northern Ireland, Sept. 24, 2005.

———. *Hermeneutics and the Psychoanalysis of Religion*. Oxford: Lang, 2010.

———. *Ignatian Mysticism: Exploring the Spiritual Exercises*. Cambridge, UK: Clarke, 2024.

———. "Meaning at the Crossroads: A Jig with Bernard Lonergan and Phil McShane." *Divyadaan* 33 (2022) 39–44.

———. *The Nine Faces of Fear: Ego, Enneatype, Essence*. Postmodern Ethics 11. Eugene, OR: Pickwick, 2022.

———. *The Pale Criminal: Psychoanalytic Perspectives*. New York: Karnac, 2002.

———. *Philosophy and the Flow of Presence: Desire, Drama, and the Divine Ground of Being*. Newcastle upon Tyne, UK: Cambridge Scholars, 2013.

———, ed. *The Search for Spirituality: Seven Paths Within the Catholic Tradition*. Dublin: Liffey, 2002.

Delio, Ilia. "Atonement and Evolution." Center for Christogenesis, Feb. 17, 2019. https://christogenesis.org/atonement-and-evolution/.

———. *The Not-Yet God: Carl Jung, Teilhard de Chardin, and the Relational Whole*. Maryknoll, NY: Orbis, 2023.

De Mello, Anthony. *Seek God Everywhere: Reflections on the Spiritual Exercises of St. Ignatius*. New York: Doubleday, 2010.

Doran, Robert M. *Subject and Psyche*. 2nd ed. Marquette Studies in Theology 3. Milwaukie: Marquette University Press, 1994.

Dreher, Rod. *The Benedict Option: A Strategy for Christians in a Post-Christian Nation*. New York: Random House, 2017.

Dunne, Tad. *Enneatypes: Method and Spirit; Our Nine Basic Compulsions*. USA: Universal, 1999.

Egan, Desmond. *Hopeful Hopkins: Essays*. Newbridge, Ire.: Goldsmith, 2017.

Egan, Harvey. *Ignatius Loyola the Mystic*. The Way of the Christian Mystics. Collegeville, MN: Liturgical, 1991.

Eliot, T. S. *East Coker*. Vol. 2 of *Four Quartets*. London: Faber and Faber, 1941.

Ellsberg, Margaret R., ed. *The Gospel in Gerard Manley Hopkins: Selections from His Poems, Letters, Journals, and Spiritual Writings*. The Gospel in Great Writers. New York: Plough, 2017.

Engelland, Chad. *Phenomenology*. MIT Press Essential Knowledge. Cambridge, MA: MIT Press, 2020.

Evagrius Ponticus. *"The Praktikos" and "Chapters on Prayer."* Translated by John Eudes Bamberger. Cistercian Studies. Trappist, KY: Cistercian, 1972.

Flanagan, Joseph. *Quest for Self-Knowledge: An Essay in Lonergan's Philosophy*. Toronto: University of Toronto Press, 1997.

Foley, Marc. *The Dark Night: Psychological Experience and Spiritual Reality*. Washington: ICD, 2018.

Francis. "*Dilexit Nos*: On the Human and Divine Love of the Heart of Jesus Christ." Vatican, Oct. 24, 2024. https://www.vatican.va/content/francesco/en/encyclicals/documents/20241024-enciclica-dilexit-nos.html.

———. "*Laudato Si'*: On Care for Our Common Home." Vatican, May 24, 2015. https://www.vatican.va/content/francesco/en/encyclicals/documents/papa-francesco_20150524_enciclica-laudato-si.html.

———. "*Traditionis Custodes*: On the Use of the Roman Liturgy Prior to the Reform of 1970." Vatican, July 16, 2021. https://www.vatican.va/content/francesco/en/motu_proprio/documents/20210716-motu-proprio-traditionis-custodes.html.
Frankl, Viktor E. *The Doctor and the Soul: From Psychotherapy to Logotherapy*. London: Souvenir, 2004.
———. *Man's Search for Meaning*. London: Rider, 2004.
———. *Man's Search for Ultimate Meaning*. New York: Basic, 2000.
———. *On the Theory and Therapy of Mental Disorders: An Introduction to Logotherapy and Existential Analysis*. Routledge Mental Health Classic Editions. New York: Brunner-Routledge, 2004.
———. *The Rediscovery of the Human: Psychological Writings of Viktor E. Frankl on the Human in the Image of the Divine*. Translated by Shimon Cowen and Liesl Kosma. Melbourne: Hybrid, 2020.
———. *The Will to Meaning: Foundations and Applications of Logotherapy*. Harmondsworth, UK: Meridian, 1988.
Franz, Marie-Louise von. *Alchemical Active Imagination*. Rev. ed. C. G. Jung Foundation Books. Boulder: Shambhala, 1997.
Gaultier, Alyse. *The Little Book of Dalí*. Paris: Flammarion, 2004.
Gorman, Jonathan. *Rights and Reason: An Introduction to the Philosophy of Rights*. UK: Acumen, 2003.
Goujon, Patrick. *Counsels of the Holy Spirit: A Reading of Saint Ignatius' Letters*. Dublin: Messenger, 2021.
Griffiths, Bede. *The Golden String: An Autobiography*. London: Fount, 1979.
Grogan, Brian. *Alone and on Foot: Ignatius of Loyola*. Dublin: Veritas, 2008.
Guardini, Romano. "The Meaning of Melancholy." In *The Human Experience: Essays on Providence, Melancholy, Community, and Freedom*, 33–81. Translated by Gregory Roettger. Providence: Cluny, 2018.
Hadot, Pierre. *Philosophy as a Way of Life: Spiritual Exercises from Socrates to Foucault*. Edited by Arnold I. Davidson. Translated by Michael Chase. Oxford: Blackwell, 1995.
Hammarskjöld, Dag. *Markings*. New York: Vintage, 2006.
Hannan, Peter. *Nine Faces of God*. Dublin: Columba, 1992.
Harpur, Patrick. *The Philosophers' Secret Fire: A History of the Imagination*. London: Squeeze, 2002.
Hart, David Bentley. "Three Cheers for Socialism: Christian Love and Political Practice." *Commonweal*, Feb. 24, 2020. https://www.commonwealmagazine.org/three-cheers-socialism.
Havel, Václav. *Letters to Olga*. New York: Knopf, 1988.
Hederman, Mark Patrick. *Manikon Eros: Mad, Crazy Love*. Dublin: Veritas, 2000.
Helminiak, Daniel A. *The Human Core of Spirituality: Mind as Psyche and Spirit*. New York: State University of New York Press, 1996.
———. *Meditation Without Myth: What I Wish They'd Taught Me in Church About Prayer, Meditation, and the Quest for Peace*. New York: Crossroad, 2005.
Herrera, R. A. *Silent Music: The Life, Work, and Thought of St. John of the Cross*. Grand Rapids: Eerdmans, 2004.
Heuertz, Christopher L. *The Sacred Enneagram: Finding Your Unique Path to Spiritual Growth*. Grand Rapids: Zondervan, 2017.

———. *The Sacred Enneagram Workbook: Mapping Your Unique Path to Spiritual Growth*. Grand Rapids: Zondervan, 2019.

Hey, David. *The 9 Dimensions of the Soul: Essence and the Enneagram*. Winchester, UK: O Books, 2006.

Hillman, James. *Archetypal Psychology: A Brief Account*. Woodstock, CT: Spring, 1983.

———. *The Dream and the Underworld*. New York: Harper Perennial, 1979.

———. *Insearch: Psychology and Religion*. Woodstock, CT: Spring, 1996.

———. *Re-Visioning Psychology*. New York: Harper Perennial, 1976.

Hopkins, Gerard Manley. *The Notebooks and Papers of Gerard Manley Hopkins*. Edited by Humphrey Howe. London: Oxford University Press, 1937.

———. *Selected Poems*. Dover Thrift ed. New York: Dover, 2011.

Hughes, Glenn. *A More Beautiful Question: The Spiritual in Poetry and Art*. Columbia: University of Missouri Press, 2011.

Ignatius of Loyola, Saint. *Personal Writings: Reminiscences, Spiritual Diary, Select Letters—Including the Text of "The Spiritual Exercises."* Edited and translated by Joseph A. Munitiz and Philip Endean. Penguin Classics. London: Penguin, 1966.

———. *The Spiritual Exercises of Saint Ignatius*. Edited and translated by George E. Ganss. Bilbao: Mensajero, 2021.

Jesuit Centre for Faith and Justice. *Catholic Social Teaching in Action*. Dublin: Columba, 2005.

Jesuits in Ireland. "Naming of Deceased Jesuits: Fr Paul Andrews SJ and Fr Dermot Casey SJ." Jesuits in Ireland, Feb. 2024. https://jesuit.ie/wp-content/uploads/2024/02/Naming-of-deceased-Jesuits-Fr-Paul-Andrews-SJ-and-Fr-Dermot-Casey-SJ.pdf.

———. *Naming of Deceased Jesuits Regarding Child Sexual Abuse Complaints*. Jesuits in Ireland, Feb. 12, 2025. https://jesuit.ie/wp-content/uploads/2025/02/202502-Naming-of-Jesuits-Final.pdf.

John of the Cross, Saint. *Ascent of Mount Carmel*. Translated by David Lewis. New York: Cosimo Classics, 2007.

———. *Dark Night of the Soul*. Edited and translated by Alison E. Peers. New York: Doubleday, 1990.

Jung, C. G. *1906–1950*. Edited by Gerhard Adler and Aniela Jaffé. Translated by R. F. C. Hull. Vol. 1 of *C. G. Jung Letters*. Bollingen Series. Princeton, NJ: Princeton University Press, 1973.

———. *Jung on Active Imagination*. Edited by Joan Chodorow. Encountering Jung. Princeton, NJ: Princeton University Press, 1997.

———. *The Practice of Psychotherapy: Essays on the Psychology of Transference and Other Subjects*. Edited and translated by Gerhard Adler and R. F. C. Hull. Vol. 16 of *The Collected Works of C. G. Jung*. Bollingen Series. London: Routledge, 1954.

———. *The Structure and Dynamics of the Psyche: Including "Synchronicity: An Acausal Connecting Principal."* Edited and translated by Gerhard Adler and R. F. C. Hull. Vol. 8 of *The Collected Works of C. G. Jung*. Bollingen Series. London: Routledge, 1954.

Kearney, Richard. *The Wake of Imagination: Toward a Postmodern Culture*. London: Hutchinson, 1988.

Kugler, Paul. *Raids on the Unthinkable: Freudian and Jungian Psychoanalysis*. New Orleans: Spring, 2005.

Laporte, Jean-Marc. "A Christian Transposition of the Enneagram: With Paul of Tarsus and Ignatius Loyola." Orientations for Spiritual Growth, Oct. 9, 2017. https://orientations.jesuits.ca/ennea%20spexx.pdf.

———. "Reflections on Viktor E. Frankl's Anthropology." In *Existential Psychotherapy of Meaning*, edited by Alexander Batthyany and Jay Levinson, 177–86. Phoenix: Zeig, Tucker and Theisen, 2009.

Levinas, Emmanuel. *Entre Nous: Thinking-of-the-Other*. Translated by Michael B. Smith and Barbara Harshav. European Perspectives: A Series in Social Thought and Cultural Criticism. London: Athlone, 2000.

Lonergan, Bernard J. *Insight: A Study of Human Understanding*. Edited by Frederick Crowe and Robert Doran. 5th ed. Vol. 3 of *Collected Works of Bernard Lonergan*. Robert Mollot Collection. Toronto: University of Toronto Press, 2005.

———. *Method in Theology*. Edited by Robert Doran and John Dadosky. Vol. 14 of *Collected Works of Bernard Lonergan*. Robert Mollot Collection. Toronto: University of Toronto Press, 1971.

Lorca, Federico García. *Romancero gitano*. Madrid: Espasa-Calpe, 1983.

Loughrige, Clare. *Motions of the Soul: iEnneagram; The Enneagram and Ignatian Spirituality*. N.p.: CTR, 2016.

Lowney, Chris. *Heroic Leadership: Best Practices from a 450-Year-Old Company That Changed the World*. Chicago: Loyola, 2005.

Machado, Antonio. *Poesías completas*. Madrid: Espasa-Calpe, 1984.

MacIntyre, Alasdair. *After Virtue*. London: Duckworth, 2003.

Maitri, Sandra. *The Enneagram of Passions and Virtues: Finding the Way Home*. New York: Penguin, 2005.

———. *The Spiritual Dimension of the Enneagram: Nine Faces of the Soul*. New York: Penguin Putnam, 2000.

Malcolm, Norman. *Wittgenstein: A Religious Point of View?* Edited by Peter Winch. London: Routledge, 1993.

Mallarmé, Stéphane. *Collected Poems*. Edited and translated by Henry Weinfield. Berkeley: University of California Press, 1994.

Marinoff, Lou. *Plato, Not Prozac! Applying Philosophy to Everyday Problems*. New York: Harper, 1999.

Marlan, Stanton. *The Black Sun: The Alchemy and Art of Darkness*. College Station: Texas A&M University Press, 2024.

Martin, James. *Jesus: A Pilgrimage*. New York: HarperOne, 2014.

Matthew, Iain. *The Impact of God*. Soundings from St John of the Cross. London: Hodder, 1995.

May, Gerald G. *The Dark Night of the Soul: A Psychiatrist Explores the Connection Between Darkness and Spiritual Growth*. New York: Harper One, 2005.

McColman, Carl. "Praying with the Spanish Mystics: John of the Cross." YouTube, July 24, 2020. https://www.youtube.com/watch?v=QcXuNme5MxA.

McDermott, Brian, and Constance Fitzgerald. "Teresian and Ignatian Spiritualities Part 1." YouTube, Sept. 6, 2015. https://www.youtube.com/watch?v=LltM9Qq2Tz4.

McGarry, Patsy. "More Than 40 Jesuit Priests Accused of Child Sex Abuse, Report Discloses." *Irish Times*, Feb. 8, 2024. https://www.irishtimes.com/crime-law/2024/02/08/new-report-reveals-44-jesuit-priests-accused-of-child-sexual-abuse/.

McGinn, Bernard. *Mysticism in the Golden Age of Spain, 1500–1650*. Pt. 2. Vol. 6 of *The Presence of God: A History of Western Christian Mysticism*. New York: Crossroad, 2017.

McLean, Julienne. *The Diamond Heart: Jungian Psychology and the Christian Mystical Tradition*. Asheville, NC: Chiron, 2023.

———. *Towards Mystical Union: A Modern Commentary on the Mystical Text "The Interior Castle" by St. Teresa of Ávila*. London: St. Paul's, 2003.

McLellan, David. *Simone Weil: Utopian Pessimist*. London: Palgrave MacMillan, 1989.

McManus, Brendan. "The Manresa Method: Praying with Your Desire." Jesuits in Ireland, July 5, 2022. https://jesuit.ie/blog/praying-with-your-desire-the-manresa-method/.

McTeigue, Robert. *Christendom Lost and Found: Meditations for a Post Post-Christian Era*. San Francisco: Ignatius, 2022.

Mills, Jon, and Erik Goodwyn. *Archetypal Ontology: New Directions in Analytical Psychology*. Philosophy and Psychoanalysis. London: Routledge, 2023.

Minnich, Nelson H. "The Early Jesuits' Relations with Other Religious Orders." Jesuit Sources, Aug. 2022. https://jesuitsourcesdigital.bc.edu/isjs22n04/.

Mormando, Franco. "Ignatius the Franciscan: The Franciscan Roots of Jesuit Spirituality." YouTube, Nov. 6, 2019. https://www.youtube.com/watch?v=V6tOEmfYzgc.

Murray, Placid. "Newman the Priest: A Study of His Spirituality as a Priest in the Light of His Ministry in the Church of England and His Hitherto Unpublished Oratory Papers." PhD diss., Pontifical Institute of S. Anselm, 1968.

Naranjo, Claudio. *Character and Neurosis: An Integrative View*. Nevada City, CA: Gateways, 1994.

———. *The Enneagram of Society: Healing the Soul to Heal the World*. Consciousness Classics. Nevada City, CA: Gateways, 2004.

Nayak, Anand. *Anthony de Mello: His Life and His Spirituality*. Dublin: Columba, 2007.

Nevin, Thomas R. *Simone Weil: Portrait of a Self-Exiled Jew*. Boston: University of North Carolina Press, 1991.

Nogosek, Robert J. *Nine Portraits of Jesus: Discovering Jesus Through the Enneagram*. New York: Paulist, 2018.

Núñez, Julio. "The Charagua Manuscripts." *País*, June 18, 2024. https://english.elpais.com/society/2024-06-18/a-pedophile-priest-recorded-his-crimes-the-jesuit-order-covered-up-the-findings-of-the-investigation.html.

Obbard, Elizabeth Ruth. *A Monastic Enneagram*. Darlington, UK: Carmel College Press, n.d.

Odorisio, David. "Of Gods and Stones: Alchemy, Jung, and *The Dark Night* of St. John of the Cross." *Journal of Transpersonal Psychology* 47 (2015) 64–82.

O'Leary, Brian. *Ignatius Loyola: Christian Mystic*. Dublin: Messenger, 2023.

Otto, Andy. *God Moments: Unexpected Encounters in the Ordinary*. Notre Dame, IN: Ave Maria, 2017.

Padberg, John W., ed. *The Constitutions of the Society of Jesus and Their Complementary Norms: A Complete English Translation of the Official Latin Texts*. Jesuit Primary Sources in English Translation, 1st ser., 15. Saint Louis, MO: Institute of Jesuit Sources, 1996.

Plato. *The Republic*. Edited and translated by Desmond Lee. Penguin Classics. Middlesex, UK: Penguin, 1985.

Portal to Jesuit Studies. www.jesuitportal.bc.edu.

Progoff, Ira. *At a Journal Workshop: The Basic Text and Guide for Using the Intensive Journal*. New York: Penguin, 1975.

———. *The Symbolic and the Real: A New Psychological Approach to the Fuller Experience of Personal Existence*. New York: Julian, 1963.

Purfield, Brian. "Call and Response in St. Ignatius and St. Francis." *Way* 32 (1992) 143–50.

Raff, Jeffrey. *Jung and the Alchemical Imagination*. Jung on the Hudson Books. Berwick, ME: Nicolas-Hays, 2000.

Rahner, Karl. *The Practice of Faith: A Handbook of Contemporary Spirituality*. Edited by Karl Lehmann and Albert Raffelt. New York: Crossroad, 1986.

———. *Spiritual Exercises*. Translated by Kenneth Baker. South Bend, IN: St. Augustine's, 2014.

Ricoeur, Paul. *Oneself as Another*. Translated by Kathleen Blamey. Chicago: University of Chicago Press, 1992.

Rieff, Philip. *The Triumph of the Therapeutic: Uses of Faith After Freud*. New York: Harper and Row, 1966.

Rilke, Rainer Maria. *Poems 1906 to 1926*. Translated by J. B. Leishman. London: Read, 1976.

Riordan, Patrick. *A Politics of the Common Good*. Dublin: Institute of Public Administration, 1996.

Rohr, Richard, and Andreas Ebert. *The Enneagram: A Christian Perspective*. New York: Crossroad, 2021.

Ruefli, Paul. "Via Intention to Personal Authenticity: Incorporating Lonergan's Method of Self-Appropriation and Doran's Psychic Conversion into the Clinical Practice of Depth Psychology." PhD diss., Western Sydney University, 2009. http://handle.uws.edu.au:8081/1959.7/47025.

Saint-Jean, Patrick. *The Spirituality of Transformation, Joy, and Justice: The Ignatian Way for Everyone*. Minneapolis: Broadleaf, 2023.

Sartre, Jean-Paul. *Nausea*. Translated by Robert Baldick. Penguin Modern Classics. London: Penguin, 2000.

Schumacher, E. F. *A Guide for the Perplexed*. London: Vintage, 1995.

Scruton, Roger. *How to Be a Conservative*. London: Bloomsbury Continuum, 2014.

Severson, Randolph. *A Catholic Soul Psychology*. Benson, NC: Goldenstone, 2013.

Shakespeare, William. *The Tempest*. OpenSourceShakespeare, n.d. https://www.opensourceshakespeare.org/views/plays/play_view.php?WorkID=tempest&Scope=entire&pleasewait=1&msg=pl.

Silva, Walter Sánchez. "Prominent Jesuit: The Society of Jesus Is in 'Profound Decline.'" Catholic News Agency, May 24, 2024. https://www.catholicnewsagency.com/news/257795/prominent-jesuit-the-society-of-jesus-is-in-profound-decline.

Sintobin, Nikolaas. *Living with Ignatius: On the Compass of Joy*. Dublin: Messenger, 2023.

———. *Praying with the Bible: An Ignatian Guide*. Dublin: Messenger, 2024.

———. *Trust Your Feelings: Learning How to Make Choices with Ignatius of Loyola*. Dublin: Messenger, 2022.

Snell, R. J. *Acedia and Its Discontents: Metaphysical Boredom in an Empire of Desire*. Kettering, OH: Angelico, 2015.

Stein, Edith [Saint Teresa Benedicta of the Cross]. *The Science of the Cross*. Edited by L. Gelber and Romaeus Leuven. Translated by Josephine Koeppel. Vol. 6 of *The Collected Works of Edith Stein*. Washington, DC: ICS, 2002.
Storr, Anthony. *Feet of Clay: A Study of Genius*. London: HarperCollins, 1997.
Taylor, Charles. *Cosmic Connections: Poetry in the Age of Disenchantment*. Cambridge, MA: Belknap, 2024.
———. *A Secular Age*. Cambridge, MA: Harvard University Press, 2007.
———. *Sources of the Self: The Making of the Modern Identity*. Cambridge, UK: Cambridge University Press, 1989.
Teresa of Ávila. *The Life of Saint Teresa of Ávila by Herself*. Translated by J. M. Cohen. Penguin Classics. London: Penguin, 1957.
Thérèse of Lisieux. *The Story of a Soul: The Autobiography of St. Thérèse of Lisieux*. Edited by Mother Agnes of Jesus. Translated by Michael Day. Tan Classics. Gastonia, NC: Tan, 2010.
Thibodeaux, Mark E. *Discern: Listening for God's Whispers*. Chicago: Loyola, 2024.
———. *Ignatian Discernment of Spirits for Spiritual Direction and Pastoral Care*. Chicago: Loyola, 2020.
———. *Reimagining the Ignatian Examen: Fresh Ways to Pray from Your Day*. Chicago: Loyola, 2015.
Torkington, David. "Ignatian and Carmelite Spirituality—Complementary or Contradictory?" David Torkington, Nov. 20, 2021. https://davidtorkington.com/ignatian-and-carmelite-spirituality-complementary-or-contradictory/.
Tyler, Peter. *The Living Philosophy of Edith Stein*. London: Bloomsbury Academic, 2024.
———. *The Pursuit of the Soul: Psychoanalysis, Soul-Making and the Christian Tradition*. London: T&T Clark, 2016.
———. *The Return to the Mystical: Ludwig Wittgenstein, Teresa of Avila, and the Christian Mystical Tradition*. New York: Continuum, 2011.
Udías, Augustín. *The Spiritual Exercises with Teilhard de Chardin*. New York: Paulist, 2024.
Voegelin, Eric. *Plato and Aristotle*. Edited by Dante Germino. Vol. 3 of *Order and History*. Vol. 16 of *Collected Works of Eric Voegelin*. Columbia: University of Missouri Press, 2000.
———. *Published Essays: 1966–1985*. Edited by Ellis Sandoz. Vol. 12 of *The Collected Works of Eric Voegelin*. Baton Rouge: Louisiana State University Press, 1990.
Volz, Jon. "Melchior Cano." New Advent, 1908. From *The Catholic Encyclopedia*, vol. 3 (New York: Appleton). https://www.newadvent.org/cathen/03251a.htm.
Wallenfang, Donald, and Megan Wallenfang. *Shoeless: Carmelite Spirituality in a Disquieted World*. Eugene, OR: Wipf & Stock, 2021.
Walsh, David. *The Growth of the Liberal Soul*. Columbia: University of Missouri Press, 1997.
———. *The Third Millennium: Reflections on Faith and Reason*. Washington, DC: Georgetown University Press, 1999.
Weil, Simone. *The Need for Roots: Prelude to a Declaration of Duties Towards Mankind*. Translated by Arthur Wells. London: Ark, 1987.
———. "On Human Personality." In *Selected Essays, 1934–1943: Historical, Political, and Moral Writings*, translated by Richard Rees, 9–34. Oxford: Oxford University Press, 1962.
Welch, John. *Spiritual Pilgrims: Carl Jung and Teresa of Avila*. New York: Paulist, 1982.

White, Norman. *Hopkins in Ireland*. Dublin: University College Dublin Press, 2002.

Wikipedia. "Alfonso Pedrajas." Wikipedia, last updated Feb. 13, 2025. https://es.wikipedia.org/wiki/Alfonso_Pedrajas.

Wittgenstein, Ludwig. *Culture and Value*. Translated by Peter Winch. Oxford: Blackwell, 2002.

———. *Lectures and Conversations: On Aesthetics, Psychology, and Religious Belief*. Edited by Cyril Barrett. Berkeley: University of California Press, 1967.

———. *Private Notebooks, 1914–1916*. Edited and translated by Marjorie Perloff. New York: Norton, 2022.

Wong, Simon. "Bernard Lonergan's Cognitional Theory and the Ignatian Examen of Consciousness." *Universitas—Monthly Review of Philosophy and Culture* 41 (2014) 59–76.

Wood, Mary Antonia. *The Archetypal Artist: Reimagining Creativity and the Call to Create*. London: Routledge, 2022.

Index

acedia, 85, 112, 113, 119, 120, 123, 179, 234
active imagination, 99, 153, 156, 157, 158, 159, 160, 163, 164, 165, 171, 174, 219, 230, 231
alchemical, 133, 135, 164, 165, 230, 234
Allers, Rudolf, 12
Andrews, Paul, 220, 221, 231
Antwerp, 33
application of the senses, 11, 22, 48, 152
Aquinas, Thomas St, 50, 85, 107, 119
Aristotle, 8, 44, 83, 106, 155, 162, 214, 215, 216, 227, 235
Augustine, St, 87, 100, 137, 180, 206, 223, 224
Autobiography, 21, 23, 60, 83, 112, 167, 230, 235
Avens, Robert, 167, 168, 169, 227
Azpeitia, 10, 11, 21, 24, 25, 35

Barcelona, 1, 24, 29, 31, 33, 37
Benedictine, 19, 29, 47, 83, 119, 177, 178, 205, 222, 225
Betz, John, 12, 170, 227
Boethius vii, 5, 98, 99, 100, 101, 102, 103, 104, 105, 106, 107, 108, 142, 147, 227, 228
Bourgeault, Cynthia, 137, 138, 175, 223
Bruno, 155
bullet journalling, 149, 228

Camus, Albert, 88, 90, 119

Carmelites, 8, 12, 14, 15, 134, 222
Carthusians, 15
Catholic vii, ix, 5, 12, 16, 100, 113, 115, 119, 120, 140, 168, 170, 171, 177, 190, 198, 199, 201, 203, 204, 205, 208, 219, 220, 221, 227, 228, 229, 231, 234, 235
chain of being vii, 5, 198, 199
Cheetham, Tom, 172, 174, 228
childhood, 25, 101, 121, 182, 185, 218
Christianity vii, 5, 17, 82, 87, 90, 91, 100, 101, 139, 145, 176, 177, 182, 187, 191, 204, 205, 210
Christou, Evangelos, 134, 228
church ix, 1, 5, 6, 8, 9, 11, 13, 15, 16, 17, 25, 29, 31, 34, 37, 39, 40, 42, 44, 54, 55, 113, 114, 139, 171, 179, 201, 203, 204, 208, 217, 219, 221, 222, 223, 225, 226, 230, 233
Clark-Stern, Elizabeth, 12, 228
colloquy, 22, 40, 42, 47, 153
Comerford, Brendan, 40, 228
consciousness vii, 3, 5, 9, 22, 46, 56, 57, 58, 60, 61, 63, 64, 65, 66, 68, 69, 70, 71, 72, 76, 84, 91, 94, 95, 96, 133, 138, 139, 141, 158, 161, 162, 164, 165, 169, 200, 216, 233, 236
consolation *passim*
Constitutions, 5, 6, 7, 8, 9, 10, 11, 15, 17, 36, 38, 48, 233

contemplation, 1, 3, 13, 14, 22, 29, 42, 48, 51, 55, 61, 65, 67, 75, 97, 120, 127, 128, 129, 131, 137, 140, 152, 153, 198, 214, 216, 225
conversion vii, 3, 3, 5, 10, 15, 24, 27, 35, 61, 63, 64, 67, 77, 82, 83, 84, 85, 91, 93, 94, 95, 96, 97, 98, 101, 113, 174, 184, 187, 190, 194, 195, 197, 202, 215, 228, 234
Costello, Stephen J, 1, 40, 59, 79, 83, 106, 114, 154, 177, 228
creation vii, 5, 11, 22, 38, 46, 51, 55, 72, 73, 74, 75, 77, 85, 117, 120, 137, 155, 157, 158, 170, 180, 198, 199, 201, 202, 203, 209, 227

dark night *passim*
de Chardin, Pierre Teilhard, 14, 44, 46, 71, 75, 137, 200, 229, 235
de Mello, Anthony, 44, 45, 46, 47, 48, 49, 50, 51, 229, 233
depression vii, ix, 49, 79, 80, 110, 112, 113, 114, 116, 117, 118, 119, 121, 129, 130, 130, 133, 141, 142, 143, 144, 145, 146, 158, 218
Derrida, Jaques, 86, 135, 136, 170, 214
desire, 2, 3, 22, 25, 31, 34, 38, 44, 45, 46, 47, 54, 57, 58, 61, 62, 63, 64, 65, 66, 67, 68, 77, 78, 79, 85, 91, 93, 95, 97, 105, 107, 111, 119, 122, 123, 126, 127, 130, 136, 144, 146, 153, 160, 186, 188, 212, 214, 225, 226, 228, 229, 233, 234
desolation *passim*
Doran, Robert, 95, 172, 173, 174, 229, 232, 234
Dreher, Rod, 205, 223, 229
Dunne, Tad, 176, 192, 229

Ebert, Andreas, 177, 178, 179, 180, 181, 182, 234
enneagram *passim*
essence, 6, 41, 52, 70, 76, 102, 107, 117, 160, 168, 170, 176, 181, 182, 183, 184, 185, 189, 190, 191, 194, 229, 231

Evagrius, 118, 177, 178, 179, 180, 181, 229
Examen vii, 9, 22, 23, 42, 46, 47, 57, 60, 68, 69, 71, 76, 113, 139, 141, 142, 149, 150, 224, 225, 235, 236

Ficino, Marsilio, 155
first principle and foundation, 45, 46, 150, 223
flourishing, 83, 86, 87, 88, 89, 90, 91, 96, 202, 228
Formula of the Institute, 5, 6
Franciscans, 7, 8, 9, 10, 11, 31, 180
Frankl, Viktor xi, 12, 84, 101, 102, 106, 109, 119, 124, 125, 150, 151, 166, 170, 207, 228
Freud, Sigmund ix, x, xi, 93, 125, 130, 154, 157, 164, 169, 174, 217, 231, 234
fullness, 4, 71, 82, 83, 84, 85, 86, 87, 88, 89, 90, 91, 93, 95, 96, 97, 118, 120, 122, 124, 128, 159, 197, 228

God *passim*
Goodwyn, Erik, 165, 233
Guardini, Romano vii, 5, 110, 112, 121, 122, 123, 230

Hadot, Piere, 56, 230
Harpur, Patrick, 154, 155, 230
Havel, Vaclav, 92, 93, 230
Herrera, R.A., 137, 230
Hillman, James vii, 51, 134, 135, 152, 154, 162, 163, 164, 165, 166, 167, 168, 169, 170, 171, 172, 173, 227, 228
Holy Ideas, 183, 184, 185, 194
hope xi, 14, 35, 49, 50, 79, 98, 102, 104, 106, 108, 112, 113, 115, 118, 131, 142, 144, 150, 179, 189, 196, 201, 223, 224, 227, 228
Hopkins, Gerard Manley *passim*

Ignatian *passim*
Ignatius, St *passim*
imagination *passim*
intelligence, 188, 198, 199

INDEX

Jerusalem, 27, 28, 31, 34, 36, 153, 203
Jesuit *passim*
John of the Cross, St vii, 5, 12, 49, 80,
    92, 110, 111, 112, 113, 118, 123,
    135, 126, 127, 131, 133, 134,
    136, 174, 227, 230, 231, 232, 233
Jung, Carl *passim*

Kant, Immanuel, 154, 155, 168, 169,
    207, 214
Keating, Thomas, 137, 178, 227

labyrinth, 2, 3, 4, 124
Laporte, Jean-Marc, 190, 191, 192, 193,
    232
Laudato Si vii, 5, 198, 199, 200, 201,
    202, 203, 206, 229
Levinas, Emmanuel, 86, 212, 232
Lonergan, Bernard *passim*
Lorca, Federico García, 110, 232
Loyola vii, ix, 1, 10, 12, 16, 21, 23, 24,
    26, 27, 43, 75, 92, 112, 114, 131,
    174, 190, 195, 218, 219, 225,
    229, 230, 231, 232, 233, 234, 235

Machado, Antonio, 4, 232
MacIntyre, Alisdair, 210, 212, 213, 232
McGinn, Bernard, 9, 136, 233
McLean, Julienne, 12, 125, 233
McTeigue, Robert, 223, 224, 233
Maitri, Sandra, 184, 185, 232
Manresa ,2, 3, 10, 23, 24, 29, 30, 176, 233
Marlan, Stanton, 135, 136, 232
meditation, 1, 13, 14, 22, 48, 52, 53, 54,
    55, 59, 62, 63, 72, 73, 99, 128,
    129, 131, 149, 156, 169, 192,
    198, 223, 226, 230, 233
melancholy, 103, 107, 112, 114, 115,
    116, 118, 121, 122, 123, 194, 230
method *passim*
Mills, Jon, 165, 233
Montmartre, 34
Montserrat, 1, 11, 24, 28, 29
Murray, Placid, 17, 18, 19, 233

Naranjo, Claudio, 178, 181, 184, 233
Newman, John Henry St, 16, 17, 18, 19,
    113, 233

Nogosek, Robert, 187, 188, 193, 195, 233
Notebooks, 75, 76, 77, 78, 140, 141, 142,
    143, 144, 145, 146, 147, 149,
    231, 236

obligations, 206, 209, 211, 212, 213,
    214, 229
Ochs, Robert, 176, 178, 181, 190
Odorisio, David, 133, 233
O'Leary, Brian, 114, 174, 193, 195, 233
Oratorian, 16, 17, 18, 19

Pamplona, 24, 26
Paracelsus, 155
path vii, 3, 4, 5, 13, 14, 21, 28, 40, 43,
    51, 55, 86, 87, 100, 106, 112,
    145, 157, 192, 197, 201, 203,
    217, 229, 230, 231
perspective vii, x, xi, 14, 43, 44, 56, 68,
    71, 77, 89, 93, 95, 106, 142, 145,
    161, 162, 163, 166, 167, 169,
    174, 184, 185, 199, 200, 206,
    207, 213, 229, 232, 234
philosophy *passim*
pilgrim vii, 1, 7, 18, 21, 22, 23, 24, 29,
    34, 39, 40, 43, 123, 153, 197,
    214, 216, 227, 228, 232, 235
Plato, 4, 5, 8, 60, 64, 85, 99, 100, 101,
    108, 133, 154, 155, 162, 164,
    165, 166, 167, 170, 171, 183,
    199, 204, 206, 207, 211, 214,
    215, 216, 232, 233, 235
Pope Francis, 11, 16, 24, 121, 199, 200,
    202, 206, 225
Progoff, Ira vii, 5, 40, 60, 152, 159, 160,
    161, 162, 234
psyche *passim*

Rahner, Karl, 14, 44, 51, 52, 53, 54, 55,
    58, 95, 117, 234
Ricoeur, Paul x, 212, 234
rights *passim*
Riordan, Patrick, 213, 234
Rohr, Richard, 177, 178, 179, 180, 181,
    182, 234
Rome, 6, 11, 21, 29, 36, 38, 39, 51, 98,
    176

Salamanca, 10, 32, 34
Schumacher, E.F. vii, 5, 198, 199, 200, 234
Select Letters, 43, 44, 231
self-transcendence, 5, 56, 61, 63, 66, 67, 68, 84, 91, 95, 173
senses, 10, 11, 23, 37, 42, 48, 49, 53, 61, 78, 119, 124, 126, 128, 137, 152
Severson, Randolph, 170, 171, 234
sex, 5, 130, 140, 144, 156, 190, 217, 219, 220, 221, 222, 231, 232
Sintobin, Nikolaas, 42, 234
Snell, R.J., 119, 120, 234
Society of Jesus, 5, 6, 15, 21, 23, 33, 37, 39, 40, 219, 225, 233, 234
sonnets, 113, 114, 115
soul *passim*
spirit *passim*
Spiritual Diary, 21, 39, 40, 41, 231
Spiritual Exercises passim
Storr, Anthony, 217, 218, 219, 235
Suscipe, 51, 60

Teresa of Avila, 12, 43, 48, 92, 125, 126, 128, 131, 134, 166, 167, 199, 233, 235
Thérèse of Lisieux, 12, 112, 113, 134, 202, 227, 235

Thibodeaux, Mark, 1, 79, 80, 81, 150, 235
three degrees of humility, 48, 54, 63, 72
Torkington, David, 13, 14, 15, 235
two standards, 48, 54, 69, 61, 72, 192
Tyler, Peter, 12, 165, 166, 167, 235
types, 94, 95, 96, 118, 128, 131, 154, 155, 165, 168, 169, 178, 180, 181, 182, 185, 186, 188, 189, 192, 193, 194, 196, 229

Venice, 35, 39, 43
Voegelin, Eric, 65, 83, 88, 90, 96, 214, 215, 216, 235
von Balthasar, Hans Urs, 11, 14
von Franz, Marie-Louise, 164

Wagner, Jerome, 176
Wallenfang, Donald, 131, 132, 235
Walsh, David, 82, 83, 205, 235
week x, 10, 36, 43, 46, 47, 48, 50, 51, 52, 53, 54, 55, 59, 67, 68, 69, 72, 73, 74, 81, 152, 153, 198
Weil, Simone vii, 5, 85, 129, 198, 206, 207, 208, 209, 210, 211, 212, 214, 227, 229
Wittgenstein, Ludwig *passim*
Wong, Simon, 68, 71, 236

www.ingramcontent.com/pod-product-compliance
Lightning Source LLC
Chambersburg PA
CBHW031731230426
43669CB00007B/318